THE

KAFIRS OF NATAL,

ETC.

THE

KAFIRS OF NATAL

AND

THE ZULU COUNTRY.

BY THE

REV. JOSEPH SHOOTER,

CURATE OF HOLY TRINITY AND SAINT MARY'S, GUILDFORD,
AND FORMERLY OF ALBERT, NATAL.

NEGRO UNIVERSITIES PRESS
NEW YORK

Originally published in 1857
by E. Stanford

Reprinted 1969 by
Negro Universities Press
A Division of Greenwood Publishing Corp.
New York

SBN 8371-1538-8

PRINTED IN UNITED STATES OF AMERICA

PREFACE.

THE natives of Africa south of the equator may be divided into two classes — those, namely, whose language is characterized by Clicks, and those who speak what have been called the Alliteral languages. The former class embraces the Hottentots and Bushmen. The latter includes the Kafirs, Bechuanas, Damaras (of the Plain), the people of Congo, the Suaheli, and other tribes less known.

The Kafirs—a name borrowed from the Arabs—lie on the east coast between the Cape Colony and Delagoa Bay. The Amaxosa, who extend to the Bashee River, consist of three divisions, known in Colonial phraseology as the Galekas, Gaikas, and Hlambies. The Abatembu (Tambookies) lie N.W. of the Amaxosa, and are supposed to be a few generations older. The Amampondo, under Faku, live on the Umzimvubu and beyond. N.E. of the Amampondo are Natal and the Zulu-country—a region some years ago inhabited by two divisions of the Kafir race. The one, called by their neighbours AMALALA (apparently an opprobrious term), occupied a great part of Natal. The OTHER reached from the Amalala towards Delagoa Bay, and included the *Zulus, Dwandwes, Tetwas, Quabies*. A more particular account of these tribes (whose names it has been thought best to give in an English form) will be found in the Appendix. Each embraced a number of smaller tribes or families—the chief of the parent-family being regarded as head of all.

The Zulus were comparatively unimportant before the time of their celebrated chieftain Tshaka (Chaka). That extraordinary man, having adopted a new system of warfare, became the terror of all the people from Delagoa Bay to the Amaxosa. Some of his more immediate neighbours submitted; but others, including most of the Dwandwes, fled. When the tribes living in the present Colony of Natal were attacked, a few received permission to remain as tributaries; many were taken captive; others sought refuge in the bush or among more distant people. Some of the last found their way to the Amaxosa, among whom they lived in a state of abject bondage until 1835, when they were liberated by Sir Benjamin D'Urban. Their masters had denominated them Amafengu, "destitute people in search of service"—a name which has been corrupted into Fingoes.

During Tshaka's reign, a few Europeans established themselves at Port Natal, and laid the foundation of a settlement which subsequently became a British Colony. Their presence encouraged some of the frightened natives to leave the bush; others subsequently returned to the country they had been obliged to quit; while many have sought refuge there from the tyranny of the Zulu kings. The consequence is that a district found by the white men almost without inhabitants now possesses a native population of one hundred and twenty or thirty thousand souls.

The author lived above four years in Natal, where he made some researches into the manners of the people. His enquiries were primarily addressed to his native servants, and especially to a young man of about twenty-four, who was in his employment half the time that he resided in the country, and never gave him any reason to doubt his truthfulness. His veracity however was not the only point to be considered. The mental habits of a barbarian had to be taken into account, as well as the uncertainty which attaches to all statements respecting the past made by people without written documents. To obviate the difficulties arising from these sources (as well as to test his informant's truthfulness) it was the author's practice to write down the result of every conversation; and, at some future period, to go over the same subject, again committing the information to paper. The two accounts were then compared. In the vicinity of the writer's abode were several kraals, which not only afforded

an opportunity of witnessing native customs, but
enabled him to procure information from men of
standing and respectability. A stranger's questions might have been regarded with suspicion;
but the author was well acquainted with his neighbours and found them ready to help him in his
investigations. Other Kafirs, especially the members of his servant's tribe, frequently called at his
residence. From some of these knowledge was
occasionally obtained; but, generally speaking, the
author placed no reliance on the testimony of
natives whom he did not know. Information
was also acquired from several Europeans.

Great use has been made in the following pages
of the "Travels" of Mr. Isaacs, one of the first
settlers at Natal. Reference also occurs to the
Evidence taken by a Commission appointed to enquire into some matters connected with the Kafirs
of Natal. Of the witnesses examined, Mr. Fynn,
from his long acquaintance with the people, is especially entttled to consideration, and has been freely
quoted. Reference is also made to the evidence of the
Rev. C. L. Dohne, a native of Germany, but con-
connected with the American Mission. The Commissioners' Report is cited. The MSS. referred
to are those of the unfortunate traveller Green and
a gentleman who visited Natal from the Cape. They
were kindly shown to the author by J. C. Chase,
Esq., Civil Commissioner of Uitenhage, with permission to make extracts.

CONTENTS.

ILLUSTRATIONS.

THE PLATES.

The plates, executed by Mr. M'Lean, are from sketches for which the author is indebted to the kindness and facile pencil of Mr. E. Redinger of Natal. PLATE I (Frontispiece) is a "man" with shield and assagai, on a journey. PLATE II (facing p. 17) is a married woman going to work in the garden. PLATE III (facing p. 151) is a young wife. An unthatched hut in the distance. PLATE IV (facing p. 61). An unmarried woman. In the distance a thatched hut.

THE WOOD CUTS.

Page 3. Three squatting figures; viz., a "boy" smoking hemp through a cow's-horn containing water; a "man," distinguished by the ring on his head, expectorating through a tube, after smoking; another "man," producing fire by means of two sticks. *Page* 9. A portrait. *Page* 12. A kraal. *Page* 173. A prophet. *Page* 238. An unmarried woman; a "boy;" a child; a "man" with a blanket wrapped round him. *Page* 356. Utensils, &c. In the background, two large baskets, in front of them a large earthenware pot with cover, a rolled mat on one side, and a bottle-shaped basket on the other; next to that a milk pail, between which and the shield is a wide-mouthed basket. A hoe lies against the basket; near that a knob-stick;

then a beer strainer, a "pillow" (like a stool), a bag, a dancing spear and sticks overlying a wide basket, which stands on a mat; an axe and the blade of a hoe are on the same mat; snuff boxes on another mat; a knife, spoons, sections of calabashes, and a cooking pot in front. (The above are from drawings of Mr. Redinger.) *Page* 88. A woman suckling a child. *Page* 153. A "man" creeping out of a hut. *Page* 134. Two of the author's servants. *Page* 218. Interior of a hut. *Page* 248. Blacksmith with bellows, a table mountain in the distance. *Page* 304. A young woman grinding corn.

ERRATA.

Page   34, line 25, *Read,* "of the gods."
  „   78, „   2, *For* smallest *read* largest.
  „   86, „ 26, *For* mothers *read* mother.
  „   117, „ 22, *For* place *read* palace.
  „   121, „   3, *For* them *read* then.
  „   307, „ 26, *For* Thaba, 'Nchu *read* Thaba 'Nchu.

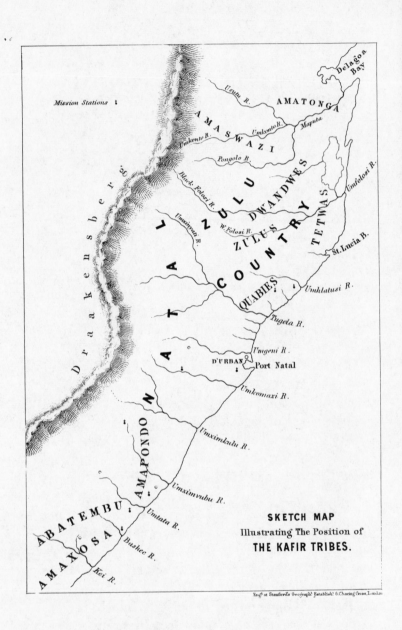

Mission Stations

Delagoa Bay

U'sutu R. AMATONGA

AMASWAZI

Umkonto R. Maputa

Umkonto R.

Pongolo R.

Black-Folosi R. DWANDWES

Umfolosi R.

Umxinwaa R. *W.Folosi R.*

ZULUS TETWAS

ZULU COUNTRY

St. Lucia B.

QUABIES *Umhlatusi R.*

Tugela R.

U'mgeni R.

D'URBAN Port Natal

Umkomaxi R.

NATAL

Umximkulu R.

AMAPONDO

Umximvubu R.

ABATEMBU *Umtata R.*

AMAXOSA *Bashee R.*

Kei R.

SKETCH MAP
Illustrating The Position of
THE KAFIR TRIBES.

Eng.d at Stanford's Geograph.l Establish.t 6.Charing Cross, London

THE KAFIRS OF NATAL, &c.

CHAP. I.—PERSONAL APPEARANCE.

I.—PHYSICAL CHARACTER. II.—DRESS AND ORNAMENTS.

I.—THOUGH the Kafirs belong to the Negro variety
of mankind, their features differ much from those
popularly ascribed to the race; and instances occur
in which, but for its colour, the countenance might
be taken for that of a European.[1] The illustrations
accompanying the present work, will give the
reader a better idea of this subject than could be
conveyed by any verbal explanation.

Except among the tribes near Delagoa Bay,[2]
the skin is not usually black. The prevailing
colour is a mixture of black and red, the most
common shade being chocolate. Lighter colours
are met with, an olive, for example, not darker than
the complexion of a Spaniard, and occasionally an
instance of copper colour. Generally, the hair is
black, while the eyes are dark; but in some cases
the former is of a red hue. Albinos are not
unknown.[3] Dark complexions, as being most common, are naturally held in highest esteem. To
be told that he is light coloured, or like a white
man, would be deemed a very poor compliment by
a Kafir. I have heard of one unfortunate person,
who was so very fair that no girl would marry

him; and it may have been the dread of such a
dire calamity, which made a young man vehemently indignant, when told that he was as fair as
a European : his colour was a light olive. A
modest gentleman, whose opinion I asked respecting the most approved complexion, assured
me that it was *just his own, black with a little red.*
One of the Zulu king's titles is "You who are black."

A new-born infant is not so dark as when a
few days old. It is said that when a native has
been wounded, the new skin is at first light
coloured. Hunger deepens the colour; I have heard
the Zulu soldiers, when they have returned from a
long expedition and suffered much want of food,
described as peculiarly black. The same thing
has been observed among the Hottentots in the Cape
Colony, who sometimes come back to service, after
a period of idleness and privation, with a skin much
darker than usual. This illustrates the passage in
Jeremiah: "Our skin was black like an oven, because of the terrible famine."[4]

When a Kafir squats on the ground, as he ordinarily does while at rest, his appearance is by no
means imposing; but when standing, or in motion,
he is "altogether graceful." Mr. Isaacs, who had
the opportunity of comparing these people with
others, thought them the finest African race that
he had seen; while another author records his impression of the Frontier tribes in terms of absolute
enthusiasm. "Their figures," says he, "are the
noblest that my eye ever gazed upon; their move-

ments the most grace-
ful; and their atti-
tudes the proudest,
standing-like forms of
monumental bronze.
I was much struck
with the strong re-
semblance that a
group of Kafirs bear
to the Greek and Etru-
scan antique remains,
except that the savage
drapery is more scanty
and falls in simpler
folds." Instances of
deformity are rare.
I do not remember to
have met with more
than three in which
the malformation was
conspicuous, but have
heard of two others
sufficiently curious to
be described. The one
had a body of the

usual size, and when my informant saw him sitting
on an ant-hill he had the appearance of an ordinary
man, but his legs were very short, and, except that
he had large feet, he might have served for the
original of some of Punch's caricatures. The
other was a dwarf, about four and a half feet high
and singularly ugly: his chin was long, his forehead

large and flat, the rest of his face was small, while his teeth were large; his thighs were flat, and curved outwards, and he had scarcely any heel. Though examples of deformity be seldom observed, it must not be altogether attributed to the regularity with which nature performs her functions; for we shall see that infanticide is practised, and that a child born with any very great defect, would hardly be allowed to live.

Corpulence, though much admired, is not very common. It is probably as a proof of good feeding, and therefore as an evidence of riches, that this uncomfortable condition is so highly esteemed; but another reason was given me by a Kafir, viz. that in case of famine a fat person might survive till the next season, while a lean one would die. Obesity has its accidental advantages. A very corpulent man had incurred the displeasure of the Zulu king, who summoned him to the Great Place, and after treating him with some indignities ordered him to be thrown down a precipice. The victim was heavy, and his descent rapid; but his fat protected his bones, and he was not much worse for the fall. His executioners then removed him to the bush, where he was left for the wild beasts to kill; but in the mean time his son sought out the place and conveyed him safe home. This man was a chief, and it is to persons of exalted station that the distinction of unwieldly proportions is principally confined. Common people are more or less limited in the matter of food and beer; but a chief's superior wealth enables him to eat and drink without stint, and when thus situated a Kafir is tolerably certain to make the most of his privilege. If the reader will go upon his knees and peep into a hut in one of the Zulu monarch's kraals, he will see how natural it is for people of rank to grow fat. Crawling through the small entrance, we see a large lady—one of many queens—reclining on a mat, and supporting her head with her hand. A pot, containing porridge of white millet, stands near her; a vessel of bruized corn and curds keeps it company; while a third, no small one, holds a supply of native beer. Of these she partakes during the intervals of sleep, a female being in attendance to hand her now the one and now the other, as her majesty may feel inclined. Before the day is over a supply of beef will probably be brought in, nor will she fail to do it justice, notwithstanding that she complains of being unwell. We cannot wonder at the lady's ailments; to which we are indebted for this glance at a scene as jealously guarded as those of the Grand Seignior's harem; it is described on the authority of a European who officiated as her physician. The bulk to which chiefs and rich men attain is sometimes enormous. Dingan was estimated to weigh twenty stones; and others have been described to me as unable to walk. I have heard, however, of one chief in the Zulu-country notorious for his leanness. He differs from the rest of the people in several respects, but especially in this, that he eats only when hungry and does not care to drink much beer. But, though a petty chief, he is also a blacksmith; and his leanness may be owing to his exertions at the anvil.

II.—A MAN's ordinary dress is very simple, and consists of two parts. The one is a square piece of skin hanging behind, the other a few strips of the same material in front; both being suspended from a small string round the hips. For grand occasions, as wedding feasts, they are of more showy materials and more ample dimensions; the former is then made of strips of goat or monkey's skin; the latter of the tails of a small feline animal, or of its skin cut into strips (*pl.* 1). To protect themselves from cold the men wear blankets, which are also used for a covering at night; but before they had the opportunity of purchasing these from Europeans, they employed sheets of prepared hide. The women's principal garment is still made of hide. It is folded round the loins, and reaches to about the knee (*pl.* 2); but for dances they have a larger one, descending lower (*pl.* 3). Young wives have another piece of clothing, viz. the skin of an antelope, with the hair off down the centre, and ornamented with brass buttons or knobs; it is tied under the arms, and hangs down in front (*pl.* 3). A belt is fastened round the waist of married women, who also tie a piece of blue calico over their shoulders to protect them from the cold. Unmarried women are more scantily dressed (*pl.* 4.)

A very singular head-dress is adopted by the married men among the Zulus. A piece of thong or other material is formed into a ring and sewed to the hair on the top of the head; when it is covered with a glutinous substance obtained from the bush, and blackened with charcoal. The hair is then shaved off, both inside and outside the ring, which now appears like a crown of solid leather surmounting the bare skull. When the hair grows again, the ring is carried up with it and gives the individual a still more singular aspect. But I believe it is contrary to strict etiquette to allow it to do so; the head ought to be frequently shaved, and the ring periodically removed and sewed on again close to the head. The barber sometimes works by contract, receiving perhaps a goat for attending to a rich man's poll for half a year. The married women also among the Zulus are distinguished by a shaven head. But, in place of the ring, they leave a small tuft of hair, and colour it red.[5]

Ornaments are worn by all classes. Rings for the fingers, arms, and ankles, are made of brass or copper. Beads of the same metal were formerly manufactured by the natives; but glass ones of various colours and sizes are now bought from the traders. The small beads are fastened to their clothes; an ornament of red and white beads is sometimes suspended from the neck; a band of beads is worn round the head; and I have seen several strings of small white ones worn over each shoulder, so as to form a cross on the back and front. Large beads are worn as necklaces. Tails of cattle, that is, the tufted ends, are worn by the men. The tufts are opened and made to form a fringe, which is tied round the arms, knees, and ankles, and sometimes several are fastened together and tied round the breast like a tippet (*pl.* 1). Feathers are conspicuous among the decorations of the men. These various ornaments are displayed on grand occasions, as at wedding feasts, when a Kafir is sure to be arrayed in all his finery. Ordinarily little more is worn than the rings, of which two or three may be seen on a young man's finger; but, generally speaking, a wealthy man would wear only one or two armlets or anklets.

Besides his ornaments there are some articles which a Kafir wears, and without a knowledge of which we cannot form a just idea of his personal appearance. Of these, his snuff-box is the most indispensable. It usually consists of a small round calabash, in which is a hole fitted with a stopper, and opposite to it another hole with a piece of string inserted, and by means of which it is suspended from the string round his body. When he can afford it, he carries an ivory spoon, with which to apply the snuff to his nostrils. The size of this spoon would astonish a Highlander. The operation of snuff taking is, with a Kafir, one of great importance. Having first squatted on the ground, he shakes a quantity out of the calabash into his left hand; and then taking up a spoonful (or in default of a spoon, using his finger and thumb) he applies it to his nose, and inhales it slowly. After a while, tears roll down his face; but before they flow, and apparently to excite them, he draws the ends of his fingers from the eyes downwards, as if to make a channel for them. The flowing of the tears is a necessary part of his enjoyment; and so completely is he entranced that it is almost impossi-

ble to induce him to move until the operation is
completed. This excessive use of snuff has necessarily a great effect on the nerves; and the Kafir
seems to be as dependent on its excitement as
many civilized people are on other sorts of stimula-
tion equally needless and more baneful. All classes
and both sexes indulge in the excitement; and there
are perhaps very few individuals who abstain from
it.

A Kafir usually carries something in his hand.
If he is going far from home he takes his weapons,
and perhaps a long stick to assist him in fording
rivers, unless he be a rich man and have a servant
to bear his arms.

GILKS   Jack

CHAPTER II.—MODE OF LIFE.

I.—THE Kafirs live in small communities and occupy what Europeans denominate KRAALS.[1] In its most simple form, a kraal consists of a circular cattle fold, with huts disposed around it; but in bushy districts, where the materials can be easily procured, an external fence is added and made to enclose the whole. Kraals of this latter description occur near the coast, and when built on the side of a hill form a conspicuous and characteristic feature of the landscape. The accompanying illustration shows one in such a position, as seen from an opposite elevation and at some distance.

Perhaps the reader would like to take a nearer view, and examine it more closely. We will therefore descend into the valley and cross that small stream which is just visible where the woman is filling her waterpot, but elsewhere is concealed by the trees and bushes which grow on its margin. A narrow crooked path will conduct us to the ford, where the water will cool our feet while we stand for a moment to examine the plants which it nourishes. Further down the valley there might be little to attract our notice, save high grass and taller reeds; but here the vegetation is of a more interesting character; a wild date is conspicuous among the varied foliage, while at a little distance a strelitzia

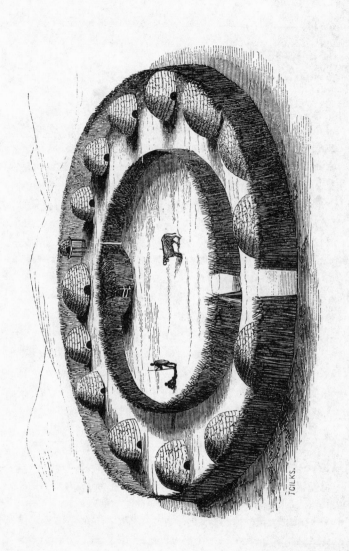

TCILKS.

displays its broad leaves beside a clump of water-booms. We must not however tarry too long, but proceed, taking care to select the right path, for several converge at this ford. The ascent before us is rather tough; but the kraal now comes in sight (never mind the noisy dogs while you have a stick to show them) and the outer fence appears a really formidable barrier. We will not stay to examine its construction, but proceed at once to the entrance, which is here of a respectable width, though in some cases it is so narrow that one cannot help wondering how the cattle get through. The poles of which it is formed give it the aspect of a rude and not ill looking gateway, and which would be the more complete if, as is sometimes done, others had been laid across the top and surmounted with small sticks. At night it is closed by means of other poles and strong sticks, at present lying inside. We have now passed the entrance and will examine the huts. These about the gateway are appropriated to the servants; but they will answer our purpose as well as others, for all have the same beehive form and are constructed of the same materials. On an average, they are about fourteen feet in diameter and six or eight feet high, and consist of a frame work of sticks, covered with thatch. The door-way is semicircular, and so very small that, though the supple Kafir manages it more easily, a European crawls through with difficulty. If however the reader be willing to try the experiment, and care not for certain insectile annoyances which he may bring away, we will enter one of these dark abodes and take a brief glance at its penetralia. But though we are now inside, we must wait awhile that the eye may, after suddenly leaving the bright light without, adapt itself to the obscurity of a windowless hut. A few moments will suffice, and we may now observe the hard smooth floor on which we are sitting, and which has the additional merit of being quite clean. A circular ridge (for most things are of that form here) raised a few inches above the floor, and situate between the entrance and the centre, contains wood ashes, which bespeak its use as a fire-place, the smoke escaping wherever it can, as the blackened roof testifies. Cooking-pots and other earthenware utensils are disposed around the circumference of the floor ; the calabashes standing near them contain milk, which is being converted into *ama-si* or curds, the condition in which it is usually taken ; others empty are hanging from the sides or roof of the hut ; here is a large basket for carrying corn ; there a small one, so close in its texture as to be used for a drinking vessel; that rolled-up mat serves the purpose of a bed, while the singular looking article, so like a wooden stool, is a pillow. The large stone, which has been left inside, is the woman's mill; that ponderous implement is the rude hoe, with which she cultivates the ground. The man's assagais need not be pointed out, though it is not very obvious that the cow's horn near them is a native hookah. There are several other articles that might be noticed, but our limbs are cramped, and we will crawl out again, noticing as we pass the frame of basket work which is used to close the doorway.

Once more in the open air, we will enter the *isi-baya* or central enclosure, and proceed towards the top of the kraal. The *isi-baya* is a very important part of a Kafir's homestead. It is here that his beloved cattle are secured by night, and his idolized cows milked by day. The herd is now at pasture, and there is nothing to represent the live stock of the kraal, except those fowls, which are being closely watched by a thievish hawk that cares little for the missiles of a native. The *isi-baya* is also the usual scene of those dances which form the chief part of the wedding ceremonies, and of which we shall speak hereafter. We are now approaching the top, and may inspect the small enclosure where the larger calves are confined at night, the smaller ones being kept in the huts. Near this is a narrow passage through the fence, which brings us once more among the houses. We remarked that those near the gate belong to the servants; this, at the head of the kraal, and a little larger than the rest, is for the *umnumzana,* a compound word signifying the owner of a place ;[2] while those which occupy the intermediate space are appropriated to his family—each wife, as the general rule, having a separate hut; married sons occupying others; and one being set apart for unmarried men. The dimensions of a kraal are therefore determined by the number of a man's family and dependants. This, which is eighty yards across, contains about fourteen huts ; but there are many smaller. Some of these may be seen from our present position. Those two which lie conspicuously on the opposite

slope, belong to men dependent on our *umnumzana*,
but not so absolutely as those living inside his
kraal. A third, at the bottom of that broad valley,
is probably occupied by one of his married sons, who
has left the paternal kraal, and will in due time be
followed by others.[3]

II.—The PLANTS cultivated by this people are
more numerous than might be expected. The most
prominent are maize, millet, and some cucurbitace-
ous plants. These last include the calabash,
which when ripe is so easily converted into a
bottle as to render it invaluable to a barbarous nation
—the water melon—and the pumpkin.[3]

A Kafir's garden, the usual translation of *in-simi*
(plural *ama-simi*) is irregular in shape—not always
enclosed—and sometimes so small as to look like a
mere patch amid the surrounding wilderness of natural vegetation. A Kafir is by no means restricted
to a single garden; for, as custom does not recognize private property in the soil beyond that of actual possession, he may break up whatever land he
finds unoccupied, and cultivate as many *ama-simi*
as he pleases. He can thus select his soil to suit
his crop; and when an old garden is worn out, can
easily make a new one—a circumstance specially
important, since his ancestors have not taught him
to use manure. It may therefore happen that several
gardens belong to one kraal; close at hand may be
a plot of sweet potatoes; down in the valley a garden
of maize, with pumpkins running among the plants;
and on the opposite hill another field of corn.

When a piece of land has been selected for cultivation, the task of clearing it belongs to the men. If the ground be much encumbered, this becomes a laborious undertaking, for their axe is very small, and when a large tree has to be encountered, they can only lop the branches; fire is employed when it is needful to remove the trunk. The reader will therefore not be surprised that the people usually avoid bush-land, though they seem to be aware of its superior fertility. As a general rule the men take no further share in the labour of cultivation; and, as the site chosen is seldom much encumbered and frequently bears nothing but grass, their part of the work is very slight. The women are the real labourers; for (except in some particular cases) the entire business of digging, planting, and weeding devolves on them; and, if we regard the assagai and shield as symbolical of the man, the hoe may be looked upon as emblematic of the woman. The form of this implement, which is of a most unfeminine character and in striking contrast with the small axe of the men, will be best understood from the accompanying illustration (pl. 2). The iron blade is now generally purchased of European traders; but, though made in England, it must correspond to the African model. A merchant, not aware of this necessity, paid rather dearly for his inexperience. He had introduced a quantity of these blades, made after a new shape and better adapted to penetrate the ground than those of the old fashioned form; but the Kafir would not tolerate the innovation, and the "improved" hoes were unsaleable, until they had been restored to the shape sanctioned by ancestral usage. With this rude and heavy instrument the woman digs, plants, and weeds her garden. Digging and sowing are generally one operation, which is thus performed; the seed is first scattered on the ground, when the soil is dug or picked up with the hoe, to the depth of three or four inches, the larger roots and tufts of grass being gathered out, but all the rest left in or on the ground. The seed, as may be imagined, is only imperfectly covered ; and as a consequence (though this may be owing also to the careless mode of sowing) you may see considerable patches of bare soil, when the corn appears above ground. When the corn-plants are about a month old, and the weeds have attained a height that would astonish an English farmer, the ground is again hoed ; and this terminates the process of cultivation.[4]

Superstition is sometimes resorted to when the plants do not thrive. Among other devices, medicine is burned on a fire placed to windward of the garden, the fumigation which the plants in consequence receive being held to improve the crop. It is believed that what thus benefits one man's corn would injure that of an adjoining proprietor, unless he burned it at the same time. Custom, therefore, requires that when a man uses this mysterious medicine he must give some to his neighbour, unless he would run the risk of being deemed an " evil doer."[5]

The crops are subject to great depredations; quadrupeds, birds, and insects conspire to destroy them.

To protect the gardens from four footed depredators, two methods are employed, viz. fences and watching. The former—designed especially for protection against the wild pig—sometimes surround the gardens; but they also appear in the form of a barrier between the cultivated lands and a pig-infested region. When two or three kraals are situated near an extensive bush, the owners may agree to carry a fence along that side of the country where the pigs approach, and so exclude them from the neighbourhood generally. These barriers are sometimes very long, and not always finished in one season; but their length is needlessly increased by the irregular direction given them; for, though a Kafir is marvellously clever at describing a circle, he cannot draw a right line. The labour of constructing these fences devolves on the men, who also cut the materials; but the task of carrying these from the bush falls upon the women. When watching is resorted to, a platform of poles and strong sticks is erected in the garden, with a small hut on the top. This structure, which corresponds in use to the "lodge" mentioned by Isaiah, is for the accommodation of the watchers. In an extensive garden two or three are necessary, and the women have sometimes to assist the men in defending their crops against nocturnal depredators.

Though we have mentioned the pig as the especial enemy of the crops, he is by no means the only beast that assails them. The "fretful porcupine" is a most undesirable visitor and not easy to exclude. Antelopes eat the young plants; and baboons, where they prevail, steal the ripe maize. In bushy districts the buffalo does mischief; and when a garden is situate near a river occupied by hippopotami, it is liable to their visitations. Of all four footed depredators the elephant is the most destructive, not only from the great capacity of his appetite, but because of his huge feet and ponderous body, which crush more than he consumes. Nor is it safe to disturb him at his unbidden repast, for he is a touchy irritable brute, and must be treated with great caution. It is said by the natives that the shrill voice of a child alarms him— a circumstance by no means favourable to the juveniles, for it occasions them more beatings than they deserve; it is generally considered, however, that a noise excites him, and that if a man were to raise his voice and attempt by that means to drive him out of the garden, it would only make him more furious. It seems also that, instead of being repelled by a fire, he is attracted by it. Two men, who were engaged in watching a garden, had a very narrow escape. There was a platform, but no hut had been placed upon it; they therefore lay down beneath the incomplete structure and went to sleep, having previously kindled a small fire, not so much perhaps to warm themselves, as to scare the hyenas and "evil doers." Meanwhile an elephant enters the garden, catches sight of the smouldering embers, goes straight to the fire, and while disturbing it with his trunk scorches one of the watchers. The man was fortunately but half asleep, and was not therefore aroused with that sudden start which might have proved fatal to them both.   His position was appalling; but he had sufficient presence of mind, not only to avoid making a noise, but also to arouse his companion and prevent *his* doing so, while he communicated in a whisper their fearful danger. By this means they escaped; for the elephant, having dispersed the fire without discovering them, returned to his supper and left them to breathe more freely. On another occasion, an elephant walked over or through the fence of a kraal, attracted by some millet lying there. His enjoyment of the dainty being interrupted by the glowing of a fire in one of the huts, he rushed to the spot, overturned the house and trampled to death a sleeping woman, her husband managing to creep away between the legs of the huge beast.

We need not say more to show the danger of interfering with these herculean thieves, and cannot wonder that a man should sometimes prefer to contemplate the entire destruction of his crops, to hazarding his life in defending them. But the women, who have all the labour of the garden, are not always so passive. I have heard of one who rated her husband soundly because he would not attempt to drive a troop of elephants away. He had distinctly heard the brutes and knew that they would destroy everything; but he was well aware that he could do nothing to expel them, and that it would be extremely hazardous to attempt it. It was in vain to urge this upon his wife—visions of hunger flitted before her eyes—the beasts were destroying her corn—her children would have to starve; and

she became so frantically violent, that he was forced
to creep out of the hut and pretend at least to
comply with her wishes. He soon returned faster
than he had gone and brought the terrible intelligence that the elephants were coming towards the
kraal, and that they must all escape for their lives.
They accordingly made a hasty retreat to the top
of a neighbouring eminence (elephants run badly up-
hill) and remained there until they discovered that
it was safe to return. They found the huts standing,
but the crops were utterly ruined; what had not
been eaten was trampled down, and the garden was
as bare as a cattle-fold.[6]

The feathered enemies of agriculture are beautiful but most destructive; and the boys, to
whom the task of scaring them is allotted, have
no sinecure. Sometimes, when the birds are very
troublesome, the doctor is called in, and medicine resorted to. The mode in which it is applied
is singular. The practitioner, having obtained a
small tortoise, cuts off its head, stuffs the animal with
corn and medicine, and buries it. A fire is then made
over the grave, and some of the heads of corn which
had been partially eaten by the birds, together with
medicine, are burned in it. A chameleon also is
stuffed with corn and medicine, and when scarcely
able to move is placed in a tree. On the following
day medicine is again burned in the garden; and
until this has been done, the people of the kraal are
placed under some restriction as to food. If the
birds still come, no noise is to be made, though missiles may be thrown at them; but if they persist in

their visits after a certain time, the remedy is considered to have failed, and the doctor must return the whole or greater part of his fee. When crows attack the maize, it is believed that if one of the cobs which have been partially eaten be thrown among another man's corn, the birds will follow it, and devote their attention to the garden where it lies. This unneighbourly act must be performed in secret, if the malefactor would escape punishment. It is said that Tshaka, the mighty chief already spoken of, not only employed his warriors against the beasts of the field, but frequently declared war against the feathered tribes themselves. Knobsticks do not appear very formidable weapons to use in the chase of birds; but a Kafir throws them with great precision; and if it be true that the whole disposable part of the male population was turned out in these strange forays, the birds if not killed must have been terribly frightened and driven to more quiet regions. At all events their numbers were very considerably thinned, for a traveller to whose MSS. I have had access, noticed the scarceness of finches and other grain-destroying birds, and gives the above circumstance in explanation of it.

The locust is by far the most terrible enemy of agriculture. "It is a singular fact that these insects were not known in this quarter before 1829 or early in 1830; and the Zulus superstitiously attribute their visitations to the power of Sotshangana, whom the Zulus were sent to attack by Tshaka in the district of Delagoa, and whom they followed on their retreat after having been defeated by that chieftain."[7]

This statement, though extraordinary, agrees with what I have heard—the account given to me being only more full and particular. When they had reached Sotshangana's country, the Zulus were in great want of food; and a detachment of them coming to a deserted kraal begin, as usual, to search for it. In so doing, they discover some large baskets used for storing corn, and their hungry stomachs rejoice at the prospect of a meal. But when a famished warrior has impatiently removed the cover from one of them, out rush a multitude of insects and the anticipated feast flies about their ears. Astonishment seizes the host, for they had never beheld such an apparition before; every man asks his neighbour, but none can "tell its quality or name." One of their number at length throws some light on the mystery; he had seen the same insects in Makazana's country; and perhaps he tells his wondering companions that they had been collected for food. But they soon learn this from the people of the kraal, who had only retired to escape the enemy, and whose voices are now heard from a neighbouring rock. In no case would the fugitives have been likely to spare their lungs, since they could rail and boast and threaten the invaders with impunity ; but when they see their food is in danger, they lift up their voices with desperate energy, and utter the terrible threat that if the invaders eat their locusts, others should follow them home and carry famine in their train. The Zulus were too hungry to heed the woe or be very discriminating in the choice of victuals, and the locusts were devoured. But when the army had returned home, the scourge appeared, and the threatening was fulfilled.

The locusts being a new evil, the doctors had no remedy to employ against them. One ventured to try his art, but without success; when, as I have been told, Dingan killed him for promising what he could not perform. I have heard that application was made to Makazana, in whose territory the locusts were first seen by the Zulu, and that he sent a doctor of reputed power to work his enchantments on the foe. But his medicine produced no better effect than that of the indigenous artist, and the insects continued their ravages. Superstition having failed, the people have adopted the only rational means which can be employed when these formidable insects appear—viz. to make all the noise they can, and produce as much smoke as possible by kindling fires to windward of the garden and heaping green grass upon them. We have seen that Tshaka waged war against the birds, and must now mention that Dingan once turned out a regiment " and ordered them to destroy some myriads of locusts infesting his fields."[8]

A ceremony, which has been called the Feast of First Fruits, appears to have been common to all the tribes in their original state. The primitive institution was doubtless an act of thanksgiving for the fruits of the earth; but Tshaka added to it certain military rites, and gave it much more the aspect of a war-feast. The following are the principal circumstances which occur in its celebration at the Zulu court.

About the end of December the people assemble at the Great Place, where a black bull having been brought from the herd, the young men twist the animal's neck, and throw it on the ground. The doctor then makes an incision in the side of the groaning beast; and, having taken out the gall bladder, squeezes part of its contents into a vessel containing medicine previously boiled. The king dips his fingers into the decoction, and applies them to his mouth. Whether he swallows any of the mixture I know not, but a portion at least he squirts over his person. Other medicine is prepared, into which bruized corn and various productions of the garden are put. This is taken by the king in the same manner as before. Powders of various colours having been rubbed on his breast and face, he takes some of the first mentioned mixture into his mouth, and squirting it on an assagai, points the weapon towards the sun. The doctor now kills the bull by striking it on the head with an axe. It is then skinned and the flesh thrown on a large fire. Towards evening "boys" assemble to eat the beef—a privilege considerably impaired by the fact that they may not drink till morning. It is believed that if this rule were violated, the king would suffer defeat in war or be visited by some personal misfortune; the doctor and others therefore keep a strict watch over the thirsty soldiers, and with their sticks beat back whoever may attempt to leave the fire.

Next day another bull, of a different colour, is slaughtered with an assagai in the usual way. Some of the gall is put into a decoction of medicine, which

the men take with their fingers. They then go to the
stream and wash. Having returned, they assemble
round the doctor, who is provided with pieces of the
bull's flesh previously cooked and rolled in pounded
medicine. Taking one of these in his hand he throws
it into the air, when it is caught by the nearest person, who applies it to his mouth, and throws it up
again for another to catch. In this way it goes
round the circle, unless it fall to the ground, in which
case the doctor throws up another piece in its stead.

Next day the king comes into the fold arrayed in
grass, when a dance called *umkosi* takes place. This
being ended, he retires to resume his proper dress.
When he returns, some further ceremony takes
place—the chief feature of which consists in his
dashing a calabash to the ground. The people go
and wash, while the doctor and the king's chief
officers pick up the fragments of the calabash. These,
together with the grass in which the chief had been
clothed, are burned where the black bull had been
roasted. The ashes are then scattered about, and
cattle afterwards introduced to tread them into the
ground. At the conclusion of the ceremony the king
addresses the people, speaks of their various duties,
and gives them permission to reap their harvest. As
the general rule no crop can be gathered previously
to the celebration of this feast.[9]

III.—The Kafir sets a high value on his CATTLE.
An English dairyman would not think them deserv-
ing of the admiration they receive, but a Kafir does
not view his herd with the eyes of a European. To

his mind they represent several ideas. Cattle enable him to procure wives; cows are needful to rear a family; oxen furnish sacrifices wherewith to propitiate the spirits; while, if he have more cows than are requisite for his own use, he can lend them to others, and thus acquire dependants, over whom he exercises the authority of a petty chief. To a Kafir, therefore, his cattle are most important, and we cannot wonder that he esteems them highly. It must not be supposed, however, that he regards them merely as a means to an end, and loves them only for the benefits they place within his reach; he has learned to set his heart on them as property; he values them for their own sake, and delights " to boast himself in the multitude of his riches." They are, as it has been rather quaintly expressed, the very idol which he worships.

The Zulu cattle are usually small, the average weight of a cow, in good condition, being not more than about 400 lbs. They yield little milk, though what they give is peculiarly rich. Milk forms a favourite part of a Kafir's diet, and is preferred to all other food except flesh. Generally it is used only in a curdled state, young people and very old ones alone drinking fresh milk. A Kafir does not often slaughter his cattle, except for sacrifices or to celebrate a marriage. Rich men sometimes kill an ox for the purpose of giving a feast, but common people cannot afford to do so. The native appetite for beef is very excessive, nor is the quantity sometimes eaten less surprising. Captain Gardiner's servants told him that five men would eat an ox in a day and a half; "and this," he says, "I firmly believe, from the specimen they have already given of their carnivorous powers." I have heard a Kafir say that he could eat a sheep in two days, and that four men would finish a cow in three days.[10] With so great a passion for beef, we cannot feel surprised that they should eat animals which have died from disease. Nor does it much signify how long they may have been dead, provided they are not absolutely putrid. The man just mentioned told me that he would eat a cow which had been lying in the bush three days; but he did not think that the beef would be palatable on the fourth. Very rich men are nicer, for they do not generally condescend to eat cattle which have died a natural death. If an animal appear likely to do so, they usually "save its life by killing it," and so secure themselves a creditable indulgence.

The Kafirs attach great importance to the appearance of their cattle, and take much pains to improve it, as they think. With this view, they cut the ears so as to give them a jagged look; pieces of skin are partially cut from the face and suffered to hang down; incisions are made through the dewlap, portions of which are also partially severed and left hanging towards the ground. The horns—at least those of the oxen—are sometimes modified, and made to assume a most unnatural aspect. Means are occasionally employed to cause one horn to bend downwards while the other remains upright. Among the herds of the Zulu king, horns of most extraordinary shapes may be seen. One ox, for instance,

will have his horns bent backwards towards the
shoulders, while a second stands by with one horn
crumpled in front, and the other tending downwards.
Not far off are several beasts whose horns meet at
the tips like an arch over the head; and before you
have done wondering how this was accomplished,
your attention is attracted by what seems a veritable
unicorn, for his two natural horns have been brought
together on the top of the head, and made to grow
up in contact.   But Monoceros is not the greatest
marvel, for while he has been deprived of an antler,
there stands a beast with more than nature gave
him, and you stare at a three-horned monster!"

A Kafir does not confine his attention to the mere
physical aspect of his cattle.   They are the joy of
his heart and the pride of his life, and so far as he
can he makes them his companions.   He talks to
them—he addresses them by name—he praises them,
as if they could comprehend his meaning; and indeed I have known a cow acknowledge the compliment and sustain her part in the conversation, by
the utterance of those peculiar sounds which naturally express a cow's satisfaction.   The skill with
which these people manage their cattle is calculated
to surprise an Englishman; but it is said that, in
this respect, they are inferior to the Frontier tribes.[12]

It has been stated that the cattle are secured at
night in the *isi-baya* or central enclosure of the kraal,
the larger calves being placed in a separate pen.   In
the morning the herd is sent out to pasture under
the care of a boy, who brings them home about ten
o'clock, when the cows are milked.   That process is

singular and not calculated to find favour with an English nymph of the pail; it requires strong lungs as well as vigorous fingers, and is altogether a rough and barbarous proceeding. The Kafir engages in it with enthusiasm, and it is about the only kind of work he really likes. The first thing he does is to introduce the calf and allow it to suck a short time; he then squats on his heels, pushes away the calf, and with a wooden vessel between his knees draws as much milk as he can obtain. Meanwhile, the calf makes vigorous efforts to share it with him, and receives sundry monitory blows from a young boy who keeps watch and ward over the precious fountain with a stick. When the cow will yield no more, the calf is again allowed to suck, and again obliged to give place to the man. The process of milking is thus a contest between the calf and the milker, in which the cow is umpire. This is a very imperfect sketch of the scene, and the reader must imagine that he hears the operator talking to the cow and whistling in a manner incomprehensible to civilized ears, as if she required to be wheedled into benevolence, and would give her milk only when coaxed to do so by screams and ear piercing notes. And so it is, for the cows have been so uniformly accustomed to the savage accompaniment, that it is almost impossible for a white man to milk his own cattle. When the milking is over, the calves remain some time with their mothers; after which they are separated from them, and the herd is again driven to pasture. At sunset the cattle are brought home and the cows milked a second time. The herd is then fastened in the kraal for the night.

The Kafir has no difficulty in providing food for his cattle, during winter as well as summer; for he occupies a favoured country, and may rejoice in his goodly climate. The only exertion required of him to secure green pasture all the year, is to remove the old grass, which he does by setting fire to it. It is needful however to exercise some judgment in the matter and not burn " all at once, but in sections, so that the numerous flocks and herds may always have abundance of fresh grass." The burning usually takes place at night; and, if you are so situated as to command a good view of the conflagration, it is a sight worth beholding. Let the reader imagine himself on an eminence sufficiently elevated to over-look a plain, where the grass is dry and ready to burn. Before sunset we observe a dark figure moving among the white herbage, and, except that he is a mile off, we might see the brand which he carries. Now he stops, and presently a wreath of smoke appears to indicate what he has been doing. But, though the grass is dry, the air is still and the flame spreads slowly. Soon a gentle breeze springs up, and the fire burns more brightly, extending it-self laterally while it advances forward. Meanwhile the sun has gone down, and now that the brief twi-light also has expired, darkness overspreads the earth, and the lengthening fire becomes conspicuous amid the gloom. Generally the flame is of a tolerably uniform height, but now and then it finds more sub-stantial fuel in a patch of tall grass or a small clump of bush, and "grows by what it feeds on." Gradu-ally but surely the fiery line proceeds, disturbing the

fleet antelope and terrifying the cowardly hyena;
the slower reptiles are scorched and not unfrequently
killed, while multitudes of disagreeable and noxious
insects are swept away by the destructive element.
The fire is now approaching a morass, where it will
surely die out; but no! it creeps down to the edge
of the marsh, and laying hold of the dry reeds, extends over the very surface of the water. The frogs
cease their croaking, and we hear instead the loud
crackling of the canes. Beyond the bog, is a ridge
of hills, which the fire now ascends. In this position it becomes more conspicuous and imposing. Its
long crooked length is distinctly visible, as it proceeds
towards the crest of the ridge and crowns itself with
clouds of vapour. Now and then we catch a view
of trees looming through the lurid spectacle; and
may imagine, if we cannot see, the timid birds, as they
rush in terror from their perch, and fly bewildered
among the smoke. The fire is much more irregular
here than it was on the plain; for, while the ground
is generally open and presents only grass, there are
some places in which the "vehement flame" is consuming the larger herbage of deserted gardens, while
in other situations it is raging amid considerable
patches of bush. Its general advance, however,
is steady; and the two extremeties of the line,
having reached the top of the ridge, disappear and
descend into the valley beyond. The central parts
are detained about the base of a more elevated summit, where the "fire devours briars and thorns, and is
kindled among the thickets of the grove." Tall
flames mount upwards to the sky, enclosing the hill

as by a wall of fire, and surmounting it with a coronal of smoke.

This practice of burning the grass being essential to secure permanent pasturage, is no doubt coeval with the pastoral habits of the people of Africa. It was to it apparently that the Carthaginians owed their fright when, sailing along the Western Coast under the command of Hanno, "a remarkable phenomenon arrested their attention. During the day a profound silence reigned, and nothing appeared but a vast world of wood. But when night arrived, the shore blazed with fire, and echoed with tumultuous shouts, as well as with the sound of cymbals, trumpets and musical instruments of every description. The Carthaginians, appalled, passed hastily along these shores, and came to another region, which struck them with no less surprise. Here the land appeared all on fire; torrents of flame rushed into the sea; and if they attempted to land, the soil was too hot for the foot to tread upon. One object particularly struck them, which at night appeared a greater fire, mingling with the stars; but in the daytime proved to be a mountain of prodigious height, to which they gave the appellation of the chariot of gods."[13] After these burnings the ground presents a dreary aspect; and, if a stranger were to make his first acquaintance with the country during the season when they chiefly occur, he would receive no very favourable impression of its fertility. But in a short time the scene changes—the grass gradually springs up, and the blackened soil is covered with a lovely green.

When cattle are sick, the following remedy is sometimes resorted to. The doctor having come to the kraal (where the herd had been previously collected) makes a fire in the *isi-baya* and burns medicine on it, so as to fumigate the cattle. They are then sprinkled with a decoction of medicine. After this the doctor, having melted some of the fat of the deceased cattle, introduces it into his mouth, and then squirts it on a fire-brand held before the face of one of the animals. The beast of course rushes away from so unceremonious a salutation; and as the process goes on the herd becomes much excited. When the operation has been completed, the gateway is opened and the frightened brutes require no urging to make their exit. Their persecution however is not ended; the entire kraal rushes after them, the men beating shields, the women rattling calabashes, and all shouting at the top of their voices, to drive away the " evil-doer." The terrified brutes bellow and gallop; but the chase is mercilessly continued for a mile or two, when they are left to ruminate on a treatment so different from the gentleness they usually experience. The doctor forfeits his fee if the remedy prove unsuccessful.

Cattle, like the crops, have their enemies—the most destructive being the lion.[14] The mode which the people adopt to defend their cattle from his nocturnal depredations, is not very formidable. A platform is erected in the *isi-baya*, similar in structure to that built in the garden, and on which a watchman is placed when there is reason to antici-

pate a visit from the king of beasts. "The voice
of the fierce lion" can be heard from a long distance; and, when by a growl or a roar he reveals
his presence (for he comes only on dark nights), the
watcher endeavours to deter him by shouting and
otherwise making a noise. I have been told that
the top of the platform is sometimes covered with
earth, and a fire kindled on it as an additional
determent. If the lion approach, stones and
other missiles are discharged at him. But it is not
always possible to induce him to turn aside; and,
in spite of shouts and stones and flames he sometimes springs into the *isi-baya* and "rends the panting prey." An Englishman, who was staying at
a kraal, told me that a lion entered while he was
there; when the natives, in addition to other means,
burned torches of grass and fat, and thus endeavoured to scare him away. But he continued to
devour his meal and only growled at their harmless
display; nor was he more moved by the report of
a gun several times discharged from the platform.

> " So watchful shepherds strive to force in vain,
> The hungry lion from the carcase slain."

Where lions abound, the platform is a permanent
appendage of the kraal; but in other districts it is
constructed only when a lion visits the neighbourhood, and has perhaps already committed considerable ravages. The following anecdote will show
how serious a penalty is sometimes paid for negli-
gence in this matter.

Two men lived about half a mile apart, and were

possessed of goodly herds. The country which they occupied abounded with hyenas and some other ravenous animals; but it was not inhabited by the king of beasts. It happened, however, that a lion paid the district a visit, when one of the two men provided a platform, and prepared to receive him with due honour. Nor was it long before the royal plunderer approached the kraal, and the cattle, scenting him from a distance, became restless and noisy. This awoke the man, if indeed he had given sleep to his eyes, when he rushed out of his hut with a glowing brand, mounted the platform as quickly as a baboon, set fire to some dry fuel previously collected, and lifting up his voice yelled mightily. The noise and flame combined, brought the beast to a stand, not many yards from the kraal; and a volley of missiles, discharged in quick succession, confirmed his doubts as to the propriety of storming a place apparently so well defended. He growled fiercely, as the stones were hurled; but, deeming discretion the better part of valour, he turned his steps in another direction. Perceiving this, the man lifted up his voice again and shouted a warning to his neighbour's people, telling them that the enemy was near. A dependant, the only man in the kraal, came out of his hut and demanded where the beast might be. This being indicated, he began to beat his shield and make an unmelodious use of his lungs, for there was no platform; but he was lazy or cowardly, and soon crept into his house, saying that he could not discover any trace of the lion. He had scarcely drawn his feet through the low doorway, when the beast leaped into the *isi-baya*, and the cattle rushed about in terror and distraction. The owner's chief wife came out of her hut, shrieked desperately to the man, and called on him to drive the intruder away. The only response was from the lion, who did not like the interruption, and gave her an admonitory growl, when she plunged into the hut and was silent in the darkness thereof. She did not however long remain so; it was too painful to contemplate what was taking place in the *isi-baya*, and breaking out into frantic exclamations, she upbraided the man with cowardice. This probably touched his pride, for he began to make a loud noise, but without venturing through his doorway, and ceased only when the lion had intimated, in a manner not to be mistaken, that the unmusical accompaniment was disagreeable and that he wished to eat his supper in silence. Next morning there was a great lamentation, for the beast had been very rapacious; the remains of two carcases lay in the kraal; and, while the women were weeping over these, it was found that he had chased the cattle after they had escaped through the fence, and left some of them dead among the grass. It being confidently expected that he would return the following night, every effort was made to construct a platform; but the wood was difficult to obtain, or the labourers were few, and the sun went down upon the unfinished structure. When the lion reappeared in the evening, he again sprang into the *isi-baya* to commit fresh destruction.

These circumstances being reported to the king he ordered the depredator to be killed; and a body of warriors went out to execute the command. Guided by the lion's footprints, they discovered his lair among some reeds. The officers and rich men mounted a high tree, when the signal was given and means were employed to induce the beast to come forth, the soldiers having previously arranged themselves in a semicircle, that they might, as far as possible, enclose him. When the lion was at length driven out, he bounded towards the warriors, who received him with a shower of assagais. Two of these took effect, but did not disable him from doing mischief, for he sprang among his assailants and killed three or four. The warriors were now in full retreat, and the king's commands likely to be unfulfilled. The brave men in the tree therefore shouted vehemently, and called on the fugitives to return to the charge; if the lion escaped, they should have no beef to eat—if the lion escaped, the king would kill them all. These were powerful considerations, and put new courage into the fear-stricken host. The lion, partially suffering from loss of blood, was again attacked, and this time successfully. He died hardly however, and almost in the act of expiring bit off a man's foot. Danger being past, the officers and rich men descended from the tree, and plunging their assagais into the prostrate beast, exclaimed "we have killed him, we have killed him;" when the others testified their assent, and replied that it was done exceedingly well.

The Zulu soldiers have been ordered not to kill

but to catch a ravenous beast. Pande directed a
lion, which had been destroying his cattle, to be
caught; and the command would doubtless have
been obeyed, if a missionary resident in the country
had not poisoned the beast. Dingan gave a similar
command to one of his regiments; four men were
killed in the attack, when Umpahlana seized the
lion's tail, Tapuza jumped to one of his jaws, a third
person laid hold of the other, and the animal was
taken alive into the king's presence.[15]

IV.—It is only as a means of obtaining food
that HUNTING requires a distinct notice. When
the unfortunate traveller Green passed through
Natal and the Zulu-country, he remarked that the
people were "indifferent about hunting." Since
then, many Colonial Kafirs have been employed by
Europeans to hunt the elephant; and it cannot be
doubted that the occupation has given them more
relish for the chase than they might otherwise have
possessed. The people however seem generally to
regard it as an amusement rather than a business—
as a thing to be occasionally engaged in and not to
be followed as a principal means of support.

I have heard of a bold young man who was in the
habit of attacking buffaloes single-handed. When
he had discovered one, he contrived to get in advance and conceal himself until the beast came up;
then, springing to his feet, he plunged an assagai
into the animal's side. The sport was dangerous
and in the end proved fatal. He had waylaid an
old bull; but the beast was too acute or his hide too

thick, and the hunter was obliged to run. He fled towards a tree, and had nearly found refuge in its friendly arms; but the pursuer was at his heels, and while laying hold of the lower branches he received a deadly wound from the brute's horns. When the enemy had withdrawn, he descended and with great difficulty reached home, where he died in a few days.

This mode of hunting is an exception to the rule. Usually a party is formed, and as many assagais as possible are simultaneously discharged at the animal. If, for instance, the hunters come to a clump of bush, where a small antelope or a pig is likely to be found, they surround it; and by shouting, beating the bushes, and sending in the dogs, endeavour to draw the animal forth. When it appears, all who are within reach throw their weapons. In some cases, " they endeavour," says Isaacs, " to get the animals into narrow passes, where they previously station some of the party, concealed, who spear them as they pass."

The wild pig frequently makes an attack on some of the assailants, who usually carry small shields to protect their nether limbs from its formidable tusks. The eland sometimes turns upon its pursuers and makes them glad to mount a tree. The gnu justifies the praise given him by the Bechuanas: " the gnu," say they, " is a man; it is a man; we fight together. But we overcome the father of greatness amongst the rocks, and his strength yields to ours." A European told me that the father of greatness attempted to charge him after he had broken two of its legs. The zebra sometimes bites his assailants. The buffalo is especially dangerous, though he probably bears a worse character than he deserves.[13] In hunting the elephant they try to get him "into defiles where they can assail him with less danger from the bushes around him, provided these are not too thick; and in this position they do not fail to make their assagais effectual. The elephant however in these situations will often escape from his pursuers, who at times feel the effect of his rage."[16]

Mechanical contrivances are employed for the capture of wild animals. Pitfalls are made principally by the Tetwas, who use them to take the hippopotamus and buffalo. A white man, who fell into one of these excavations, described it as six feet deep, exclusive of two feet of mud. If designed to take the hippopotamus, the pits are dug " in his tracks, with a large stake in the centre. When he emerges from the water to graze on the river banks, the natives endeavour to drive him into the paths in which the pit is prepared, covered over to elude his vigilance, when he is precipitated into it, and the stake pierces his body." In some localities these pitfalls are numerous, and present serious danger to travellers. When pits are made for the capture of buffaloes, a long fence is constructed, with openings or passages leading through it, and near to which the pits are placed. These having been covered, people watch for the animals and contrive to drive them towards the fence, when they naturally pro-

ceed to the openings and pass over the treacherous
holes. Snares of a peculiar construction are used
for the capture of the smaller animals. The Amatonga use poison.

Fish is held in almost universal abhorrence; it is
eaten only by the degraded people just mentioned
and the Amatuli. When the latter resided near
Natal, they formed enclosures of reeds in the bed
of the bay and placed bait in them; as the water
flowed, the fish were attracted into the pens; and if
the bait were large enough to detain them until the
water had sunk below the top of the reeds, they
were unable to escape.[17]

Wild honey is plentiful and much sought after.
The bees build their nests in hollow trees, in crevices
of the rocks, in holes in the ground, or any other
convenient place. I have known a swarm select a
large box standing in an inhabited house; honey has
been found in a human skull; and, as Samson found
it in the carcase of a lion, so a European told me
that he had discovered a bees' nest in the skeleton
of an elephant. When a Kafir finds a nest, he
sometimes takes it without adopting any precaution
against the stings of the insects. It may be that
smoke is occasionally used to stupify them, as among
the natives of the interior; but, in the only two instances which I have seen, nothing was done in the
one case, and in the other the operator only chewed
the root of a particular grass and spattered it over
his shoulders and breast.

In seeking honey the natives are assisted by a
small bird, which is extremely fond of the contents

of bees' nests. An extraordinary instinct enables
it to discover these; but, as it cannot obtain access, it possesses the more singular instinct of
calling other animals to its aid. "It usually sits
on a tree by the wayside, and when any passenger
approaches, greets him with its peculiar cry of
cherr-a-cherr, cherr-a-cherr. If he shows any disposition to attend to its call, it flies on before him,
in short flights from tree to tree, till it leads him to
the spot where it knows a beehive to be concealed.
It then sits still and silent till he has extracted the
honeycomb, of which it expects a portion as its
share of the spoil; and this share the natives, who
profit by its guidance, never fail to leave it. Sparr-
man states that the Ratel or Honey Badger (*Gulo
Mellivorus*) avails itself of the help of this bird to
discover the retreat of those bees that build their
nests in the ground, and shares with it the plunder
of them. Some of the Hottentots assert also that
to obtain access to the hives in hollow trees, the
honey-bird sometimes calls to its aid the wood-
pecker—a bird which finds in the larvæ or young
bees, a treat as enticing to its taste as the honey is
to that of its ingenious associate."[18]

CHAPTER III.—DOMESTIC INSTITUTIONS.

I.—RESTRICTIONS ON MARRIAGE. II.—THE PURCHASE OF WOMEN. III.—PRELIMINARIES TO MARRIAGE. IV.—MARRIAGE CEREMONIES. V.—THE MATRIMONIAL RELATION. VI.—PARENTS AND CHILDREN. VII.—DEPENDANTS.

I.— THE ties of consanguinity are very highly respected among the Kafirs. If a man were to take a wife within the degrees prohibited by custom, he would be denounced as an "evildoer," the "marriage would be dissolved, and the general belief entertained that the offspring of it would be a monster—a punishment inflicted by the ancestral spirit."[1] Mr. Fynn says that "a man cannot marry any female who is related by blood." The Commissioners observe that "no Kafir can marry a blood relation;" and they illustrate this by adding that he "cannot marry a cousin, for instance." Mr. Isaacs' language is more precise, but still indefinite; for, after stating that "no intermarriages take place between persons who are descended from the same line of progenitors," he qualifies the remark by adding, "except they be of very remote degree." When authorities like these speak with so much reserve, it may be easily believed that there is some difficulty in fixing the exact point where consanguinity ceases to be a restriction on marriage. All that I am able to add is that, according to the testimony of a native, a man does not marry one of

his own tribe—the word being understood in the
more limited sense of *family*, as before explained—
nor of any tribe (or family) descended from it; but
if the chief of the elder tribe were to take a wife
from the inferior one, his people would be at liberty
to do the same.[2]

So much for consanguinity, which, as the Commissioners remark, " forms a bar to marriage even
more strict than among the white races." Affinity,
however, does not impose the restraints which prevail among ourselves. A man, for example, may
marry two sisters; and it is the ordinary custom for
him to take his deceased brother's wife.[3] But if the
Kafirs differ from us in this respect, they do not
disregard the ties of affinity. In some cases they
impose very extraordinary restrictions on parties
connected by marriage. Thus a man is required to
be *ashamed* of his wife's mother—that is to say, he
must altogether avoid her society : he does not enter
the same hut with her; if they chance to meet on
the road, one or the other turns away— she perhaps
hiding herself behind a bush, while he screens his
face with his shield. It matters not that they may
have occasion to speak to each other—the custom
is inexorable and they must keep apart. Their communications must be made at a distance—shouting
is certainly no hardship to a Kafir—or with something to separate them, as a kraal-fence. Another
and perhaps more singular restriction is laid upon
them, for they may not even pronounce each other's
i-gama or proper name.

This is only an example, for the custom applies

to other relationships than the one just mentioned. It is not however equally rigorous in all cases. Thus, while a man cannot enter a house in which his son's wife may happen to be, but must wait until she has retired, and leave before she can return, I am not aware that any further restriction is imposed on him. And, considering that a man generally lives in his father's kraal until he has married his second wife, and that the eldest son seldom leaves, it is manifestly impossible that it should be otherwise. The custom must, in fact, prove generally inconvenient; and it may be this circumstance which has introduced another singular usage, viz. that the present of an ox or cow, made by the man to the woman, would remove this restriction of *uku-hlonipa*.[4]

In the Zulu-country, bachelors require the king's permission to take wives—a permission sometimes not given until they are thirty or thirty-five years old. The reason of its being so long withheld is that unmarried men are thought to make better soldiers than those who have wives and families to attach them to life. Tshaka permitted very few of his people to marry, but his successors have found it politic to be more indulgent. This unnatural practice, introduced by Tshaka, seems to have been based on an existing institution. My idea is that, in the normal condition of the people, no man can marry until he belongs to the class of *ama-doda* or men, the sign of which is the head-ring; but, as he cannot enter that class without the chief's consent, he is virtually unable to marry without it. When therefore he wishes to do so for the first time, he solicits permission to become an *in-doda* or man; but if the chief think him too young he probably withholds it, though a sufficient present might influence his judgment. When a person has become a "man," there is no further restriction on him in this respect, and he may marry as many wives as he pleases.[5]

II.—Though "it is publicly known" (as asserted by Mr. Dohne) "that the Kafirs have the custom of purchasing and paying for their wives," we are not, it seems, to look upon this as one of the original usages of the people. I do not mean that their customs or traditions warrant us in asserting that marriage has not always been attended with some transfer of cattle or other property; but it appears that the barbarous idea of selling women is of comparatively modern origin.

The word employed to express the act of buying a wife, supports this opinion. The verb for buy is *tenga;* but when a Kafir speaks of "buying" a wife, he uses the verb *lobola,* which means to take away a cutting, and figuratively to remove a pain.[6] It would seem therefore that the word, when applied to the act of giving cattle for a girl, refers to the pains which the mother endured in bearing and nurturing her; and that they were originally given to remove those pains—that is, to reward her for them. According to this view the cattle should belong to the mother, and so they do in one sense, as we shall see.

The practice of making an express bargain can hardly be said to have prevailed thirty years ago. "In the evidence I now give," says Mr. Fynn, "I wish to be understood as showing those Kafir customs as they prevailed prior to Europeans coming among them. If cases ever occurred in the tribes of a stipulated amount of cattle being given by a bridegroom for his bride, it was not a common occurrence. The general mode is that on the ceremony being concluded, the male friends of the bride make their demand for cattle, but not for any particular number. The bridegroom having previously arranged as to the number he will give on the occasion, presents them with apologies for the smallness of the number, or as the case may be; and is desired to come on some future occasion. The number of cattle given depends more on the wealth of the bridegroom than on any other circumstance."

There can be no doubt that the people are now impressed with the idea that, as regards marriage, woman is a legitimate article of merchandize, though they have not descended so low as to permit the purchaser to sell her again. Whether the usage mentioned by Mr. Fynn still prevails, I know not. A strict interpretation of his language would perhaps require us to understand him as saying so; but it does not appear to be common in Natal. "The general rule is, not to let the girl go before the whole payment is disposed of (a few exceptions there are; payment for widows remarried commences with a few or one head of cattle). This done to satisfaction, the purchaser demands the girl

to be brought to him." Sometimes a man delivers
to the girl's father whatever cattle he possesses,
and all others subsequently acquired until he thinks
the number given sufficient. He then requires his
bride to be sent to him, though the father may not
yet be willing to comply with his request. There
are cases in which an express bargain is made.

The price is paid in cattle, the amount varying
with the qualifications of the bride. Good looks
have their value, and a reasonable amount of corpulence is admired; but a woman's most important
recommendation is the ability to work hard. Rank
is taken into account; a rich man would expect
more than a poor one, and a chief more than his
councillor. The bridegroom's condition also would
be considered, and a less price accepted from a man
of high standing, for the sake of his alliance, than
from one of an inferior position. In Natal (where
the men easily procure cattle by working for Europeans) a tolerably good-looking spinster could hardly
be obtained, even from a poor person, for less than
six cows; while the daughters of rich men may
command twelve. Prices are much lower in the
Zulu-country.[7]

III.—It is said that the young women prefer
bachelor-beaux. I do not mean that married men
never pay them attention and are never accepted;
but have been assured that they are not general
favourites, and usually apply in the first instance to
the father. We will therefore exclude them from

consideration while treating of courtship as one of the PRELIMINARIES TO MARRIAGE, and suppose the suitor to be single. Most likely he has already had considerable experience in the art of wooing, and would make no difficulty in telling us how largely his good looks and gallant speeches had subdued maidens' hearts. Possibly he may have used unlawful as well as lawful weapons, and tried the efficacy of "spells and medicines;" for the Kafir believes in the power of philters and employs them when he deems it necessary.

Courtship is often concealed from the girl's father, and it may be in consequence of this that interviews sometimes take place at night. It is very dangerous however to enter a kraal during that season, all well-minded people being supposed to be then at home. A young man, who had acquired the good opinion of a maiden, went to visit her after sunset. When he reached the kraal, the gate was closed and everything beyond the fence abandoned to "evildoers" and wild beasts. He contrived to get inside without disturbing the dogs, and crept stealthily to the door of a hut, against which he made a preconcerted signal. It happened that he had mistaken the house; and, instead of bringing forth his favourite, the noise aroused a man, who assailed him with an assagai. The intruder uttered a fearful cry and attempted to escape, but he had received a mortal wound and was soon overtaken. When the girl came out of her hut, she burst into a fit of frantic raving, and exclaimed that they had killed her lover; but, though the discovery protected him from further violence, he died in a short time. The king, on becoming acquainted with the case, said that it was quite right to kill any person found under such circumstances in a kraal. Young men were advised to abstain from nocturnal assignations.

Courtship does not always begin with the men. A certain chief in Natal, who is generally admired by the young women, visited a friend of his own rank; when a sister of the latter fell in love with him, as he displayed his fine figure and barbaric graces in a dance. The chief was unaware of the impression he had made, until the damsel presented herself at his kraal and avowed the state of her heart. Not reciprocating the admiration, he told her to go home. She flatly refused; and, having no alternative, he permitted her to remain and sent a messenger to her brother. That personage caused her to be brought back; but she soon reappeared before the handsome chief, and begged him to kill her if he would not make her his wife. He was still unmoved, and despatched a second message to his friend, who ordered a severe beating to be administered to the girl after her return. The stripes, however, were as ineffectual as remonstrances; and ere a week had elapsed, she was a third time in the chief's presence, reiterating her protestations, but without success. When the communication reached her brother, he lost all patience and answered that his neighbour had better marry her. The chief persisted in his refusal, and there was a great interchange of messages; but, yielding at length to his councillors, he consented to negotiate. Under the circumstances, he might expect to obtain the girl at a reduced price; but five cows— the number he sent—were a very small offer, and the brother was exceedingly indignant—his sister, he said, was not a poor man's daughter—he must have at least ten cattle. When the messenger returned, the chief declined to give more, and ordered those already transmitted to be sent for. A councillor remonstrated in vain; the chief would not be reasoned with, and said that, if no one else was to do it, he would go for the cows himself. Accordingly he set off, but his advisers persuaded him to return; and he was ultimately prevailed on to make a proposal worthy of his dignity. The brother was satisfied, and a time appointed for the wedding.

In some cases, when the suitor wishes to bring his courtship to a crisis, he asks the maiden to come to his kraal. The fact of her arrival being communicated to her father, he expresses great indignation and protests that unfair means have been employed to induce his daughter to take such a step—she must return—he will not marry her to a "boy"— boys do not know how to manage their wives properly—besides how can a "boy" give him the cattle he will require—she shall be given to a married man. If he be determined, she must go home; but the prospect of a good bargain may induce him to relent. If a treaty be entered on, he takes care to ask enough, and does not forget to enumerate his child's excellencies—she is handsome—she is fat—

her arms are strong—her garden will be large—he must have plenty of cattle. On the other hand, the suitor and his friends endeavour to keep the price low.

Arrangements having been concluded with the father, a goat is killed at the suitor's kraal; or, if that animal cannot be obtained (for no other may be substituted), a present of beads is made to the girl. Until the one or the other has been done, she eats no food belonging to the kraal—a rule which occasionally proves inconvenient, for a goat is not always easy to procure, while it may be still more difficult to obtain beads. A girl has been thus obliged to fast several days. Though now at liberty to eat, the promised bride may not partake of the slaughtered goat, but must confine herself to other food. The ceremony of bethrothal being ended, she remains a few days at the kraal, and then returns home to await the celebration of the marriage.

It has been already stated that married men, not being favourites with the young women, usually make their first application to the father. A rejected suitor occasionally repairs to him, and seeks to buy a wife whose affections he has failed to obtain. If the applicant be rich and willing to pay a good price, he will have little difficulty in concluding an arrangement. When there are several candidates for the same girl, the father sometimes refuses to make an immediate bargain with any of them; and thus it may happen that " several lovers, if I may use the expression, send cattle to her father commencing paying for her. In such an instance the girl is asked to decide for herself which of those she chooses for her husband. This however is merely formal; for, if she should happen to choose one who is known to possess few cattle, the father recommends to her that one of whom he calculated to get the greatest price, and as soon as " the bridegroom is selected "the number of cattle also is fixed he has to pay."[8] Marriages are frequently " effected," says Mr. Fynn, " by the father of the female proposing to the intended husband or his parents." If a man have a particularly attractive daughter, he will take care to acquaint some rich man with the circumstance, "lest the rich should engage the girl of another;" and when young women do not receive early proposals they "are usually offered by their fathers, brothers, or friends, who go from one kraal to another until they have met with somebody who accepted of their offer."[9]

When a husband has been selected for a girl, she may be delivered to him without any previous notice; and Mr. Fynn acknowledges that in some cases this is done. But usually, he says, she is informed of her parents' intention a month or some longer time beforehand—in order, I imagine, that she may, if possible, be persuaded to think favourably of the man. Barbarians as they are, the Kafirs are aware that it is better to reason with a woman than to beat her; and I am inclined to think that moral means are usually employed to induce a girl to adopt her parents' choice, before physical arguments are resorted to. Sometimes very elaborate efforts are made, as I have been told, to produce this result.

The first step is to speak well of the man in her presence; the kraal conspire to praise him—her mother praises him—her sisters praise him—all the admirers of his cattle praise him—he was never so praised before. Unless she is very resolute, the girl may now perhaps be prevailed on to see him, when a messenger is despatched to communicate the hopeful fact and summon him to the kraal. Without loss of time, he prepares to show himself to the best advantage; he goes down to the river, and, having carefully washed his dark person, comes up again dripping and shining like a dusky Triton; but the sun soon dries his skin, and now he shines again with grease. His dancing attire is put on, a vessel of water serving for a mirror; and thus clothed in his best, and carrying shield and assagai, he sets forth, with beating heart and gallant step, to do battle with the scornful belle. Having reached the kraal, he is received with a hearty welcome; and, squatting down in the family "circle" (which is here something more than a figure of speech) he awaits the lady's appearance. Presently she comes, and sitting down near the door stares at him in silence. Then, having surveyed him sufficiently in his present attitude, she desires him through her brother (for she will not speak to him) to stand up and exhibit his proportions. The modest man is embarrassed; but the mother encourages him, and while the young ones laugh and jeer, he rises before the damsel. She now scrutinizes him in this position; and, having balanced the merits and defects of a front-view, desires him (through the same medium as before) to turn round and favour her with a different aspect. At length he receives permission to squat again, when she retires as mute as she came. The family-troop rush after her, impatient to learn her decision; but she declines to be hasty—she has not yet seen him walk, and perhaps he limps. So, next morning, the unfortunate man appears in the cattle-fold, to exhibit his paces before a larger assembly. A volley of praises is showered upon him by the interested spectators; and perhaps the girl has come to think as they think, and signifies her approval. In this case, arrangements are made for the betrothal. If, however, she is not pleased with her parents' choice, she continues silent, and probably sheds tears. She has now to encounter the wrath of her enraged father, who declares that she shall have no other husband, but remain unmarried till her hair grows white. It is in vain to protest that she cannot like the man—that it makes her sick to look at him; her furious parent will hear nothing—go with her husband she must—if she return home she shall be slain. With sobs and tears she begs him to kill her at once, for she would rather die than go with a man she cannot bear to look at.

It not unfrequently happens that the girl "elopes with the man of her own choice; from whom she may be forcibly brought back and sent to the one chosen by her father."[10] A graybeard, wishing to make an addition to his harem, arranged with a neigh-

bouring patriarch for one of his numerous daughters.
It did not occur to either of the reverend seigniors
to consult the damsel, a merry good-looking girl
of about fourteen; but she was told her destiny,
and the ceremony of betrothal having been performed, a time was appointed for the wedding.
She did not however acquiesce in her father's
disposal of her; the man was already married—
he was old—he was ugly, whereas she knew one
who was unmarried, young, handsome; and her
heart counselled her feet to run. Her purpose was
suspected or discovered; and, while sufficient care
was taken to prevent her absconding, the marriage
was hastened and some usual preparations omitted
that she might be the sooner handed over to the
custody of her husband. Another girl was more
resolute, but she had perhaps more reason; for her
husband elect, being particularly ill-favoured, had
never been able to obtain a wife; the women had
uniformly repelled his advances, and he grew so old
in singleness that Dingan told him to put on the
head-ring and take his place among the "men,"
without being married. This was only a mitigation
of his disgrace; and he was so ashamed to own
himself a bachelor, that when I once asked him how
many wives he had he mentioned some considerable
number, well knowing that I should eventually
discover he was fibbing. Though thus unfortunate, he was wealthy, and applying to a chief
offered him a very large price for one of his wards.
That worthy personage did not hesitate, and received
payment in advance; but, when the victim was

advertized of the matter, she proved rebellious and refused to go to the ugly man; chastisement having no effect, her arms were bound and she was delivered like a captive. The violence was useless, for within a few hours she escaped—not to return to the affectionate care of her guardian, but to claim the protection of a rival chief. No attempt, I believe, was made to recover her, and it was said that the royal vendor declined to return the cattle.

A man, who wished to take a certain damsel to wife, applied to her brother and guardian, and was referred to the lady. He said that he had already obtained her consent; but the brother thought it prudent to summon her, when she immediately confirmed the statement. The suitor was delighted, and went home a happy man. The damsel, however, had been acting deceitfully; and, before the day appointed for the betrothal, she left the kraal. In a short time she reappeared, accompanied by a handsome youth, to whom she was attached, and who brought a cow and calf as an earnest of his willingness to procure more. He met with a bad reception; for, when they had entered the kraal, no one offered him shelter, though the day being cloudy was very cold. He was obliged therefore to sit outside alone and shivering, until a woman invited him into a hut and made a fire to warm him. The girl's brother (to whom the kraal belonged) having discovered this, was exceedingly wroth, and rushing into the house dashed water on the fire, drove out the young man, and sent him away with his cattle. Thus ended our bachelor's

suit, but not his misfortunes; a violent thunderstorm
overtook him on the road and his cattle were lost in
the deluging rain.   When he reached home, he
found his mother weeping over the cow, which had
been torn by the hyenas and had returned without
her calf.   The unfortunate girl, whom he left at
her brother's kraal, was condemned to receive an
unmerciful beating.   From this, however, she was
sheltered by one of the women; and her brother
contented himself with ordering her to go next day
and be betrothed to the husband he had chosen.
She went, the goat was killed, and in due time
she was married.

If a girl, after being brought back, continue
to elope, "it generally happens (according to Mr.
Fynn) that her father, either of his own will or at
the intercession of the girl's mother, gives up his
original intention; and he does so, frequently, when
the amount of cattle which he receives from the
husband chosen by the girl is much less than he
would have obtained from the other party; and this
is a point of serious consideration with a Kafir."[11]

The following story will show not only how a
woman may avoid a forced marriage, but how she
may initiate a courtship, and triumph over many
difficulties.   Our heroine (for she deserves the name)
was the daughter of a man who had been comparatively wealthy; but war or other misfortune had
swept away his cattle, and he was obliged to become
a dependant.   In time his circumstances improved;
the sale of his daughters replaced a part of his herd;

and he began once more to indulge the feelings
of independence. He had yet two girls unmarried,
and his master proposed to buy them. The price
offered was very small—too small even for a poor
man's children; and he refused to accept it. The
master was indignant, and waxing exceedingly
wrathful upbraided his servant with black ingrati-
tude—he had received him when a beggar—he had
given him food to eat—and now he might not have
his daughters! The servant could storm as well
as the master; he thought his services more than
an equivalent for his food—such food at least as he
had eaten—it was nothing—when had he eaten his
master's beef? The latter threatened to carry a
complaint to the king, and as the servant persisted
in his refusal he journeyed to the Great Place and
obtained an interview with the monarch. His
appeal was not in vain; for he took back a piece of
information which quickly changed the servant's
tone, and made him glad to deliver the girls. They
were as unwilling to go, as he had been to take
them; he therefore begged that they would be
dutiful and not jeopardize their parents' safety—if
they ran away, the whole family would be killed.
His counsels were ineffectual; for, after he had
placed them in his master's kraal and was returning, they attempted to accompany him, and
would certainly have done so, if he had not driven
them back with his stick. Thus compelled to
remain, the girls sat down in the cattle-fold, and
utterly disregarded their "husband's" order to go
into a hut. The command was repeated to no

purpose; they did not even vouchsafe him a word
of refusal, but sat in sullen silence. At length he
directed them to be bound and carried into the
house, saying that unless they remained with him
quietly he should again go to the king, and kill
them and all their family. They were not to be
intimidated, and breaking silence boldly bade him
go at once—they would rather be killed than be
his wives—they wished to die; then snapping
their fingers they added, as if the man were obtuse
enough not to know it, " We don't like you—can't
you hear us ?—we don't like you." The threat was
repeated, and they were carried into the hut.

It was now night, and one of the girls, worn out
with distress and weeping, had fallen asleep. She
would have been glad to escape, but where was she
to go to? Her father would bring her back, no
neighbour would dare to shelter her, nor indeed
could any subject of Pande give her protection.
Perhaps her thoughts had wandered to the white
man's country, where many of her people had found
refuge; but the journey was long, and she could
hardly expect to reach that distant asylum. We
could scarcely therefore be surprised if she dismissed the idea, and resigned herself to the necessity of remaining where she was. But, if she slept,
her sister was awake and determined to be free.
She knew well that she could find no safety in the
Zulu-country, and that it would be difficult to reach
Natal; she was resolved, however, to brave every
danger rather than continue with her " husband."
She was drawn as well as driven towards Natal, for

among those of her tribe, who had taken refuge there, was a certain young man with whom she had been acquainted from childhood, and who had obtained possession of her heart before that evil day which compelled him to run for his life.

When she thought that the fit moment had arrived, Uzinto released herself from her bonds, and taking up her mat crept out of the hut. If she had attempted to open the entrance of the kraal, the dogs might have been disturbed or the men aroused; she determined therefore to make a way over or through the fence; and, this being done, ran across the dewy grass and began her journey. For the present she felt safe, except from hyenas and "evil-doers," but knew that when the sun arose and the people began to leave the kraals, she would incur the risk of being taken back—to say nothing of the pursuit to be expected. Soon after daylight she met a party of men, who asked where she was going. She replied, without hesitation, that she was going to see a relative amongst the Amakoba; but there were the marks of tears upon her face, and her questioners wished to know why she had been weeping. It was easy to say that she had been taking snuff, which, as the reader knows, is a lachrymal process; but they were not satisfied with the explanation, and said that the marks on her face had been produced by tears of another sort. They expressed their conviction that she was a fugitive, on the forbidden journey to Natal. Her denial of this assertion being vehement and vigorous, she was allowed to proceed.

When Uzinto reached the country of the Amakoba, the sun was setting, and she had no choice but to enter a kraal and solicit permission to remain for the night. The events of the last few days were known here; and the people, being acquainted with her, easily divined that she was absconding. When they charged her with doing so, she replied, as before, that she was going to see a relative, whose residence she now placed among another people. This was not believed, and they asked why she carried a mat (in reality a bed) if she were going to visit her relatives. She replied that it was to protect her from the rain; but they were not deceived, and said plainly that they should send a messenger to her "husband" in the morning, and detain her until an answer had been received. On hearing this, Uzinto became very desperate, wept, raved, screamed, and begged them to fetch their assagais and kill her at once. This was perhaps a piece of acting, for she shortly afterwards displayed a very good appetite when food was set before her. She was too well secured to escape during the night; and next morning, after a messenger had been sent to her "husband," she was committed to the custody of the women of the kraal. These had their own business to attend to, and contented themselves with leaving her bound in the hut. Her bonds, not being very strong, were soon severed; and, having left the kraal, she was again free. But she was not out of danger; for, before she had gone far, a boy in charge of the cattle saw her, and immediately ran to inform the women. These, who were at work in the garden, uttered exclamations of surprise and indignation, threw down their picks, and commenced a hot pursuit. They had not much difficulty in catching the fugitive, but it was another thing to manage her; she wept again, again begged them to kill her, declared that she would submit to anything rather than return, and altogether her conduct was so extraordinary that the women allowed her to escape.

She now determined to avoid the kraals and travel as much as possible in the bush—a step which obliged her to dispense with food, and exposed her to danger from the wild beasts. A terrible fright caused by a leopard was however the only accident she met with; and at the end of the fourth day, she forded the river Tugela, very tired and very hungry. But she forgot this in the thought that she was free, and beyond the reach of Pande himself.

Being now in Natal, our heroine went to a kraal not only to obtain food, but to discover where her people lived. The owner saw that she was a fugitive, and thought it a fine opportunity to gain a wife without expense. He therefore said that he knew nothing about them, and invited her to stay with him. She declined to become an inmate of his kraal, but was glad to abide with one of his wives for the night. So soon as she had the opportunity of doing so, the woman communicated privately the information which Uzinto wanted, and said that the man wished to deceive her. When our heroine departed in the morning, the master of the kraal met her in the path, and again endeavoured to prevail on her to remain. He was very liberal in his promises, he was a rich man (he said) and pointed to a herd of cattle, possibly not his own, in proof of his assertion—she should have plenty of milk, and plenty of beef—she had only to become his wife, to be happy and honoured. She listened in silence, and went on her way. A comparatively short journey brought her to the locality occupied by her people, where she was received by the chief as one of his wards.

Though our heroine had escaped from her "husband," she had yet to find the young man before mentioned. This was not very difficult, his brother's kraal being in the neighbourhood of her new home, and both families drinking of one stream. It was not singular, therefore, and may have been accidental, that while fetching water she met her favourite's young nephew. Affecting not to know him, she said that his face was not altogether strange to her, and wondered where she had seen him. The boy did not think he had seen her anywhere, and when she suggested the Folosi (a river in the Zulu-country) he observed that she was plainly mistaken, for he had never been there. The truth was that he knew her very well, and had been born at the Folosi; but he chose to deny it—partly, perhaps, because lying is a sort of second nature with some Kafirs. He may, however, have had another reason. It often falls to the lot of young boys to be entrusted with delicate commissions, when their seniors have not the courage to make a declaration in person; and the shrewd urchin, seeing the girl conceal her own knowledge of himself, probably suspected that she wished to employ him as an internuncio. But, whatever his motive, he persevered in his denial, thereby compelling her to be more explicit and say whose nephew he was. He then laughed mischievously, and confessed that she was right.

The way being now clear, she could ask after his uncle, and was not altogether pleased to find him many miles away in the service of a white man. It is possible that she knew this before, and only wanted the boy to tell his uncle that she was there and had been making enquiries about him. At all events he lost no time in carrying the important message, which his uncle received with astonishment. He had not expected her to follow him, and, I am afraid, had forgotten many of the honeyed words which he had poured into her attentive ears on the banks of the Folosi. Still he could not but feel pleased, and his reply was favourable; no present however accompanied it, and when Uzinto thought thereon her heart was sad. She resolved nevertheless not to be discouraged and patiently to bide her time. Meanwhile two suitors pay her unremitting attention; but she steadfastly repels them both, and will listen to no one until she shall have failed to subdue her old lover. One of the two, learning how matters stood, either from the girl herself or, as I suspect, from a certain garrulous confidante, immediately repaired to the favoured bachelor, and begged him

to make up his mind, for that none of them had
any chance while he remained undecided. I know
not how he answered; but sometime after, when he
had returned home and there was a gathering of
the tribe to plant the chief's corn, he sought an
interview with her. She was hoeing in a distant
part of the garden; but he contrived to find her
out, and saluted her with a friendly greeting. She
gave him no reply, nor deigned even to turn her
head. "Why don't you speak to me?" said the
puzzled bachelor; but she remained silent and
continued to work. He then advanced nearer, and
lifting up her head, looked and perhaps spoke
straight in her face. Still Uzinto made no remark,
though perhaps she might have done so, if an officer
of the chief had not espied the idlers and put a
very unromantic termination to the scene, by a
liberal use of his stick. I cannot say whether any
other interview took place until the young man
became ill; when she testified her sympathy by
paying him a visit. But she contented herself
with this mute expression of her feelings; while a
girl, who had accompanied her, uttered words of
kindness to the patient, she sat by in silence and
went away without having spoken. After his recovery, she took a little girl and set off for his
kraal under cover of the night, that she might
have an interview without exciting suspicion. The
entrance was closed, but she knew the hut appropriated to the young men, and threw a stone upon
it. The veracious urchin previously mentioned,
when he heard the signal, imagined that some

"evildoer" was near; and, had he been alone, would probably have taken the red embers from the fire and cast them over the fence to scare him away. His uncle knew better, such signals being not uncommon in the Zulu-country; but perhaps he was not altogether free from apprehension, seeing that he deputed the boy to reconnoitre and awaited the result. When he discovered who was outside, he moved with some alacrity, and admitted his persevering admirer. She was silent still, and paid no regard to his salutation. "Why don't you speak?" said he; "you deceived me when you were young; I see you don't love me." This appeal opened her lips and she answered vigorously: "No; *you* deceived *me*; I am not blind—I can see; you don't care about me; when you see me you don't feel it there" (pointing to her throat); "I can see." The young man declared that he *did* feel it there, and that she didn't, for why had she always refused to speak? Having confessed enough to satisfy her, he now asked how the chief was in the habit of addressing her; and, finding that he did not use a term which would have implied an intention to make her one of his own wives, our bachelor took courage and hoped that he might succeed. But alas—the cattle—where was he to get the cattle. It was very certain that a large price would be required (her guardian being of such high rank) while he was about as poor as poor could be. The lady, however, had a way and will of her own; and, fixing her value at ten cows, told him that when he had worked long enough to

obtain that number, she would come to his kraal
and be betrothed; if they attempted to take her
away, she would throw herself on the ground—she
knew that people were not killed in *this* country—
if everything failed, and she were violently given
to somebody else, there was plenty of water in the
river and she would drown herself. With this
decisive declaration of her mind, she left the young
man to meditate and dream.

Some time afterwards, but before he had obtained
the ten cattle, she appeared unexpectedly at the
young man's kraal, during his absence, and demanded to be betrothed. The people were afraid
to kill the goat without the chief's approval, and a
messenger was sent to acquaint him with the circumstances. His anger was aroused—she must
have been persuaded, he said, to commit the impru-
dence—it was ridiculous to think of marrying a
man without cattle—he should expect to receive a
large number—he did not wish to "beat" the
master of the kraal, but the girl must come home.
She was persuaded to submit to her guardian's will,
and returned in tears and sullenness. When entering her hut, she pitched her mat through the door-
way in a heedless but very vigorous manner;
the chief, who happened to be inside, was somewhat
inconvenienced by the unexpected projectile, and
asked whether she wished to kill them all. For
several days Uzinto continued to weep and appeared
so thoroughly miserable that the chief relented, and
promised, if she would wait, to send her to be betrothed. She dried her tears and became cheerful;

but her hope was deferred, and having long waited
to be sent she resolved to go of her own accord.
When she appeared the second time at the young
man's kraal, the people would not permit her to
enter a hut—she was the chief's girl, they said,
and he would "beat" them. Our heroine therefore
sat shivering in the cold (it was a cloudy day) until
some of the family, inspired with more courage
than the rest, said that she ought to be properly
received—she preferred one of themselves, and the
chief might say what he pleased. Uzinto was now
admitted into a hut, and before evening a goat was
slain. Next morning an unwilling messenger went
to her guardian, who stormed outrageously at the
despisers of his authority. He felt however that it
was useless to hold out against so impracticable
a girl, and required cattle to be immediately
brought. There were none forthcoming, but that
did not signify—he must have some at once; and
some were produced. The young man had four,
his brother added another by way of loan, and the
five being handed over, the chief was in a better
humour. Others were subsequently earned, and the
girl obtained her wish.

IV.—In addition to the cattle which a man pays
for his wife, he must provide others before the
actual celebration of the marriage. One of these is
described by Mr. Fynn as a cow or ox "given for
slaughter to the bride's mother and her attendants,
which is called *ukutu*, meaning the long leather
thongs for which a beast was slaughtered for the

purpose of procuring the thongs or entrails which, according to custom, were hung about the bride during her infancy. The beast referred to was probably a sacrifice to the ancestral spirit of the family. This head of cattle is always repaid by the bridegroom, and is not recoverable by law in case of divorce." Sometimes an ox, called *um-qoliswa*, is given to the father, though, as Mr. Fynn does not mention it, we must conclude that it is not common to the tribes. Another, to be slain at the marriage, is universally required. This, which I have heard denominated the Ox of the Girl, is provided by the bridegroom.

The bride's father must present at least one ox to the bridegroom. It is termed the Ox which has a Surplus, and "is a representative of several ideas: 1st, it shall represent the value of the girl, which her father places upon her; consequently the purchaser must not think that he paid too much for the girl; 2nd, and most particularly, it shall give assurance to the purchaser that the spirit of the father (*i-hloze*) after death shall not come to disturb the place where his daughter is married to, and that his girl shall bring many children. When this ox comes to the kraal of him who purchased the girl, it gets another name," and is called the Ox for Opening the Cattle-fold—the idea denoted being this, viz. that "in consequence of the purchaser's paying many cattle for the girl, his fold had been emptied almost to be shut up; but receiving now the first ox by his purchased wife, she opens the fold by this ox, and shall eventually fill it by bringing him many girls with whom he can trade in the same manner."[10]

"Marriages," says Mr. Fynn, "are conducted after various fashions, as the Kafir tribes differ from each other in some minor points in almost all their proceedings; but in the principal points they generally correspond. Without entering into unimportant particulars, the general custom is that the bride, attended by all the young women of her neighbourhood, proceeds to the kraal of the bridegroom, escorted by her male relatives and friends bearing their assagais and shields. She is also attended by her mother, and other married women. The ceremony may commence immediately on the arrival of the bride, or on the following day, as may be arranged."

"When it commences, the bridegroom and his companions seat themselves on the ground, while the bride and her attendants approach within a short distance, dancing in a semicircle. The young men connected with the bridegroom soon unite in the dance; the old women, who are related to the latter, dance around at a distance, addressing the bride in songs of a depressing nature, that she may not feel too highly elated, or assume too much importance in her new position. On the other hand, the old women who accompany her boast of her beauty and chastity, extolling her goodness of heart, and proclaiming how carefully she has been reared by her parents. The dance having continued for some time, the bride leaves her position and dances by herself in front of her companions. She then proceeds, accompanied by two of her bridesmaids, towards the bridegroom who is surrounded by his nearest relatives, and dances directly in front of him. It most frequently happens that the bride will take some liberty with the bridegroom just at this time, such as addressing him by some opprobrious term, or kicking dust in his face—thus intimating that the moment of her submission has not yet arrived.

" Her attendants then come forward with the unshafted assagais, beads, and picks, which are distributed by one of the bridesmaids to the nearest relatives of the bridegroom. An ox is slaughtered by the bridegroom, and feasting commences. This appears to be the fixing point of the ceremony. An ox or cow is then given for slaughter to the bride's mother," as before mentioned.

" Although dancing and other amusements be continued, the bridegroom and bride may from that moment be regarded as man and wife (so long as the relations of the bride remain at the bridegroom's kraal, the bride remains with her relatives), but she is not designated a wife until she has borne a child or has a house under her charge."

I have given Mr. Fynn's statement because it professes to be a general one. The following account supplies some facts which prevail among a particular tribe.

According to my own information, when the bridegroom wishes the marriage to take place, he sends the cow before mentioned to the girl's mother. The bride's head is now shaved; and in due time she proceeds to her husband's kraal, attended by male and female relatives. She reaches the gate about sunset, and gives the man a present of beads, but does not speak. She also receives a present from him, and hands it to her brother. A hut is assigned to the party, where they pass the night; but at sunrise, they leave the kraal and station themselves at some distance, like gypsies, in the grass. The day having considerably advanced, the male friends of the bride go to the bridegroom's kraal to claim the ox called *um-qoliswa*. In a case which I witnessed, they proceeded in a long file, with a step difficult to describe, being a sort of slow and measured stamping—an imitation of their dancing movement. Wearing the dress and ornaments previously mentioned as appropriated to occasions of festivity, they brandished shields and sticks—the usual equipment of a wedding-dance— while their tongues were occupied with a monotonous and unsentimental chaunt:

> " Give us the *um-qoliswa*,
> We desire the *um-qoliswa*."

In this way they entered the kraal, and turning to the right reached the principal hut. The father of the girl now called on the bridegroom, who was inside, to come forth and give them *um-qoliswa*. The latter replied that he had no ox to present them. He was then assured that the bride would be taken home; but he remained invisible until other members of the party had required him to

appear. Having left the house, he hurried to the
gateway and attempted to pass it. His exit however was barred by a company of women already in
possession of the entrance, while a smile on his face
showed that his efforts to escape were merely formal,
and that he was going through an amusing ceremony. The *um-qoliswa* was now fetched from the
herd and driven to the bride's party, who were
bivouacing under the lee of a clump of bush. Her
sisters affected to despise it as a paltry thing, and
bade the owner produce a better. He told them
that it was the largest and the fattest he could procure; but they were not satisfied—they would not
eat it. Presently the father put an end to their
noisy by-play, and accepted the beast. The bride
then ran towards the kraal, and after a while the
dances commenced.

These usually take place in the cattle-fold, and are
sometimes two in number. The one is performed
by the bride's party, the bridegroom and *his* people
sitting down near the calves' pen to witness it, and
refreshing themselves occasionally with beer. The
other is performed by the bridegroom's party,
the bride's friends in their turn sitting down.
The old women are occupied in praising and de-
preciating the bride, as before mentioned; while,
at the conclusion of each dance or during its
continuance, the leader of it makes a speech. The
father of the girl will counsel the bridegroom to
behave well to his daughter. If the swain be a
bachelor, he will be lectured on the impropriety of
beating his wife, and reminded that "boys" are too

fond of doing so; but, if already married, he may
be complimented on his wisdom, and told that
" men" know how to manage their wives without
resorting to corporal punishment. An ancient
patriarch, whose daughter had attempted to run
away before the marriage, discoursed largely on
that head, and assured her that if she absconded
now she need not come to him. He reminded the
bridegroom that, being his friend, he had accepted
a smaller price than he might have expected to
receive—when his bride wished to run away, he had
secured her and hastened the marriage—if she now
absconded, he should have another of his daughters.
The toothless man replied that he would certainly not beat the girl, and made a sensible remark
that it was of little use to give him a wife who did
not like him. The husband of our heroine, when told
not to chastise his bride, gave a conditional promise,
and undertook not to beat her if she did not beat him
—a contingency by no means unlikely to occur.
Any unpleasant circumstance, which may have
taken place in connexion with the preliminaries to
the marriage, is pretty sure to be mentioned in these
speeches, and in a way not calculated to heal the
wound occasioned.

After the dances follows the slaughter of the Ox
of the Girl—the "fixing point of the ceremony"
the real matrimonial tie. Previously to this, the
bride might be removed—a rule of which the chief
wished to take advantage when Uzinto was married.
His speech had provoked a very disrespectful reply
from the bridegroom's brother; and his wrath was

exceedingly fierce. It had not cooled when a very
small animal was produced—the smallest which the
bridegroom's means had enabled him to procure,
but utterly unfit, as he thought, to celebrate the
marriage of his ward. This fresh insult to his
dignity was intolerable, and he would have taken
the bride from the very threshold of matrimony.
Her father however (who had found it necessary
to seek refuge in Natal) was particularly desirous
to retain the cattle which had been paid; the
chief's wish therefore was disregarded, the animal
died, and our heroine was married.[11]

V.—Polygamy produces jealousy and discord.
The women are more reconciled to it than might
have been expected; and, if we were to judge by
the sociability which a man's wives display in
public, we might conclude them to be a loving
sisterhood. In reality however they are not very
harmonious; and what indeed can be expected, under
a system so unnatural, but disagreement? I have
heard it said by a native that quarrels are of frequent occurrence, and sometimes issue in actual
fights. The remedy for these disturbances of the
domestic peace is very simple; the husband generally seizes the first stick that lies in his way and
quiets the disputants by putting them to flight.
Nor does he trouble himself to enquire who gave
the first offence, but deals his blows impartially,
knowing that if he chastises all, the guilty will not
escape.

The new wife, being of course the especial object

of jealousy, is sometimes very roughly treated by the others. When particularly bitter, they will try to injure her personal appearance, as by scratching her face or tearing open the holes in the lobes of her ears, that she might be less attractive in the eyes of their common husband. If she were about to tread unwittingly on a serpent, no warning would be given; poison has been put into her food; and I have heard of one instance in which she was violently murdered. The victim was the youngest of three wives, and having been married about twelve months, had no doubt endured much previous persecution. On her husband's return home one day, he found her absent, and anxiously enquired of the others where she was. They replied that they did not know—when they went to the bush for fire-wood they left her at the kraal—when they came back they did not see her; but, on being more closely questioned, they stated that she had gone to her father's. As soon as the morning dawned he set off to follow her, and found that he had been duped. The perplexed husband now went to the prophet, who told him that the two elder wives had killed her. The information was correct; for, before he reached home, the herd boy had discovered her body. She had accompanied the others when they went to the bush, and been hanged with the string used for tying the wood in bundles.

Besides her domestic duties, the woman has to perform all the hard work; she is her husband's ox, as a Kafir once said to me,—she has been bought, he argued, and must therefore labour. When I reminded him how Europeans treat their wives, he would not acknowledge the cases to be parallel— white men did not *pay* for their wives.

The housewifery of a Kafir woman is comparatively light; a hut does not require much keeping; her cookery is very simple; she has no laundry to attend to; her children are easily scolded and as easily beaten, when she can catch them; nor has she far to go for water, though procuring fire-wood is a more difficult task; mats and pots have to be made only occasionally. Her other duties however are heavy; she has to dig the ground, weed the crops, gather the harvest, and in fact do all the ordinary work of agriculture. Besides this, the bearing of heavy burdens is generally imposed upon her; she has to fetch the materials for building the kraal, except the wood for the outer fence—an exception which seems to indicate that this fence was not an original feature of the habitations of this people. She has also to convey the wood for making fences to protect the crops. In Natal, when maize is carried to the houses of Europeans for sale, the bearers are invariably females. A man or boy probably accompanies them, but he simply marches at the head of the procession, and carries nothing heavier than his own dignity. I have known one of these supercilious idlers refuse to assist his wife to lift a basket of corn, and stand quietly by while my own servant placed it on her head.

It seems that this extremely barbarous treatment of the female sex prevails only among the Zulus, and those tribes whom they have influenced. Mr. Fynn says that among the Amampondo and Amaswazi, the fields are cultivated by the men as well as the women; and I have been told that the same thing may be seen among the Amatonga. It would appear also that the coast tribes in the Zulu-country were accustomed to this better practice; a Dwandwe man told me that his father worked in the garden during the reign of Dingane, and that old men among the Tetwas did it still. He added that these representatives of the ancient usage very much lamented a change which had diminished the supply of food, and ascribed it to Tshaka and the Zulus.

Other facts may be mentioned as illustrating the haughty contempt with which the Zulus regard their women. When the head-servant of a particular regiment met his aunt, "he gave her his hand, which she kissed with much apparent affection; but even this dignified salute was not returned." Captain Gardiner, who had observed Dingane receive similar salutations from a near relative, concluded that it was court-etiquette; but subsequently found that it was an invariable custom for women to salute their male relations, sometimes on the hand, sometimes on the cheek, the compliment never being returned. If a man were going to the bush to cut fire-wood for his wives, he and they would take different paths, and neither go nor return in company. If he were going to visit a neighbour, and wished his wife also to go, she would follow at some distance; though, if going to a wedding, they might travel together. If a man were at a feast and the master of the kraal gave him a piece of beef to carry home, he would be told to take it for his children, though it would be meant for his wives. On the other hand, if a woman were to beg a piece of meat at her father's, she would say that she wanted it for her children.

The Amalala seem to treat their wives differently; and I have heard that the Amatonga accompany them both on visits and to fetch wood. It may be mentioned, as indicating the general feelings of this latter people, that one of them who came to Natal with the view of settling there, left in disgust, because the roads (in the district where he wished to fix his residence) were too stony for his wives' feet. Perhaps it was to purchase them a present that he defrauded a fellow-servant of some money before he left.

When a woman is disobedient, it is considered by the ancient men that she ought in the first instance to be reasoned with; and that blows should be resorted to only when arguments fail. This rule is not always observed, especially by the young men, whom the elders regard as very unwise. Whether he resort to the practice in the first or second instance, a man may undoubtedly beat his wife, if he please; nor is this always done in the most gentle manner. A stick is deemed the proper instrument of punishment; but some men,

when excited, will seize anything which happens to
lie in their way—a piece of wood, for instance, a
kerie, or even a stone.

Death sometimes results from such barbarous
violence. The dependant of a rich man received a
small ration of food, during a season of scarcity.
His wife having cooked the daily allowance and
given him his share, he spoke very angrily, and
said that she had retained too much for herself.
She replied that his accusation was unjust, and that
he really could not see how much porridge the
vessel contained, owing to the steam arising from
it. This did not appease him; but he was called
away at the moment and remained some time in
the cattle-fold. Returning, he renewed the accusation; and having, in the height of his passion,
seized the heavy handle of a pick, he hurled it at
his wife and killed her on the spot. Mr. Isaacs
writes as if, in his time, it was no rare circumstance
for women to fall a sacrifice to the ferocious passions of their husbands; he had known many
instances in which a man had appointed a time
for his wife to come and meet her fate, but prior to
which she had fled to the Europeans. In this
event they would send for the husband, and, by
the joint influence of reasoning and a string or two
of beads, succeed in saving her life. Their principal chief had told his wife that she must die, for
no heavier an offence than cutting off a piece of his
kaross; expostulation and a few beads induced
him to change his mind.

A man, according to Mr. Dohne, is not legally

accountable, if he kill his wife; " she is his lawful property, just like his ox, cow, or dog, or anything he bought. It follows then that none but himself has to dispose of it. He may kill his wife, just as he does his dog, without being guilty, since he can defend himself by saying, 'I have bought her once for all.'" In partial opposition to this, an old man (the councillor of a magistrate) told me that if a person were to kill his wife without good cause, the chief would fine him a large ox.

Notwithstanding her degraded position, the woman retains a remarkable privilege. When a man takes his first wife, all the cows he possesses are regarded as her property; she uses the milk for the support of her family, and after the birth of her first son, they are called his cattle. Theoretically the husband can neither sell nor otherwise dispose of them without his wife's consent. If he wish to take a second wife and require any of these cattle for the purpose, he must obtain her concurrence. When I asked a native how this was to be procured, he said by flattery, and coaxing, or if that did not succeed, by bothering her until she yielded and told him not to do so "to-morrow."[12] Sometimes she becomes angry and tells him to take *all*, for that they are not hers but his. If she comply with her husband's polygamous desires and furnish cattle to purchase and endow a new wife, she will be entitled to her services; and will call her "my wife." She will also be entitled to the cattle received for a new wife's eldest daughter. The cattle assigned to the second wife are subject to the same rules; and so on, while fresh wives are taken. Any wife may furnish the cattle necessary to add a new member to the harem, and with the same consequences as resulted to the first wife; but it seems that the queen (as the first is called) can claim the right of refusal.

A remark of Mr. Fynn's implies that in some tribes the men disregard this privilege of the wife, and dispose of their cattle without her consent. It is more important however to know that the institution exists, than to ascertain how far it still prevails. The innovations of barbarism may have encroached on it, but enough remains to shed light on the ancient condition of the people and show that woman was not originally the degraded being she has since become.[13]

Dissolution of marriage may, in some cases, be effected by the husband. If a wife have no children, she is sent home for a time, when the father offers a sacrifice in her behalf; but if, after having returned to her husband, she continue childless, she may be dismissed and the cattle given for her recovered. Sometimes the father gives the husband another of his daughters, one or more of whose children will be accounted as belonging to her sterile sister. By this arrangement the father retains the cattle.

If a rebellious wife can be neither convinced by reasoning nor subdued by punishment, she may be dismissed, and more or less of the cattle reclaimed according to circumstances. Sometimes a woman leaves of her own accord, as in the instances of forced marriages before mentioned, or in the event of ill usage by the man or his other wives. In this case she may be reclaimed; but "if she persist in remaining at her father's kraal and can show the chief good cause, a part only of the cattle paid by the husband is returned, according to his decision. Until the cattle are repaid the husband retains the children."[14]

Adultery is of very rare occurrence—a fact which Mr. Isaacs attributes, not to the "inherent purity" of the people, but to the fear of consequences, both the offenders being punishable with death. It seems however that the husband might send the adulteress home and recover the cattle; or accept a fine and retain her. In the latter case, she would become a drudge and be treated by the other wives with the utmost contumely.[15]

Young men usually take their first wife while residing in the paternal habitation, and sometimes do not leave it until they have taken a second or third. The eldest son of the first wife seldom leaves; but when the eldest son of another does so, he takes not only the cattle of his mother's house and the dependants, but his brothers, his sisters, and his mothers. This is a complete separation of the mother from her husband.

When a man dies, those wives who have not left the kraal remain with the eldest son. If they wish to marry again, they must go to one of their late husband's brothers; in which case the children would belong to the son. If they should take any

other husband, the son might fetch them home and
claim the children, unless they had married with
his consent and cattle had been paid for them.[16]

VI.—When a child has been born, the doctor
makes small incisions on various parts of its body,
and places powdered medicine in them. Medicine is
also administered internally, while the mother is
washed with some decoction. Next day the mediciner returns; and, having cut the wounds deeper,
puts more medicine in them. The child and mother
are washed, the former being then moved about
in the smoke of a fire. Both are daubed with
a red pigment, which I have observed dis-
figuring children several months old. (Once, when
I saw this paint put on, the mother had
carefully washed a chubby boy, and made him
clean and bright; she then took up the fragment of an earthenware pot, which contained
a red fluid; and, dipping her fingers into it,
proceeded to daub her son until he became
the most grotesque looking little object it was
ever my fortune to behold. What remained,
being too precious to waste, was transferred to
her own face). The child is now permitted to
take its natural food—a privilege strangely withheld until the doctor has discharged his functions.
In one case, this important personage was at
a great distance, working with a European;
and, being unable or unwilling to attend, returned
a message, directing that the child should be
allowed to suck. The direction was misunder-

stood; and the child, receiving only the inappropriate nutriment of cow's milk, nearly died of starvation, before the mistake was rectified. For some days after the birth, the mother is secluded in her hut, no man, except the doctor, being allowed to enter. Even her husband is excluded during this period. If she have no one to work for her, and is therefore obliged to leave her house, she goes out stealthily and endeavours to avoid observation.[17]

When a woman dies in childbirth—a circumstance not uncommon—her infant is sometimes buried with her. This arises, I conceive, from the difficulty which would be experienced in bringing it up; for, as a general rule, no woman would undertake the part of wet-nurse. A person much among the people will often see a female take up a squalling infant and try to pacify it after the manner of mothers; but it never appeared to me that the child benefited by the indulgence, and I am assured that it is done only to "deceive" it. If the mother were to die a few days after the birth, when the child could  be more easily nurtured, it might be preserved and given over to the care of its paternal grandmother, or some other old woman. When twins are born, one is usually neglected and allowed to die.

Children having any great deformity are treated
in the same manner. It sometimes happens that
the mother disregards this inhuman custom.[18]

The women manifest very considerable regard
for their young children. A European, who
was in the habit of purchasing maize from the
natives, told me that if on arriving at a kraal
he anticipated any difficulty in procuring corn,
his first step was to get the children around him
and play with them. When by this means he
had ingratiated himself with the mothers, he
mentioned the object of his visit. I had in
my service a boy about ten years of age—a
good humoured merry little fellow, with whom
it was not easy to be very angry, and yet impossible to be always pleased. His thoughts
were frequently at home, and he often amused
the elder Kafirs by exclaiming that he wanted
his mother. Sometimes she came to see him,
bringing, not the "confectionary plum," but half-
a-gallon of vegetable hodge-podge, which he never
shared with others and usually finished at one
meal. When the boy had left me, I happened
to visit a kraal at some distance from my own
home, and was received by the women with a
very extraordinary welcome, one old lady seizing
my arm and kissing it. My servant explained
the mystery by saying that I was in Skafu's
kraal—the old lady being his grandmother, and
a younger one who was standing by, equally
excited but more respectful, being his mother.

When the boy left me I gave him an article worth six shillings, instead of half that sum to which he was entitled; hence my reception.

It seems to be a necessary consequence of polygamy, that the father should feel less attachment to his children than the mother. Two brothers were returning from a long journey, during which one of them had lost a child. My servant, whom they called to see, was a near relative of theirs and communicated the painful fact. I was aware that this had been done, but did not know which of the two travellers was the bereaved parent. With this uncertainty, I went into the hut, where a smoking vessel of boiled maize had been set before them. One was eating and talking loudly; the other was silent and fasting. The evidence was conclusive; and not wishing to pain the afflicted man, I addressed myself to his loquacious brother. Having obtained the information I wanted, I left the hut, sincerely pitying the pensive man, and presented him with a piece of beef—a dainty which had revived the appetite of even a despairing lover. My sympathy was misplaced and my beef ill-bestowed; the pensive man, as I discovered after their departure, was indisposed—the voracious and talkative one was the father bereft of his child. We must not however judge of all by this example; I knew a person who took great pleasure in talking of his child and describing her little tricks (he was very young and the child his first-born); while another, who had recently lost two children, might have served the sculptor for a study of Grief.

Mr. Isaacs asserts that both parents seem most attached to their female children, for (says he) an instance of severity was scarcely seen towards them, while the boys often received an immoderate share of chastisement. This preference may be explained by the superior *value* of the girls, but it must not be supposed that boys are little regarded. In the normal condition of the people, when the general practice of cattle-stealing rendered life and property insecure, a number of valiant sons would be like "the arrows in the hand of the giant." Tshaka forbade robbery, and this may have tended to make men set less value on their male children; but boys are certainly held in great esteem and desired in due proportion. A native, who was giving me an example of prayer to the spirits, introduced a petition for plenty of boys and a few girls. The former increase a man's importance in the chief's eyes; he shares the honour they may acquire in war; when they grow up and settle around him, he becomes a little chief. We can imagine the pride with which the old man goes from kraal to kraal, advising here, commending or reproving there, respected and obeyed everywhere; or with what complacency he looks around him from the hill on which his own habitation stands, and viewing those of his children, says inly, "They are all mine," and receives the congratulations of his neighbour, who praises him as a great man and flatters him with the salutation of chief. He is a

real patriarch; and, if he were to remove to an unoccupied country, would become the natural independent ruler of his people. It is in this way
doubtless that the various tribes have originated.

We have already seen that, when young women
refuse to accept husbands chosen by their parents,
they are sometimes treated with great severity.
Mr. Dohne asserts, with reference to such cases,
that a Kafir loves his cattle more than his daughter;
and, in justification of the statement mentions instances in which " the girl had become christianized
or only civilized, and would not allow herself to be
made an article of trade. She was cursed, dis-
owned—yea, if her father and friends had had it in
their power, she would have been killed without
mercy." It must be remembered that the mother
sometimes induces the father to relent.

The father's authority over his children, so long
as they continue with him, is very great. We have
seen that parents occasionally kill their young children, and I have been told that a man might put
to death even an adult son living in his kraal. A
venerable patriarch, to whom I mentioned this subject, said that no father would act with such severity;
but, if his son were very undutiful, would drive
him away and retain his cattle. Generally, murder
is punished by fine, but in case of parricide death
is usually inflicted.[19]

VII.—Necessitous persons resort to those who
are prosperous, and seek to become their DEPEND-

ANTS.[20] A man's importance being increased in proportion to the number of his followers, indigent people have little difficulty in finding a patron willing to receive them. When admitted into his service, they are attached to one or more of the houses of his wives, and "employed in servile work." I believe however that, as the general rule, men perform only such tasks as are appropriated to their class; for example, they cut wood, make fences, prepare land for cultivation, and milk the cows. Dependants build their huts near the entrance to the kraal; but some, who possess a few cattle, are allowed to have separate establishments in the neighbourhood. A man's head-servant is called his *in-duna*—a name applied to the principal officers of a chief.

Cows are usually lent to dependants to furnish milk for themselves and their families; vegetable food is supplied until, in the case of married men, their wives have been able to provide it by tillage; when beef is slaughtered they are not forgotten; if they are sick and unable to purchase medicine, it is bought for them; if a sacrifice is required in their behalf, the master would not withhold it. Mr. Fynn states that they are permitted to retain whatever they may acquire by the practice of "any healing art or handicraft with which they may be acquainted;"[21] and that, when they accompany him to war, the master not unfrequently gives them a portion of the captured cattle.

Though death has sometimes been inflicted on

dependants attempting to withdraw, it seems
generally acknowledged that they are entitled to
leave.[22] This circumstance occasions them more
independence than they might otherwise enjoy,
for a person does not like to be deserted by his
people and see them prefer the service of another.
A rich proprietor, on the occasion of his son's
marriage, asked a dependant to supply the ox
called *um-qoliswa*. The man had a tolerably
large herd, the whole or greater portion of which
belonged in reality to the other, but he would not
part with a single bullock. The master was
furious at the denial; but the servant was equally
excited, and told him to take back *all* his cattle.
He yielded at length, and surrendered the animal.

Dependants are "generally permitted to leave
with the cattle which have been given to them; or,
if not, they are allowed to leave, retaining the cattle
as a loan, whose offspring may be claimed from
time to time by the proprietor, as well as the
original stock. Such cases, however, are the causes
of extensive litigation; and the numerous cases
which exist at the present time are occasioned by
so many tribes dwelling in a peaceful condition
under British rule."[23] When a servant withdraws
from his master, he may be called upon to make
compensation for the cost of medicine purchased on
his account, for sacrifices offered in his behalf, and
for cattle furnished to enable him to marry. If he
could not do this, the master might keep one of his
daughters. The widow of a dependant being ill,
and the prophet having directed an offering to be

made, the master sacrificed a cow and the woman recovered. Subsequently she married again and left, when the husband being unable to replace the cow, one of her daughters was retained. She considered this unjust; her husband had died in his master's service and she had thrown away his corpse; she ought therefore to have received from the master a cow to sacrifice on the occasion. He did not however furnish one; and it was, she said, to the omission of this ceremony that the prophet ascribed her sickness. Isaacs recovered the child, and restored her to her mother.

An old woman, who had been reduced to want, was received into a kraal, and employed in such work as she could perform. While able to stagger under a burden of fire-wood or carry a vessel of water, she was fed; but eventually she became blind. The women who had supplied her with victuals now told her to leave—she was useless and should not eat their food—why should they be burdened to maintain a person unable to work? The helpless creature was beaten, driven away, and left to wander. She groped about, with her hard, work-worn fingers, in the hope of detecting some edible root or fruit; but the search was vain— she could not even find the water—and ere long she died.

Solitary young females, who have been received as dependants, "marry with precisely the same ceremonies as those of the tribe, and are called the daughters of their guardian, who offers sacrifices when they are attacked by sickness, as he would for his own children. Years may elapse before such a female meets with her real relations." If however they discover her retreat they may claim the cattle received from her husband, but must pay one head for her nurture, and restore those which had been sacrificed in her behalf or given at the marriage. " I have frequently known it occur," says Mr. Fynn, " that females so situated as not to know where their relatives were, rather than not have a claimant, have secretly arranged with strangers to declare relationship. I can only account for this extraordinary proceeding by attributing it to a natural impression that the husband would have more respect for one who had a parent or relatives than for an orphan."

CHAP. IV.—POLITICAL INSTITUTIONS.

I.—THE NORMAL GOVERNMENT OF THE TRIBES. II.—THE ZULU
GOVERNMENT. III.—ADVENTURES OF A CHIEF.

I.—In describing the political institutions of this people, we must distinguish between the Zulu government, and what may be called the NORMAL GOVERNMENT of the tribes generally. The latter, which obtained before Tshaka's conquests, formed the basis of that established by himself, and is naturally adopted by the tribes in Natal, so far as the action of British authority permits.

The normal government is patriarchal, a tribe being only a larger family, of which the chief may be regarded as father: *'baba*, my father, is, in fact, one of the titles by which he is addressed. His relationship to the people is therefore more intimate than that of a mere governor; for, while they obey his commands, they seek his advice, and in some cases obtain more substantial help. "He is the centre of their thoughts and actions; with him rest their prospects and even their lives; they are entirely dependent on him and their parents for counsel and aid, not only in marrying but in every emergency."[1]

Though the chief be thus theoretically absolute, in practice he is not so, being "obliged," says Mr. Fynn, "to consider what effect his commands will have on the minds of his followers. Even Tshaka, one of the greatest despots who ever governed any nation, constantly kept this consideration in view, being perfectly aware that his reign would soon terminate, if he opposed the general will of his people." If then the will of the people was thus potent under the iron sway of the great Zulu king, we can imagine the position of a normal chief, and believe that it requires more than hereditary title to ensure submission to his will. The principal means which he employs for that purpose is the prophet or seer, of whom it has been said that he is the great lever by which the chief exercises his power.

It must be acknowledged, however, that, notwithstanding their democratic tendency, these people entertain great respect for authority. They are trained to it by that reverence which custom requires them to show towards their parents, and which the " men " exact from the " boys." A chief therefore who succeeded in corroborating his hereditary title, and possessed a good reputation for wisdom and courage, might acquire great influence over his followers.

There are three classes of officers connected with the government of a tribe. The most important are *izin-duna* (the literal meaning of the word being bulls of a year old) divided into great and small. The former are the chief's councillors and principal ministers of state; the latter are of inferior rank, and perform subordinate duties. The two other classes are *aba-yisa* (which should mean cattle herds) and *ama-pini* (axe-handles). They are appointed, I believe, by the *izin-duna*, and are promoted to the lower division of that rank, if they discharge their office well, and appear worthy of the advancement.

The Great Place (as the chief's residence is termed) is the resort of all the principal men of the tribe, who attend "for the purpose of paying their respects to the chief." Their "visits may extend from one week to four or five months, when they return to their petty chieftainships or kraals, and others arrive. The followers of a chief, while in attendance upon him at his kraal, are generally designated *ama-pakati*," those within (the chief's circle). "He generally occupies each day with his *ama-pakati*; the topics of the time engage their attention; trials of criminal and civil cases employ a portion of their time."[2]

The chief's wives are more numerous than a subject's; and in the Zulu-country are carefully secluded from view, not only at the king's court, but at those of the dependent chiefs. The influential position which they occupy in the government of the tribe will be subsequently referred to. The chief's mother is also of great consequence, and is treated with much respect. She shares what I suppose to be one of his highest titles, and is called the Elephantess, while his great wife is called the Lioness.

Though a considerable amount of authority

is exercised by the owner of a kraal over his children and dependants, important causes must be referred to the chief, who investigates them, it has been already said, in the presence of his *ama-pakati*. " As there are no professional lawyers, every *um-pakati* may enter freely into the case; and, from the ridicule which would result from the interference of one incompetent to argue the cause, it seldom happens that any display of incompetency occurs. Thus the chief's residence may be termed the school where law is taught, and its rules transmitted from one generation to another."

It is in forensic debates that the Kafir's mind appears to most advantage; and no one can witness the intellectual gladiatorship displayed on such occasions " without being convinced that in their case intellect has not been affected by the distinction of colour or clime."[3] But, though their pleading is acute, it is very tedious and almost interminable; they have no idea of separating relevant from irrelevant matter, ʹbut go on from beginning to end, detailing every circumstance, whether important to the question or not. " If you cut them short and tell them to get to the point, they will begin all over again. It is of no use being impatient; you cannot hurry them; a Kafir can always talk against time."[4] He also possesses the art of making the worse appear the better cause. " Without minutely examining him, you might be led to conclude that everything he says is indisputable, and that he has been grievously wronged; but, on interrogating him closely, you will soon discover that the fellow's tale has been a fabrication, designed to get you to punish his enemy, or to exact something as a peace-offering for himself. Nothing can be more common than impositions of this kind, which required our attention to guard against."[5]

The parties, in a cause, and the witnesses are sworn—Mr. Isaacs says by the spirit of their forefathers, but I suspect there is some mistake in this part of the statement. Oaths are sworn (1) by living persons. The most common is a mere invocation of the chief, sometimes by that general title, sometimes by his proper name. They are sworn also by an ornament belonging to the chief, and by his palace. A man sometimes swears by his father and sometimes by his wife's mother, while a woman will swear by her husband's father.[6] (2.) Oaths are sworn by deceased chiefs, as by Tshaka and Dingane; and by a deceased father. (3.) A third class of oaths consist in the person's declaring that he will do something peculiarly enormous; he may say, for instance, "let me eat my father's bones," or "I will enter the seraglio." Oaths of the first class are not entitled to much regard, nor perhaps are those of the second; but it is otherwise as to those of the third, and I am disposed to think that these are the oaths required to be taken before the chief in all important causes.

The Kafirs "may be said in their customs to

possess laws which meet every crime that may
be committed." The administration of them is
however rendered very corrupt by the injustice
of the judges; for (says Mr. Fynn) " cupidity,
which is a strongly developed feature of the
Kafir character, will not permit either the chief
or those who surround him, and between whom
the fine is generally distributed, to forego the
advantage to be derived from the infliction of
heavy fines." The Commissioners say that bribery
is nearly universal. In what may be called
civil causes, justice is done by restoring the
property, and making an allowance or not according to circumstances. These causes are chiefly
connected with marriage-questions and disputes
between a man and his dependants. If cattle
trespass in a corn-field, the owner must " make
reparation by giving a cow or a calf, according
to the extent of the damage done."

The following list of crimes and their punish-
ments is based on Mr. Fynn's evidence.

Theft	Restitution and fine.
Injuring cattle . .	Death or fine, according to circumstances.
Causing cattle to abort.	Heavy fine.
Arson	Fine.
False witness . . .	Heavy fine.
Maiming . . .	Fine.
Adultery . . .	Fine; sometimes death.
Rape	Fine; sometimes death.
Using love philters .	Death or fine, according to circumstances.
Poisoning and practices with an evil intent (termed " witchcraft ")	Death and confiscation.

Murder	Death or fine, according to circumstances. (When a chief or parent is murdered, death is usually inflicted. In other cases only a fine is levied).
Treason, as contriving the death of a chief; conveying information to the enemy. . .	Death and confiscation.
Desertion from the Tribe	Death and confiscation.

A husband's authority being absolute, he may inflict capital punishment on his wife without reference to the chief. A woman, carrying her infant, went to visit a married sister. The latter having taken the child and kissed him, he cried lustily, and continued to do so for some time. The mother returned home, and within two days the child died. It was suspected that the aunt had administered poison, and her husband was applied to. He denied that his wife was an "evildoer;" nevertheless—to satisfy the accuser, who was rich, and his brother, who was an *in-duna*—he would kill her, and she was forthwith strangled. In the following instance a wife was killed by her husband's brother. A wealthy man, having lost one of his wives, was assured by the prophet that she had been poisoned by a wife of his brother. That person was of a different opinion and attributed her death to the anger of the spirits. Sumali was therefore spared, but afterwards, when another wife died, suspicion again fell on her, and the bereaved husband determined that she should be slain. Accompanied by some of his people, he went to his brother's kraal

and announced his determination to kill the alleged
"evildoer." Her husband wept, for she was a
favourite; and his mother advised him to resist.
He was afraid to do so; his wife had been accused
by the prophet, he was a poor man, he was dependent
on his brother, and thought it best to submit. Sumali, knowing that her fate was inevitable, had put
on her dancing-dress and ornaments, and was told
to accompany her executioners to the bush. She
now kissed her children; and, taking up the
youngest, requested, in vain, that it might be killed
with her. The child having been forcibly removed
from her arms, she was led out of the kraal and
strangled.

The chief's revenue consists mainly of fines and
confiscations. When a man slaughters an ox or
cow, the chief is entitled to a portion; but those
who live at a distance from the Great Place and
are in the habit of killing beef, send him a beast
annually in lieu of the occasional tribute. He also
summons the people to cultivate his gardens, reap
his crops, and make his fences; but in this, as in
other respects, he has to consult the popular will,
and hence the manual labour required by the chiefs
has always been of very limited duration.[8] This
tax is the more reasonable, as the men, when they
attend at the Great Place, are fed by the chief.

The chieftainship is hereditary, but not in the
eldest or any particular son. In some tribes, the
chief nominates his successor on the approach of

death; or, if this be omitted, he is chosen by the
great men and councillors, after the chief's death.
He must be the son of the chief by a lawful wife.
In other tribes "the arrangements are completed
by establishing the rank of the house, each wife
being looked upon as the head of a house during
the chief's lifetime; and this requires an elaborate
organization. The domestic establishment of a chief
and his tribe is usually divided into three principal
HOUSES, which may be called SECTIONS. Each of
these is again subdivided under the headship of
the particular house to which it belongs; and these
divisions are to all intents and purposes, separate
and distinct, and united only in the person of the
chief. Every section, principal and minor, is presided over by one of the chief's wives, whose son
becomes heir to it; and which has its own peculiar
rank and property descending to the heir thus born
within it, as regularly as if it were an independent
house, and unconnected with any other part of the
tribe. This inheritance reverts to one of the other
sections or houses, only on the failure of issue within
itself, and then by regular gradation. The three
principal sections are called the *Right Hand*, the
Great, and the *Left Hand* houses.

"The ranks of all the wives, who are at the head
of these principal as well as smaller houses, are
conferred by the appointment of the chief and his
"men" (as the councillors of a tribe are usually
called *par excellence*), except that of the Right hand
House, which belongs, as a matter of right, to the
wife first married; whose rank, and that of her son

are not capable of any modification. He cannot however succeed to the chieftainship, until issue from all the other houses have failed. He is hereditary regent of the tribe, and head under the chief of that part of it which belongs to his mother's house. This house, being the senior, is the depository of the family charms and medicines. It is the one which the chief inhabits during the periods of purification, or other ceremonies, which are presided over by what are commonly called witch-doctors, but whose functions appear to assimilate more with those of a priesthood. It is therefore more or less sacred in the eyes of the people, as during such times the chief may not enter any other. These immunities and its other conservative functions secure to it considerable influence in the tribe; and, for this reason, it is always more nearly connected with the Great House, although of inferior rank to that of the Left Hand. It will be remembered that the influence of this house has had the advantage of being enhanced and consolidated by time; its rank accrued the day of the woman's marriage; and in all probability she was the only wife of five or six who held any definite rank at all, because that of the others is created at or after the marriage of the wife who is to bear the heir to the chieftainship over all; and she is seldom taken to wife until the chief has passed the meridian of life, and his first-born son has attained to the age of manhood.

"The Great House is presided over by the great wife, who is to bear *the* heir. The time of her marriage is a season of great festivity with the tribe. The men assemble together at the Great Place, and witness the ceremony. A subscription of cattle from among the tribe pays for her; and thus, with her progeny, she becomes its peculiar property. Her rank is superior to all others; and, although during the chief's lifetime, her son is merely the head of the section called the Great House, he is the heir to his father's rank over the whole tribe.

"This long delay in the appointment of a successor, or rather of the wife that is to bear him, together with the almost absolute bar that is placed to the succession of the first born, appear to be arrangements made to obviate a danger which in all savage tribes is one of no ordinary character to the life of the reigning chief— viz: that of assassination or violent expulsion by an ambitious heir. This is however prevented: and the consequence is that the chief frequently dies, leaving his heir a minor, when the regency is undertaken by the first wife."[9] It is implied, in a remark of Mr. Isaacs, that in the Zulu-country the appearance of wrinkles or grey hairs would be very likely to prove fatal to the chief. I am unable to say whether this applies to the normal condition of the people, but have certainly heard it said that when a chief's hairs become grey, his sons enquire why he does not die, and often begin to plot against him.

They sometimes plot against each other, and that during their father's life. A chief in the

Zulu-country had two sons, the elder of whom
wished to be appointed his father's successor.
The old man refused his request and would listen
to no remonstrance; when the ambitious young
man determined to destroy his more fortunate
brother. Accompanied by some dependants, he
went during the night to the latter's kraal, where
he rattled a dry hide and made other noises
to disturb the cattle and alarm the people. His
brother, thinking that a wild beast had entered
the fold, crept out of his hut, and was assagai'd
before he rose to his feet; while the dependants
who left their huts more slowly, feeling less
interest in the safety of the herd, were killed in
the same manner. The fratricide, having given
his followers an ox to eat, drove the rest of the
cattle home and added them to his own herd.
When the murder came to the king's knowledge,
that personage did not think it politic to interfere;
he had himself conspired against his brother and
done his best to kill him, while Dingane had
killed Tshaka; he did not understand the customs
of the tribe. It is said however that the culprit
was fined, owing perhaps to the interposition of
the great officers.

When the old chief died, the murderer was
recognised as his successor both by the tribe
and by the King. The former regarded him
nevertheless with great dislike; and, several deaths
occurring in his family, they attributed them to the
spirits who were supposed to be punishing him
for his brother's murder. He, of course, ascribed

them to a different origin, and caused several persons to be slain as "evildoers." These proceedings were viewed with great suspicion by the king's principal councillors, one of whom declared that on the next occasion *he* should consult the prophet and ascertain the true cause of the repeated calamities. After a while, another death occurred, when the councillor fulfilled his resolution and heard the prophet ascribe the misfortune, not to an "evildoer," but to the spirits. No more people were allowed to be slain.

II.—The ZULU GOVERNMENT was established by Tshaka, who succeeded to the chieftainship of the Zulus between forty and fifty years ago, and subdued nearly all the people between Delagoa Bay and the Frontier tribes. After a reign of about twenty years, he was killed and succeeded by his brother Dingane; who, in turn, was deposed and succeeded by another brother, Pande, the present ruler of the Zulu-country.

The government established by Tshaka differs from the normal type principally in this, that the chief or king is absolute. Tshaka was as complete an autocrat as ever lived. His influence was most extraordinary, while the cruelty with which he exercised it was truly diabolical. His successor possessed less ability; but he was equally unfeeling. In his reign, and it may be said in that of Tshaka, there was no to-morrow for the Zulu, who therefore replied to every promise with the proverb, " Give it to-day; before to-morrow I may be killed."[10]   Pande, who is perhaps less blood-thirsty, has also been restrained by the knowledge that his oppressed subjects could find an asylum in the British colony of Natal.

It has been previously stated that, with all his despotism, Tshaka had to pay some regard to the will of his people. We cannot wonder, therefore, that Dingane and the still more feeble Pande have felt themselves obliged to do so. In Tshaka's time the men, being chiefly unmarried, were pervaded by a martial spirit; but, the rule of celibacy having been relaxed by his successors, they are now divided in their interests and wishes—the "men" desiring peace, while the "boys" are more inclined to the excitement of war.

It appears that Natal owes something to the elder warriors, for the security it has enjoyed. It is not to be supposed that Pande looks with any satisfaction on that colony, where so many of his people have taken refuge. It contains also an abundance of cattle, while the plunder of the merchants' stores would yield a rich harvest of blankets and beads. The young soldiers—thoughtless, reckless barbarians, individually without courage, but heedless of danger when in a body—are said to hold the white man in contempt, and represented as impatient to distinguish themselves against him. When assembled to dance, they ask the king to send them into Natal, whence they promise to bring multitudes of fine cattle, and plenty of *hats* to prove that the Englishman's gun cannot protect him

against their conquering assagai. Pande affects to
have no confidence in them; but he praises their
spirit, and seems both to approve and expect this
expression of their views. A man, who at a dance
was next to my informant, having neglected to
follow the example of his comrades and descant on
the facility of ducking to avoid a bullet, the king
reproached him with cowardice, saying that he was
evidently becoming tired of war and wished to
marry: "I see—you want a wife. I remember
your mother requested that you might be allowed
to marry, because you were her only son. I shall
kill you." Then, turning to my informant, Pande
asked what *he* had to say. Never was there a
more arrant coward than this "boy;" but boasting
was safe, and springing to his feet he spoke like a
brave: "Yes, O Elephant. You see me. I'll go
against the white man. His gun is nothing. I'll
rush upon him quickly, before he has time to shoot,
or I'll stoop down and avoid the ball. See how
I'll kill him;" and forthwith his stick did the work
of an assagai in the body of an imaginary European. Pande insinuated that his assagai was a
poor weapon with which to fight a white man; but
the "boy" protested that it was far better than a
musket, and that he would be a great deal too active
for any white man. Our brave's hereditary chief
had found refuge in Natal; and Pande now hinted
that, if an army were sent thither, the "boy"
would prove traitor and not act against his natural
governor; but he repelled the insinuation with
great vehemence, and I have no doubt denounced

his chief as an ungrateful and incorrigible scoundrel. At all events he declared that he was ready to kill him with as little hesitation as he would kill any other man whether black or white.

Though Pande and his young warriors may despise the colonists, the "men" are far from agreeing with them, and, if ordered to invade Natal, would, as I am assured, positively refuse to do so. They have had experience of warfare with Europeans, and retain a lively recollection of the guns and horses of the boers. It is true that few of the English are mounted; but they are known to possess cannon, to which, I suppose, the submission of the boers is attributed. They are not acquainted with these mighty engines from experience, but have heard of the artillery-practice at Pieter-Maritzburg, and hold them in mortal dread; they believe that the fearful *by-and-bye* eats up everything—grass, stones, rocks—and why not *ama-doda*? I have heard this given as the explanation of their unwillingness to invade Natal.[11]

I have already had occasion to speak of the division of a tribe into subordinate tribes or families, each having a chief, but all being subject to the chief of the principal or parent tribe. Of these there were some who acknowledged the authority of Tshaka's father, and who may be included under the general term of Zulus, though that name applies more particularly to the parent tribe. When, therefore, Tshaka began his career, he was a little lord paramount; but only after the normal fashion, and as many other chiefs were. The tribes whom he conquered, did not receive uniform treatment. Those who first submitted, appear to have been left very much as they were, except that they were required to obey his commands and serve in his army. They were more liable however to become the objects of violence and cruelty; and thus it has happened that nearly all have removed, some beyond the Maputa, and some to Natal. Those who remain are chiefly of the Tetwa nation.

Chiefs subject to the Zulu monarch exercise considerable authority over their own people, though, of course, liable to be controlled by the king, who sometimes sets aside the regular succession to the chieftainship, and gives it to an individual of his own choosing. The following anecdote relates to the chief of a division of the Zulu tribe. He had lost a son, when one of Pande's wives despatched a messenger to express her sorrow to the bereaved parent. The individual selected for this office was a young unmarried man, who may be pardoned if the honour made him feel unusually important, and involved him in sundry quarrels respecting the right to the path. When he reached his destination he found the gate crowded with people assembled to condole with their chief; but he made his way through the press, and appeared inside the kraal. A councillor, perceiving the stranger, sent a servant to ask his business; but our "boy" was not going to parley with a dependant, and answered gruffly, "I shan't tell you."

The humble man said that he had been ordered to make the enquiry; but this did not appal the important "boy," and the servant returned. A second who was sent, met with as little ceremony as the other; and the messenger, laying aside his weapons, went straight to the chief's hut. He did not, with all his presumption, dare to go inside; but stood at the door and pronounced the chief's titles, when he had finished the roll, a voice came from the hut:

"*Au!* where do you come from?"

From Indaba-ka-aumbi, O Elephant."

"*Au!* what do you want?"

The "boy" explained his errand.

"*Au!* go into Nongwengu's hut, and when the sun has gone down a good deal, you shall see me."

"Yes, O Elephant;" and away goes the messenger to the hut mentioned; where, having nothing else to do, he is soon asleep. By and bye a refreshment is sent, in the shape of a bundle of sweet reeds, when etiquette requires him to go again to the chief, and repeat as many of his titles as he may think the gift deserves. He then returns, and after a while receives a more substantial present of boiled beef. The sight of the smoking mess inspires him with great alacrity, and he is soon standing by the chief's door, pronouncing his titles in full tale and with much energy. Having rendered sufficient thanks for so rich a gift, he speedily returns to the savory dish, and feels himself a happy man. A bowl of beer would have completed his enjoyment, but there did not happen to be any at the kraal, or the chief was stingy, and he was content with a less potent beverage. Towards the close of the day and when the cattle had been brought home, our " boy " leaves the hut, and finds the chief sitting at the kraal-gate. He salutes him as before, and delivers his message—the substance of which was that it was very unfortunate the child had died—that they who sent him were very sorry, and that the spirits of his ancestors did not seem to take proper care of him.

The Zulus have not admitted all the people whom they conquered to the same privileges. Some were deemed unfit for anything but tributaries. The Amatonga are of this class. The low country which they occupy, is peculiarly unhealthy, at least in summer, and equally fatal to black and white visitors. Owing probably to this circumstance, they are believed by their neighbours to be especially skilled in the art of poisoning, at all events they are regarded as egregious " evildoers; " every sort of crime and abomination is attributed to them, and I doubt whether any respectable Zulu would eat in their company. Their reputation is no doubt worse than they deserve, but white visitors have given them a bad character. We cannot wonder that the Zulu kings have never incorporated them with the nation. They are simply put under tribute, which consists of skins, calico, and metal—the two last being obtained from the Portuguese.[11]

The king's residence is built of the same materi-

als, and presents the same general appearance as
that of his subjects. It is however much larger,
and the reader must imagine the outer fence to
have a diameter of from twelve hundred yards
to a mile. He may also imagine the upper part
of an ordinary kraal—namely, the space about the
chief hut—to be enclosed by a fence when he
will have an idea of the *isi-gohlo* or palace.
This, which is appropriated to the king and the
women of his family, is furnished with several
huts—the largest being constructed in a peculiar
manner. (Behind the large kraal is a smaller
one, called *ama-pota*, for the women). The remaining space between the two fences is occupied
by about one thousand huts, for the use of the
soldiers. The cattle-pens are formed at the sides
of the central enclosure, by which means a large
vacant space is left for the assembling of the
warriors. This will give the reader a sufficient
though not an exact notion of the king's kraal;
but it must not be supposed that there is only
one of the sort. There are from twelve to
fifteen such establishments, each appropriated to
a particular regiment.

The king's wives, of whose number I never
obtained any other estimate than " plenty, plenty,"
are distributed among the various kraals, and with
them are associated numerous concubines. His
mothers live in the palace, and have under their
care a large class of girls, who do the work of
servants both in the *isi-gohlo* and the garden, and
whom he sometimes marries to his great men.

Of male attendants he has (1) a sort of *valets,* who appear to wear his cast-off clothes. When he is sick they are obliged to allow themselves to be wounded, that a portion of their blood may be introduced into the king's circulation, and a portion of his into theirs. They are usually killed at their master's death, unless they take time by the forelock and escape. One who foolishly presented himself before the *ama-pakati* while they were lamenting the chief's demise, was immediately slain. When they escape it must be to a tribe among whom they are unknown, for no chief would willingly receive the *um-siya* of another.[12] (2) *Praisers,* who repeat his titles and praise him. (3) *Sentinels,* who were introduced by Tshaka at the suggestion of a Frontier Kafir. (4) *Izim-qeko,* who cook and do whatever they may be ordered to do. (5) *Milkers.* (6) *Porters,* who close the gates at night and open them in the morning.

As a general rule no man is allowed to enter the place or the *ama-pota,* unless his occupation render it necessary. The sentinels alone enter that part appropriated to the king's wives and concubines, to open and close the entrances. These officials are sometimes very ill-favoured. "The man at the Umvoti," said my servant, "with a foot turned under his leg would make a sentinel; the man with bad eyes, who never could get a wife, would do; Bambula's brother" —he had a very protuberant chest—"would be a very good one; anybody whom the girls won't like would do."

" You would do."

" No ! they all liked me."

" You lived in the sentinel's hut."

"That was only while I was very young. Pande told me to live there. I was a milker. When he gave me a shield, he sent me to live with the cooks."

" How do you know that the girls liked you ?"

"They told me so, and complained that I would never listen to them. When I took the milk into the white palace, they used to ask me for some. I told them I should not give them any and that they ought to ask a queen for it."

"Was it for refusing to give his girls milk, that you had to run away from Pande ?"

" No. A man said that Pande was going to kill me, because he had heard that I had been talking with his girls. I therefore ran as soon as I could. But it was false, and I have been told that Pande was very sorry, and said that he did not wish to kill me."

" Were you ever in the palace when you had no business there ?"

" Yes, in the white palace. One of the queens asked me to come into her hut, and gave me plenty of food. She belonged to my tribe. Before long we heard the king coming, and were in a great fright. I don't know what he wanted ; there is a gate from the black to the white *isi-gohlo*. The women hid me behind them, but when he came into the hut he saw me."

" What did he say ?"

"*Wau*! he was very angry, and my heart beat very fast, for I expected that he would order me to be killed. But the queen told him that she had invited me into her house, to hear news about her family. The king told me not to do so to-morrow. Men sometimes climb over the fence at night."

"When the girls go to work in the garden, do they talk to the men?"

"They try to do so. They begin by asking for snuff."

"What do you say to them?"

"Speak to them roughly, and say you have none. Pande likes to hear that you have treated them so. If you were to give them snuff, or only to say gently 'No, *'mtakababa*, I have none,' you are dead; the sentinels who are squatting in the grass, would pounce upon you at once, and take you to the king."

"Are the sentinels always with them?"

"They follow at a distance to watch them."[13]

III.—The following story will give the reader some idea of the character of Zulu intrigue.

The servant of a rich man wished to leave his master's kraal and build one for himself. He had been originally unwilling to take up his abode there; but his necessities at that time were urgent, and he could not afford to resist. Now however he was in better circumstances, and desired to occupy a less degraded position. But the master would not consent to his removal, the dependant having a large family, whose departure would have made his kraal appear too empty. Some angry disputation ensued; when the master at length affected to yield, but said that he was going to the king's, and directed that nothing should be done until his return. The direction seemed reasonable, but it was given craftily; for he was going, not only to complain of his servant's disobedience, but to accuse him of being an "evildoer." (He had some colour for this latter charge, several of his cattle having died, though not from poison administered at his own kraal.) Pande did not pay much attention to his complaint; and dismissed him with the sensible advice to try the effect of good words and endeavour to persuade his dependant to comply with his wishes.

Lumbo was not to be so easily disappointed; his servant had both cattle and girls, and he had made up his mind to possess them. He therefore repaired to his brother, an *in-duna*, or councillor, of high rank, who set off to employ his influence in supporting the accusation. He did not think it politic to appear too forward in the matter; and, finding the accused's own chief at Nodwenge (the master and servant belonged to different tribes) asked him to make the charge. This personage—being, for a Kafir, well disposed and humane—refused to have anything to do with the matter; but he was young and not very firm, and at last yielded to the representations of the crafty *in-duna*. He therefore sought an audience of the king, and accused the innocent man of poisoning his master's cattle. The king asked how many had died, when the chief said twenty; but, like a bad conspirator, added that he did so on the *in-duna's* authority. "Don't you know them?" was the very natural reply; to which he could only answer in the negative. The king also enquired respecting the accused's property—a point on which it was most important to the master and the *in-duna* that he should be uninformed.[14] The chief had been instructed to deny that the intended victim possessed either cattle or girls; but he replied in a bungling manner, and the king soon discovered, by his own confession, that the accused had both. The king now sent him to call the *in-duna*, who was anxious to know exactly what he had said; the chief, however, annoyed at the treatment he had just received, was in no humour to gratify him. He therefore went into the presence, unaware that Pande knew the dependant to be comparatively rich; and, in answer to the king's question, said that the accused possessed no property. Pande denied the assertion, saying that he should some day learn the truth; but, instead of dismissing the charge and disgracing the *in-duna*, he told him to have the accused slain—ordering however that some great person should be entrusted with the execution; for the "evildoer" was the son of a rich man and not poor himself.

Having thus far prospered, the *in-duna* wished to make further use of the young chief, and asked him to undertake the murder. The latter refused, and this time was firm, he would not kill one of his father's men. The *in-duna*, being chagrined, went again to the king; and, misrepresenting the chief's words, accused him of saying that he would not kill one of his *own* people (as if he had denied the king's supremacy). This had the anticipated effect of exciting the despot's rage, and the young chief was sent for. A storm of abuse awaited him; but, when he had explained, Pande's wrath was directed towards the deceitful *in-duna*, whom he swore by Tshaka to give to the vultures. The king's rage however gradually cooled, and the *in-duna* obtained his wish, the chief being ordered to take a party of soldiers and kill the " evildoer." Pande graciously added that he did not wish him to see blood—he was a young chief, and need not witness the actual execution.

Next morning the chief set off with the soldiers appointed to accompany him; and, leaving them at his own residence, proceeded to the kraal of the accused's master. Lumbo was rejoiceded to see him, for he did not doubt that his brother had managed the affair properly, and satisfied Pande that his servant had no property; but his countenance fell when the young chief informed him that the " evildoer's" daughters and other girls were to be taken to the king. Not having expected this, Lumbo delayed the execution until he had communicated with his brother, and paid another visit to court in the hope of convincing Pande that his servant was without property. He did not however succeed in his object, for the king applied to him a very uncomplimentary epithet, and told him to return with the chief when the " evildoer " had been killed.

Having reached home, he made preparation for

perpetrating that most iniquitous deed. The victim was ignorant of his fate; and it was to prevent any suspicion arising in his mind, that the soldiers had not been brought to the kraal. Still further to deceive him, it was pretended that the cattle required medicine, and a doctor was accordingly sent for; while, to account for the presence of the soldiers, it was said that the king had sent them to assist in holding the animals. When the cattle had been assembled in the *isi-baya* and the doctor had prepared his physic, the unsuspecting dependant proceeded to take his part in the ceremony, and having caught a cow endeavoured to bring it to the practitioner. While thus engaged, and consequently unable to resist, he was seized by the soldiers and overpowered. His brother rushed immediately to one of the huts, in search of an assagai; but all dangerous instruments had been secreted, and when he at length succeeded in obtaining a weapon, it was too late to render the victim help. The deed being done, the young chief (who had been sitting outside the kraal) entered the fold, and pointed out the victim's cattle. The master persisted in denying that his dependant had possessed anything; but the chief gave no heed to his protestations and selected a beast for himself. He gave the soldiers permission to take another for their customary feast; but the master's threats deterred them, and the chief, whose food they had been previously consuming, was now obliged to furnish them with beef.

Having returned to court, the chief reported

what Lumbo had said about his servant having no
property. That worthy was then sent for by his
brother, that they both might appear before the
king and confirm that statement on oath. They
did so, and Pande was satisfied. But not so the
conspirators, who asked for the restoration of the
cow which the chief had taken; and, as a sure way
of exciting the royal anger said that he had spoken
disrespectfully of the king and complained that one
of *his* people should be killed. The chief having
been summoned, Pande charged him with dis-
loyalty, and abused him in a very undignified manner. He attempted a rejoinder, but Pande would
listen to nothing—the *in-duna* HAD SWORN, and he
evidently believed him.

A month after the murder, two of the victim's
brothers, who had been meditating revenge, went
to Nodwenge. The *in-duna* was there and con-
descended to salute them; but they beheld him with
scorn, and received his compliments in silence. He
then asked their business, but they only told him
that it was with the king. He had no difficulty
in guessing what they wanted, and advised them
to go home again—the king (he said) would not
attend to boys' matters. They did not choose to
follow his advice, and he again asked what they
wanted. They were now more explicit, and told
him that they had come to inform the king that
their brother's girls had not been taken to him.
This made the *in-duna* very anxious to get them
away; and addressing the elder in a tone of

great apparent solicitude, he urged him not to think of going into the royal presence—the king would certainly kill them. They replied that they did not care—their brother had been slain. The *in-duna* then tried other arguments; but finding it impossible to turn them from their purpose, he endeavoured to discover what they intended to say, intimating at the same time that it would be dangerous to deceive the king. They told him that they were aware of the circumstance, and said something not very flattering as to the statements which *he* had made to that august personage. This was unpardonable, for was he not a rich man and a great officer, and entitled to the respect of all miserable paupers? How dared they—poor fellows with perhaps two or three cattle—talk to *him* who had hundreds, and call him a liar too? It was not to be endured; he would immediately inform the king of their insolence. They told him to go and be quick about it; when he crept out of his hut in terrible wrath, promising to return with no pleasant message. Nor was it long before he came back, saying that Pande was exceedingly angry, and had ordered him to inform the councillors that their story was altogether false, and that they might go home. They had watched his movements, and, knowing that he had not been near the king but was only trying to frighten them, received his statement with laughter. This device having failed, he went to the other principal councillors, and prevailed on them to direct the boys not to present themselves before the king until they had previously investigated the case.

Next morning the councillors assembled, and directed the elder of the two brothers to state his complaint. He repeated the history of the false accusation, and asserted that the deceased did not injure his master's cattle. The *in-duna*, who had procured his death, said in reply that he had consulted three prophets on the subject, while his brother had consulted another; and that the four had agreed in describing the deceased as an "evil-doer." If this had been true, the execution would have been legal; but the *in-duna* did not possess a very good reputation, and his statement was doubted. It was considered especially remarkable that he did not know the names of any of his prophets—a circumstance pronounced by one of the council to be unexampled and utterly incredible. The elder complainant, who had been a fellow-dependant of the deceased and Lumbo's head servant, was asked whether he knew that application had been made to any prophet before his brother's death. He replied in the negative, when the criminous *in-duna* made some remark about an Amaswazi prophet, and tried to confound this with some previous case, in which a seer of that nation had been visited. Another of the prophets, whom he professed to have consulted, resided with a person then present, but who, on being questioned, stated that his dependant had not been visited by the *in-duna* or any of his people.

Finding himself defeated, the unjust councillor became exceedingly violent; and, declaring that they were all leagued against him, left the circle, and sat down at some distance alone. He was soon accosted by a very bold "boy," who held some small office at a neighbouring military kraal, and had come to Nodwenge to see the issue of the investigation. Observing the *in-duna* sitting apart, he approached him in a rude manner, and spoke to him somewhat in this style: "You are a liar— you deceive the king—you deceive the *izin-duna*. You are a great man, and think you may do as you please. People are afraid of you, but I am not. Go and tell the king what I say. He knows you." The *in-duna* was astonished, and asked the "boy" why he did not pay him the same respect as others did. The "boy" requested to know why he should respect him: "Who are you? A dependant—you are the king's dependant. We are equal. What does it matter that you are the king's relation? You are not king—you are only a man." The councillor rose and withdrew, intimating to the "boy" that he had better take care.

When the *in-duna* had left the council, it was determined that the complainants should fetch two of their brother's daughters, and thus convince the king that he had been deceived. It being not unlikely that they would meet with opposition, a messenger was directed to accompany them. Having reached the kraal where their brother had been murdered, the elder complainant went straight to Lumbo, who was sitting in a hut, and asked his dependant whether he had returned to stay with him. "No," was the vehement reply, coupled with the remark that he was very unlikely to remain with the man who had killed his brother. When Lumbo learned his errand, he became very desperate, rushed frantically out of the house, called his people into the cattle-fold, and said with tears that he should now be slain. Taking up two of his young children, he kissed them; and then declared that he must go and consult his mother, who lived in another kraal. The sun being set, his wives persuaded him to defer the visit till morning. The people chaunted a sort of dirge, which he interrupted with such observations as these: " I shall die now—the soldiers will be here to-morrow, and we shall all be killed. The son of Bangu has been making false statements to the king. My brother was very stupid not to prevent it." The elder complainant was told that he might continue at the kraal for the night, but the younger that he must sleep elsewhere. The youth, who heard this announcement in silence, manifested no intention to remove; whereupon Lumbo exhibited great violence and threatened to kill him. His people, however, interfered, and the boy was allowed to remain. The man who had accompanied them was bountifully entertained, but the complainants went supperless to bed. Lumbo had given a loud order to prepare food for them, but it was never produced, and in all probability the direction was designed to add disappointment to their hunger.

Next day a council was held in the bush. Lumbo's mother wept over her son's misfortunes, and railed immoderately at the wicked " boys " who had deceived the king. Suddenly she changed her tone, and railed at Lumbo, upbraiding him with stupidity in not having long ago killed the elder one. He told her to be silent, that the council might proceed. The advice varied, but the issue was that Lumbo expressed his determination not to surrender the girls. The complainants, who were present, might not have found their position safe, if the young chief, attended by some followers, had not been there. The council being ended, they accompanied him to his kraal, and afterwards contrived to obtain possession of one of the girls, whom they left in the care of a relative. They then returned to Nodwenge, and told the king what they had done. He knew it already; and, giving them permission to appropriate all their brother's property, directed a great man to accompany them that they might be allowed to take it. When they arrived at Lumbo's, he wept again, and again refused to yield anything. They therefore retired to the kraal where they had left the girl.

When the complainants had left Nodwenge, the *in-duna* succeeded, by various misrepresentations, in incensing Pande against the young chief, and obtained an order for his destruction. Having been himself directed to execute the sentence, he took several soldiers and made a hasty journey to his own kraals, which were near those of the intended victim. The complainants, who had not left their relative's, soon heard of his unexpected arrival, and were not long in divining its purpose. The elder, believing that if the chief were killed they would not be allowed to escape, immediately fled to Natal; the younger thought it best to return to the king—a circumstance with which his Majesty was particularly pleased.

The *in-duna* (who endeavoured to conceal his design) left the kraal in which he had placed the soldiers, and took up his abode at another. Here he made preparation for a great feast; oxen were slaughtered, and invitations sent to all the principal men of the neighbourhood, including the young chief. The latter had no doubt that his death had been decreed, and that the feast was only a treacherous scheme intended to entrap him. His friends, being of the same opinion, strongly advised him not to go; but he resolved, in spite of their remonstrances, to be present; and, having ordered his attendants, about twenty in number, to carry not less than two assagais each, he set forth. As he approached the *in-duna's* kraal, he observed that it was already thronged, and his followers wished him to remain outside: he scorned, however, to appear timid; and, directing them to accompany him, proceeded to the principal hut and saluted the owner. The latter begged his guest to enter; but the chief prudently declined, and withdrawing to the central enclosure sat down with his followers. The *in-duna* tried to separate him from them, by making various dispositions of the assembled people, but without success. He endeavoured to accomplish the same purpose by again inviting him into his hut—it was unfit, he said, for a guest of his rank to sit outside in the heat of the sun. The chief excused himself, but said that he would come presently.

He then called one of his dependants, and bade him arrange his head-ring. This proceeding was purposely prolonged; and, when a servant announced that beef had been taken into the hut, still served as an excuse for his absence—he could not go until the operation had been completed. The *in-duna* subsequently renewed the attempt, but the chief was not to be entrapped—he was no chief, he said, to-day—he was not fat enough for the sun to hurt him—he preferred to remain where he was.

After a while beef was brought into the enclosure, and the chief, as the most important person present, requested to carve it. If he had undertaken the task and performed it in the usual way, he might have been easily seized; he therefore declined the honour, but went to cut a portion for his own followers. He was careful, in doing so, not to squat, and kept his eyes about him—a precaution which probably saved his life. The beef had been placed within a semicircle of men, the *in-duna's* people being at the extremities. Some of these, while the chief was cutting the meat, rose up and came near him. Turning hastily towards them, he demanded what they wanted. His deportment, and the assagai which served him for a knife, intimidated them, and they endeavoured to excuse themselves by saying that they had come for beef. It was not customary, he said, to do so; and they slunk back to their places. The chief very speedily cut a moderate supply for his attendants, and retired to his former position. When the *in-duna* learned that this scheme had failed, he attributed it to the folly of his "boys" who had acted with too much haste; he had instructed them to proceed stealthily and enclose the chief before he could be aware.

A present of beef being now sent expressly for the chief, etiquette required that he should go to the host, who was then in the house, and thank him; he thought it safer, however, to depute two of his attendants to perform that ceremony. A servant afterwards came to say that his master had some intelligence to communicate from the king; when the chief, taking his followers with him, went to the hut. He refused to enter—the sun was nearly set and he must return home. The *in-duna,* having repeated what the servant had said, namely, that he had a message from the king, the chief told him to deliver it; but was asked whether he usually received royal communications in the presence of his people. He replied that his followers might be trusted; and, soon after, finding that the message was only another pretext to separate him from his guard, took leave of his host. The baffled *in-duna* now came out of his hut, expressed great surprise at the chief's conduct, and regretted that he should entertain unfriendly feelings. The chief replied that it was *he* who entertained such feelings, and left the kraal.

Though the chief's prudence had thus protected him from immediate danger, he knew that it was unsafe to remain under Pande's dominion. He had previously fled from the tyranny of Dingane

and sought refuge beyond the river Maputa; but
his experience on that occasion rendered him unwilling to trust again to the hospitality of a native
chieftain. He therefore determined to avail himself of the asylum presented by the white man's
country and turn his face towards Natal. Having
assembled his followers, he pointed out their peril,
and advised them to accompany him. They agreed
to do so, and sacrifices were immediately offered to
the spirits, that they might bless the enterprise.
This done, they set forth while it was yet dark,
abandoning the women and children to their fate—
these would only have hindered their flight, and,
like the cattle left behind, could be replaced in
Natal. To elude pursuit the fugitives took a cir-
cuitous course, travelling only at night, and, when
it was possible, in the bush. This made their
journey much longer than it need otherwise have
been, and extended their wanderings to several
days. Having had no time to furnish themselves
with provisions, they would have been almost destitute of food, if they had not contrived to scare a
lion from the carcase of a buffalo. The hungry
beast was unwilling to leave his prey; but the
fugitives were famishing and therefore bold. On
one occasion, when near some huts, they wished to
revenge themselves for Pande's unjust treatment,
by destroying the helpless occupants; the chief,
however, forbade them to molest the unoffending
people—*they* were not his enemies, and he would
not permit them to be injured. This moderation was
subsequently reported to the king, and no doubt

excited his surprise, though it would hardly awaken
his admiration.

The fugitives ultimately reached Natal, where
the elder of the two "boys" mentioned in the
former part of this story had arrived before them.
The younger subsequently joined his relatives.

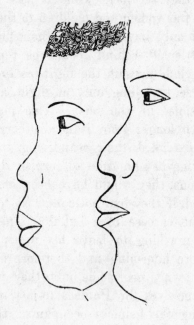

CHAPTER V.—CRIMES AGAINST LIFE AND PROPERTY.

I.—MURDER. II.—POISONING. III.—ROBBERY.

I.—THE reader has doubtless concluded, from facts previously mentioned, that these Kafirs set little value on human life. Several of the facts alluded to, having reference to normal customs, prove that this has been their manner for a long time; yet it cannot be doubted that they have become more savage since their subjection to the sanguinary rule of Tshaka and his successors. When the Zulus appeared among the Bechuanas, those people were struck with their extreme barbarity. "On seeing these men," said a Basuto, "so strong and well-made, entirely naked, of a cruel and ferocious countenance, armed with short handled but large headed assagais, and with a shield of buffalo or bullock hide twice as large as ours, we were all seized with fear, and called them *Matebeles*," those *who disappear*, or are scarcely to be seen behind their immense bucklers, "but amongst themselves they are called Amazulu." The author from whom this is quoted observes that "the neighbouring tribes say of them proverbially that *they are not men but eaters of men*, so formidable have they become." The Zulu soldiers are not all equally destitute of humanity, as the following anecdote will show. A detachment, on a marauding excursion, reached a kraal, from which the inhabitants had fled, leaving behind them an old woman hardly able to move. Being now at the mercy of the savages, she probably expected nothing but death; and this would certainly have been her fate, if one of the party had not interfered and protected her from the weapons of his ruthless associates. This man was a tender-hearted barbarian; yet he was less humane than may be thought, for he told the story as a joke, and seemed infinitely amused to describe and mimic the despairing gestures of the helpless creature.

The following description of the Kafirs in Natal was written in 1847: "Their universal character, as formed by their education, habits, and associations, is at once superstitious and warlike; their estimate of the value of human life is very low; war and bloodshed are engagements with which their circumstances have rendered them familiar from their childhood, and from which they can be restrained only by the strong arm of power; their passions are easily inflamed, while at the same time they have grown up in habits of such servile compliance to the wills of their despotic rulers, that they still show ready obedience to constituted authority."[1]

Such being the character of the people, the reader will perhaps expect to hear that murder (by which we mean violent homicide committed without the chief's command) is of frequent occurrence.

This however is not the case—a circumstance explained partly by the fact that they are not of an
extremely revengeful character, and partly perhaps
by their natural cowardice.[2] When excited, they
are very reckless; but they do not like to expose
themselves in cold blood. A proof of this is
furnished by the precautions which are taken in
executing the sanguinary decrees of the Zulu king.

Violent homicide is usually committed under the
influence of passion. The following are examples.
A number of unmarried soldiers had been sent to
procure wood, for repairing one of the Zulu
monarch's large kraals. As they returned in single
file, along the narrow path, they were met by a
" man," who ought to have paid respect to the
king's property, by giving way to the bearers of it.
As he neglected this duty, the leader of the file
ran against him with the bundle of sticks he was
carrying on his shoulder. A quarrel resulted, but
it was not very serious; the " man " contrived to
push the " boys " aside, and threatened to beat
them " to-morrow." Before this, the last member
of the procession had been left behind, engaged in a
similar dispute with a disloyal " boy." When he
joined his companions, and was asked what had
detained him so long, he replied that he had
stopped to extract a thorn from his foot. They
affected to believe that the " boy " had been beating
him; but he indignantly denied the insinuation—
he had beaten the " boy." The procession, having
gone on, was overtaken by two persons, who stated

that they had passed a "man" lying dead near the path, and observed a "boy" carrying wood, who, as they approached him, quickened his pace. Suspicion immediately fell upon the loiterer. When the soldiers reached the king's kraal he expressed himself pleased with their day's work, and ordered beef to be given them for supper. Meanwhile the two persons already mentioned communicated what they had seen to a great officer, and a council was held. The "boys" were summoned to give evidence; and, when the matter had been investigated, a report was made to Pande, who deferred the consideration of it till next morning. The "boys," instead of the promised beef, received a very small allowance of corn. On the following day, the principal councillor sent for the suspected youth, and told him that, though the king was very angry, he would nevertheless forgive him, on his confessing and saying how the murder had been done. The "boy" then stated that the deceased had refused to give way to the bearer of the king's wood—that he made use of an opprobrious epithet—and that he (the "boy") had consequently struck him with an assagai. The councillor blamed him for having used that weapon instead of a stick, repeated his assurance of the royal clemency, and directed him to leave for a neighbouring kraal. He went—but his executioner followed, and despatched him outside the gate. The *in-duna* had deceived him.

A young man, whose fine tall person rendered him a great favourite with the king, was returning from Nodwenge to the kraal where his regiment assembled. Pande had just given him a present of beads, and he walked towards Isangu with an immense idea of his own importance. While approaching a small stream he was met by a married man, to whom he ought to have given the path; but his arrogance would not suffer him to do it, and they came into collision. A quarrel ensued; in which the young man stabbed his opponent. He then wiped the blood from his assagai and walked on. Meeting some men, he remarked that he had seen a dead person in the grass but did not know who he was or what had killed him. When these reached the body, which was lying on its face, they turned it over, notwithstanding their superstitious dread of a corpse, and discovered a wound; then, proceeding to Nodwenge, they reported the circumstance. They were not the only witnesses in the matter; a boy who was washing himself in the stream, had heard the quarrel and seen the murder. He could not identify the murderer, but gave a description of his appearance, which convinced the king (when the matter was brought before him) that the criminal was no other than his favourite. He was unwilling to have the homicide slain; and, in the hope of being able to screen him, wished a prophet to be consulted. But the principal councillors were resolved that the murderer should die; and to ensure their purpose accused him of an additional crime, telling the king that he had spoken treasonably, and said that *his* chief was in Natal. This sufficed to procure an order to kill the favourite and all his kraal.

In the following instance there was "malice pre-
pense." A married man, who paid attention to a
girl, was at first favourably regarded by her; but
she eventually told him that she had changed her
mind and preferred the addresses of another. Both
men lived in one kraal; and, as the rejected suitor
believed that his rival had been slandering him to
the lady, a quarrel took place between them. Sometime afterwards the girl paid a visit to the house of
her favourite, who, as she was leaving, gave her a
small calabash of grease. Delighted with the present, and anticipating the polish it would give to
her charms, she walked trippingly away; but had
not passed the gate when the discarded lover, who
had watched her departure, and was overflowing
with jealousy and rage, attempted to beat her.
His stick was uplifted for the purpose, but she
nimbly avoided the blow, while a piercing
shriek brought the accepted suitor to her rescue.
A fight ensued, in which the rivals plied their
sticks with desperate energy, until the people of the
kraal forcibly separated them. Some time afterwards, the favoured man had an assignation with
the girl, and publicly boasted of the fact. This
circumstance added fresh fuel to the fire, and the
rejected wooer determined to be revenged upon his
rival. Observing the latter going to the river, to
perform his ablutions, he took an assagai and followed him. Having reached the stream, he said
that he had come to wash, and made some preparations as if he were about to do so; but in the meantime he renewed the quarrel, and soon stabbed his

victim in the back. A woman who was going for water witnessed the murder, and screamed so loudly that the people of the kraal imagined her in the jaws of a crocodile.

The criminal escaped to the bush; but afterwards voluntarily went to the king, and related all the circumstances of the case. That personage seems to have thought that the provocation justified the deed; but cautioned the murderer not to repeat the act, unless he wished to die.

II.—The term "witchcraft" has been applied by Europeans to a class of native crimes, partly real and partly imaginary. *Um-takati*, the word usually translated witch or wizard, signifies an evildoer, though it is perhaps limited in use to malefactors of the greatest criminality. It expresses, for instance, a murderer, an adulterer, and (as we have seen) one who violates the rules of consanguinity. It is also used to designate an individual who is doing, or supposed to be doing, secret injury to another. In effecting this hidden mischief, the "evildoer" is supposed to employ medicine, human remains, the liver of a crocodile, hyena's hair, and other means. The results attributed to these instruments are various—it being believed that an "evildoer" can, for example, injure the health, destroy life, cause cows to become dry, prevent rain, occasion lightning. It thus appears that there is a large amount of superstition and ignorance associated with this subject; but we are not therefore to conclude that the secret injuries attri-

buted to an "evildoer" are never real. There is
no doubt that poison is included among the several
means which an *um-takati* is supposed to use. "In
acquiring a knowledge of plants possessing healing
properties," says Mr. Fynn, "it is evident that the
natives would also become acquainted with others
of a poisonous nature. With several of the latter
description I have an acquaintance; and I am of
opinion that Europeans generally do not give sufficient credence to the fact that there aré many nations who possess a knowledge of poisons of a most
destructive character, perfectly unknown to themselves." There is reason for thinking that the
potent and subtle qualities of strychnine are not
unknown to these Kafirs.[3]

It is the opinion of some that poisoning prevails
to a very large extent. "The fatal practice of
using poisonous roots," Mr. Isaacs writes, "was so
prevalent among the natives that, from long experience, we found nothing but great vigour would
put an end to such a fatal custom. It became a
law therefore amongst our tribes that any persons
found with poisonous roots in their possession (except the Botwas, on their hunting excursions, who
used them for killing elephants) should suffer death."
Mr. Dohne states his belief "that there is hardly
one kraal, where there is not found either a woman
which endeavours to poison her fellow-woman, in
order to become the only one to her husband; or
even him, in order to connect herself with another;
or a husband which does not the same thing, in
order to get rid of one or more of his wives, for

the reason of reclaiming the cattle paid for them, and so marry others; or to do so to his own sex, in order to get their cattle or their wives for his own." The author of an anonymous pamphlet, published in Natal, makes the following statement: "Nearly every Kafir kraal has its poison maker, whose business it is to try experiments upon herbs, roots, and other things, as also to extract poison from serpents, in order to produce the most effectual poison by their combination, and devise the best mode of administration with the least probability of detection. And it is with them in poison as it is with us in medicine; the man who can produce the best becomes the most celebrated, and carries on the largest trade in this deadly art. A short time ago the most celebrated in Peter-Maritz-burg was a young man in the service of a white man; and no one can be certain that his servant is not employed in this traffic. I do not think that they are in the habit of injuring the white man by the use of these poisons, so that the statement of this fact need not create fear or suspicion in any breast. But amongst the Kafirs the knowledge of this fact produces constant suspicion and dread."[4]

In a case related by Mr. Isaacs, the youngest wife of a native belonging to the Europeans' settlement, lost her hair and became otherwise disfigured. It was suspected that some "pernicious preparation" had been administered to her by the elder wife, who wished to secure the enjoyment of her husband's undivided affection. The supposed

criminal was therefore arraigned before the senators; and, after an investigation of five hours'
duration, was proved to have had in her possession
certain poisonous roots, produced at the trial, " and
which, after some questions put to her, she confessed
having used to make the ornamental patch of hair
fall off and disfigure Noie, the young wife of
Nongue, so that she might enjoy more of his company and Noie less. Other similar offences were
proved against her, which left no doubt of her
guilt, and that her aim was avowedly to poison her
rival." When sentence of death was pronounced
upon her, she smiled, and said, " What a pity it is
to be friendless;" then, accompanying her executioners, she walked away with an air of the greatest
unconcern, and bade adieu to the spectators as she
passed them. Mr. Fynn applied blisters to the head
of the unfortunate Noie, and succeeded in recovering her from her dangerous condition.

The two following stories are related on native
testimony. A man, having three wives, took a
fourth, whose mother brought her, according to custom, some sour milk. The old woman sat with her
daughter until the mess was nearly consumed; and
then, leaving the hut, bade her be quick, saying that
she was in haste to return home. There were three
children in the house, to whom the bride offered the
remainder of the food: two refused it; but the
third partook, and in a short time was seized with
convulsions. The young woman hastily wiped
away all traces of milk from the child's person;
and, when some people entered, denied that she had

given her anything. The truth was afterwards revealed by the two other children, who had seen their sister take the milk. Subsequently the chief wife died, then a child, then another wife. Before this, a prophet had pronounced the bride an "evildoer:" but her husband would not believe the accusation; his suspicion rested on her parents, whom he caused to be put to death. The mortality, however, continuing in his family, she was eventually slain. It is believed that she intended to make herself mistress of the kraal, and that the poison had been supplied by her mother.

A man, who was suspected to be an "evildoer," fled to Natal, leaving his second wife and two sons of his first wife. The second wife claimed the cattle, but was told that they belonged to the eldest son of the first. Next day the neighbours were surprised to observe that the herd had not been turned out to pasture; and a rich man, to ascertain the cause of so remarkable an occurrence, sent a dependant to the kraal. The entrance being closed, the messenger called on the people by name, but received no answer. He then endeavoured to arouse them, by casting stones upon the huts; and, finding this unsuccessful, examined the outer fence. Discovering a hole of recent origin, he concluded that a hyena had entered during the night, and destroyed the inmates. Afraid to carry the investigation farther, he returned; when the master assembled his people, and having gone to the kraal ordered the gate to be opened. He then proceeded to examine the huts, in one of which were found the two sons of the first wife lying dead, with a vessel containing sour milk between them. The second wife who had claimed the cattle could not be found; but it was afterwards discovered that she had gone to her husband's brother, and had made her way through the fence, apparently to lull suspicion.

A native doctor remarked to me that the prophets, who profess to detect "evildoers," are themselves frequently poisoners. Mr. Isaacs relates a case confirmatory of this statement. Some children having died at the Europeans' settlement, suspicion fell upon a seer, who increased it by disappearing. Isaacs "went to investigate the affair and found incontestible evidence of the infamous man having administered to each of the children" two poisonous seeds sufficiently powerful, he says, to kill any grown person. "The villain had gone to Ogle's people; and, as one of our senators was absent, we sent to inform those who had the criminal that they must attend the trial, which would take place next day." The people came, but the prophet refused to appear. He was "at last taken at the kraal of Mataban by the people of that chief. Having received intimation of his offences, when he appeared among them, they secured him, and in a short time he confessed having poisoned the children. The chief and his natives, rather than risk bringing the culprit to us for trial by the senators, anticipated his sentence, and thus ended his iniquitous career." It was discovered that he had been guilty of similar crimes among the Zulus, from whom he had escaped to take refuge among the people at Port Natal.

The crops in a dependant's garden flourished, while those belonging to his master withered. This appeared singular, for the gardens were almost contiguous and the soil was similar; it was therefore suspected that the servant had burned medicine among his corn and given none to his master. When the latter accused him of so doing, he protested that he had burnt nothing except common sticks; but a prophet denounced him as an "evil-doer," and he was slain by the king's order. His wife and son were spared.

In process of time the master died, leaving the widow and her son dependent on his heir. The boy was appointed to tend the cattle; but he frequently neglected his duty, and received many severe beatings. One of the cattle eventually died, with symptoms which induced the master to send a young child to watch the herd-boy. The same day another beast died in the bush, with similar symptoms and a small wound near the shoulder. The child, when questioned by his father, denied that he had seen any one near the cow, and was punished with sundry blows. The prophet, being consulted, asserted that a wife had employed her son to administer poison to the cattle—a statement which was afterwards confirmed by the child's mother. She said that her son had observed the boy strike the cow with a stick, which he kept concealed in the bush, and that when the cow died, he was threatened with a severe beating if he mentioned the circumstance; that he had nevertheless told it to her; and that she had directed him not to divulge it to his father. She did not wish the boy to be killed on her son's evidence; but, now that the prophet had accused him, there was no reason why she should keep silence. The unfortunate child was again chastised for having told his mother; but the master took no steps to punish the "evildoer."

Other cattle died, and at length a child became sick. The master now asked the herd-boy's mother to give his son medicine; her husband, he said, had been a doctor, and she doubtless knew how to recover the child.[5] The request excited her wrath—her husband was not killed for being a doctor but an "evildoer." The master reminded her that he had not been concerned in her husband's death; but it was in vain—she was a "wife," and not a doctor. He then went to her son, and tried to get the antidote from him; but the youth said that his mother had not made him acquainted with his father's medicines. The master promised him a cow if he would obtain the antidote; and advised him to tell his mother that some other person required it. The youth did so and succeeded; the means were applied, and the child recovered. Having learned the deception practised on her, the woman became very furious; she upbraided her son for confirming the suspicion which attached to them, and especially for having healed the child of a man, who had beaten him so frequently, and whose father had caused his to be killed; she assured him that his deceased parent would punish him for so doing.

The master's mother now died, with symptoms resembling those of the cattle. Application being made to a prophet in Saduga's country, he gave a similar account to that which had been given by the prophet previously consulted; and added that the wife's husband had obtained the poison in Makazana's country. In consequence of this, the master resolved that the boy's mother should die. When asked how the poison had been obtained, she gave substantially the same account as the prophet, and added that her son was ignorant of it. She derided a request to reveal the antidote—it was not likely that she would communicate so valuable a secret to those who had slain her husband and beaten her son—if she had been afraid to die she could have gone away—she was not afraid to die—she had been revenged, and wanted to die—only she wished her son to be killed at the same time. This request was not complied with, the master believing him to be unacquainted with her medicines. The absence of mortality, for several months, confirmed his impression; and the people congratulated themselves that the knowledge of the poison had perished with the "evildoer." Suddenly, however, a boy died to dissipate the delusion. The suspected youth endeavoured to escape; but he was seized and taken to the king, who wondered that his master had suffered him to live so long. He was put to death.

A man living at the Europeans' settlement was tried on a charge of poisoning. It was stated by a woman, who resided in his kraal, that, while seeking fire-wood, she saw him in the bush feeding a wild cat called *im-paka*. It being believed that this animal is specially connected with "evildoers," the sight so terrified her that for some time she was afraid to move. Recovering herself, she walked cautiously backwards, but kept her eyes fixed on the man. When the latter perceived that he was observed, he pushed the beast aside; and, approaching the woman in a confused manner, said: "What have you to say? You have been lately picked up by me; and, when you were sick, I went to Tambuza," meaning Isaacs, "and got you medicine." He then went to the garden; and, having returned with a present of sweet reeds, told her not to mention anything which had occurred, as she was a stranger and did not yet know the customs of the place. When she reached home, her husband noticed a peculiarity in her countenance, and asked what had caused it. Suffering her bundle of wood to fall, she said, "I shall never forget this day." He thought that she referred to the fatigue she had just endured, and made no further enquiry. She then communicated what she had seen to the queen or mistress of the kraal, by whom it was made known to the chief captain. (Both persons kept the matter secret from others, under the idea that the seer, when applied to, would "smell" the "evildoer.") The woman further attested that ever after, when she met the suspected man in the gar-

dens, he gave her either corn or sweet reeds. She
had also heard it stated that he had put poison into
the calabashes of two men, whose wives had been
long sick; and said that, when he had beaten his
eldest wife, a few days before, the latter said to
him, "You are an 'evildoer,' and it is known that
you put roots into the calabashes." He replied,
"If I am killed for being one, you will meet the
same fate for assisting me."

His young wife, having been sent for, was in-
terrogated by the senators, but displayed a great
disinclination to criminate her husband. She spoke
of a conversation which she had heard between
him and his elder wife, in which he said, "I do not
think they have found us out—they only want our
corn." She also mentioned other conversations, and
gave evidence "quite enough to satisfy any un-
biassed mind that he was guilty of putting poison
into the calabashes of the people." Messengers
were now despatched to bring the elder wife to be
examined. They told her that he had been executed, when she said, smiling: "O! there are
plenty of men left for me." Having entered the
kraal, she sat down, and was examined "respecting
the statements of other persons, which were explained to her." She replied, with great levity,
that she knew nothing, when the senators referred
to the dispute which had occurred between herself
and her husband.

"Do you recollect quarrelling a few days ago
with your husband?"

"I do not remember any instance of quarrelling

with my husband."

" What did you say to your husband when he came in the night and asked for food for the child?"

" I don't know."

" What did he beat you for?"

" He never beat me."

She was urged to speak the truth, " and afterwards threatened with death, if she did not comply; but nothing made any impression. The young wife was then confronted with her. Her testimony was incontrovertible, and perfectly satisfactory to the judges," who condemned the man to death. The execution of the sentence was witnessed by his two wives. The younger could not repress her grief; but the elder seemed entirely unaffected. The senate now began to question her, when she requested that they would kill her. Some were willing to comply with her wish; others desired that she might be tortured, to extort a confession. After a short debate, they decided that she should die. When the executioners were lifting up their hands to strike her, she said, "Cajola, you can get my beads from Pambo's wife, and Tambuza can take my corn."

III.—It appears that, before Tshaka's time, cattle-stealing was very prevalent among these people. The following account of a notorious thief of the olden time, derived from one of his descendants, will illustrate the manner in which Kafir raids were then practised.

Dutulu, who was of the Xnumayo tribe, stole

principally from the Dwandwes. Before starting
on his pillaging journeys, he did not neglect to
offer sacrifice to the spirits and entreat them
to prosper his undertaking. He was careful
also to be duly prepared by a mediciner, that
the dogs might be dumb and the robber invisible.
Thus fortified, Dutulu would go forth, and, while
the inmates were asleep, approach some previously-
selected kraal. An attendant removed the cattle
from the fold; and, if pursuit were apprehended,
drove them at first in some other direction than
that of the plunderer's home. They were also
made to turn frequently and cross their course,
so as to confuse the track. In the event of an
actual chase, a beast was sometimes slain, as a
sacrifice to the spirits and perhaps as a temptation
to the pursuers. Medicine was occasionally left
on the road, in the belief that it would charm
the latter and prevent their seeing the foot-prints.
While the cattle were being driven from the *isi-
baya*, Dutulu and other attendants proceeded to the
huts; and, having made a noise to alarm the people, assagai'd them as they crept out. The men

were killed to prevent resistance; the women, as I was told, that they might not give an alarm. (Once, when his own kraal was invaded, and an attempt made to draw him from his hut, Dutulu profited by his experience; and, folding his leather kaross, thrust it through the low door-way. In the dim light, it was mistaken for a man; and, while the thief was striking it with his weapon, the owner rushed out, duly armed, and bounded to the gate to defend his cattle.) If Dutulu had reason to apprehend that the stolen herd would be chased, he remained in the neighbourhood; and endeavoured, by various feints, to mislead the pursuers.

In his old age, Dutulu determined to carry off a herd by day-light. He could not prevail on any one to join him in so hazardous an enterprise; but that circumstance failed to deter him, and he made the attempt without help. The cattle were grazing near a bush, and he succeeded in driving them away; but, before he had gone far, an alarm was raised. Several men set off in pursuit, and surrounded the thief ere he was aware. His courage and activity enabled him to find refuge in the bush; but only after a hard struggle and with many wounds. Loss of blood so reduced his strength that he did not reach home until after his family had given him up for dead. When he recovered, his chief advised him to abandon a business for which he was becoming too feeble—he had cattle enough—it was not necessary to hazard his life in obtaining more. The old robber protested that he was yet a boy, and had still a very great desire to increase his herd—he did not fear—people might wound him as they pleased—if they wished to kill him, they must cut off his arms, his legs, his head—he did not care for wounds. The chief ceased to reason; and the robber went forth on what proved to be his last adventure.

His attendants having, as usual, driven the cattle out of the fold, Dutulu, who knew that they would be followed by a strong party, went to the principal hut; and, having killed the owner, rushed away to conceal himself. When the pursuers set forth, he left his hiding-place, and decoyed them in a direction opposite to that taken by the cattle. As there was no bush to which he could fly, Dutulu dashed into a bog, where he stood with only his head above the water. The bottom being deep clay, his pursuers contented themselves with surrounding the morass and hurling their assagais from the bank. His shield protected him against the missiles; but the continued immersion gradually weakened him; and, finding his strength almost gone, he left his position and attempted to force the enemy's line. In this desperate feat, he slew more than one of his foes; but, being too feeble to run far, was quickly overtaken and killed.

Tshaka forbade cattle-stealing, among the tribes subject to his dominion, and punished it with death. The ancient practice was therefore generally abandoned; and, I have been told, the children were taught by their parents to be, in this respect,

honest.   One of Pande's councillors disregarded
the innovation.   His master, having missed two
conspicuous oxen, ordered the herd to be counted;
when not less than forty were found wanting.   A
careful search was made throughout the entire
neighbourhood—hills were scoured, valleys ex-
plored, every piece of bush was penetrated; but
without success.   No trace of the animals could
be discovered; nor, when the heavens were
scanned, could a single vulture be descried, to
indicate the position of a dead ox.   Pande did not
doubt that the cattle had been stolen, but remarked,
significantly, that *there were no Dutchmen who
could have taken them.*   Very soon after this, an
in-duna, who was also a subject chief, asked permission to visit his kraal, alleging that one of his
wives had died.   Pande refused, and told him to
perform the customary ceremonies where he was;
but he ventured to disobey the royal command,
and went home without leave.   A dependant of
Masipula, Pande's General-in-Chief, then reported
that he had seen one of the *in-duna's* servants
driving several oxen, of which he refused to give
any account.   The *in-duna* was immediately summoned to court, but sent an excuse; when he
received a second message, he promised to come
shortly.   A day or two after, he visited the Great
Place, attended by a number of followers, whom
he took armed into Pande's presence.   The king
was astonished (it being a capital crime to appear
before him with weapons) and immediately retired
behind the fence which enclosed his palace.   He

then summoned one of his principal councillors, whom he sent with a gracious and friendly message to the intruders—he was not angry with them—he should overlook their breach of etiquette—he was particularly pleased with the appearance of their assagais, which he desired to examine more closely. The device was successful, and the councillor carried the weapons to his Majesty. The day passed, and at night the offenders slept in the huts, not knowing probably that a guard was set over them. The *in-duna* hoped to escape, and ordered a follower to spread his blanket over the fence, that he might scale the barrier with less inconvenience. The servant proceeded very stealthily; but he was observed by the guard and sent back to his master. Next morning the *in-duna* was brought to trial, and accused of stealing the king's cattle. He denied the charge; but eventually admitted that he had directed them to be driven to his own kraal. Pande now referred to the fact that he had come armed into his presence; and expatiated, in no very dignified style, on the absurdity of his attempting to make war against one who had supplanted Dingane, the destroyer of the boers. The *in-duna*, who, with his attendants, was squatting in front of the king, listened in silence and dug the ground with a piece of stick, apparently indifferent to the tragical end which, he knew, awaited him. Pande turned to the culprit's brother; and, saying that *he* was now head of the tribe, gave him permission to remove as many of the *in-duna's* followers as he pleased. Knowing that those not removed would be slain, the new chief left about ten, among whom were some of his brothers and the offender's principal officers. Pande waved his hand and retired—a signal understood by the warriors present, who immediately seized the attendants, and, having dislocated their necks, carried them from the kraal. The callous *in-duna*, who had continued to dig the ground, heedless alike of his followers' cries and his own fate, was then slain in the same manner.

CHAPTER VI.—SUPERSTITIONS.

1.—THE Kafirs of Natal and the Zulu-country
have preserved the tradition of a Being whom
they call the Great-Great and the First Appearer
or Exister. He is represented as having made
all things—men, cattle, water, fire, the mountains,
and whatever else is seen. He is also said to
have appointed their names. Creation was
effected by splitting a reed, when the first man
and other things issued from the cleft. The
antiquity of this part of the tradition is attested
by the fact that *u-hlanga* signifies origin as
well as a reed, and *dabula*, to create as well as
to split. Some few Kafirs may be found who
state their belief that the Great-Great shook the
reeds with a strong wind, and there came there-
out the first man and woman.[1] When mankind
had been formed, a chameleon and a lizard called
in-tulu were sent to them—the former being
commissioned to direct men to live, while the
latter was to command them to die. The slow-
paced chameleon having tarried to eat some
berries by the way, the quicker *in-tulu* arrived
first, and delivered his message of death. Thus
mankind became mortal.[2]

This tradition of the Great-Great is not universally known among the people. War, change, and the worship of false deities have gradually darkened their minds, and obscured their remembrance of the true God. Captain Gardiner states that the generality of the people were ignorant of it, in his time. When Zikali, the present chief of the Amangwane, was asked whether he knew anything of the Great-Great, he replied in the negative; but thought that some of his old men might have heard of him. One of these said that when a child he had been told by women stooping with age, that there was a great being above, who was called by the two names previously mentioned. This was all he knew on the subject.

There is a tribe in Natal which still worships the Great-Great, though its recollection of him is very dim. "When they kill the ox they say 'Hear Unkulunkulu, may it always be so.' So when a person is sick, they say, 'Hear Unkulunkulu, may he recover.' But they never make these petitions when the shields and soldiers are present; therefore not at the feast of First Fruits; but when a person is going to eat comfortably, or is sick, or is prosperous, then when they kill the ox, they say 'Unkulunkulu, look down upon us; Baba [my Father] may I never stumble.'" Zulus have been heard to say "that in their own country, when they are going to sit down to a meal, they will send their children out and tell them to pray to Unkulunkulu, to give them all sorts of good things; and they go out and say, 'O Unkulunkulu, give us cows, give us corn.'"[3]

The Kafirs believe that, when a person dies, his *i-hloze* or *isi-tute* survives. These words are translated "spirit," and there seems no objection to the rendering. They refer to something manifestly distinguished from the body, and the nature of which the prophets endeavour to explain by saying that it is identical with the shadow. The residence of the *ama-hloze*, or spirits, seems to be beneath; the practice of breaking a man's assagais, before they are buried with him, shows that he is believed to return to earth through the grave; while it appears to be generally thought that, if the earth were removed from the grave, the ghost *would* return and frighten his descendants. When spirits have entered the future state, they are believed to possess great power; prosperity is ascribed to their favour, and misfortune to their anger; they are elevated in fact to the rank of deities, and (except where the Great-Great is worshipped concurrently with them) they are the only objects of a Kafir's adoration. Their attention (or providence) is limited to their own relatives—a father caring for the family, and a chief for the tribe, which they respectively left behind them. They are believed to occupy the same relative position as they did in the body, the departed spirit of a chief being sometimes invoked to compel a man's ancestors to bless him.

Departed spirits are believed to revisit the
earth and appear to their descendants in the
form of certain serpents. When one of these
animals appears at a kraal, it is carefully watched.
If it hiss or move away, on being approached or
gently touched with a stick, it is regarded as a
mere snake and treated accordingly. If however
it should not give these evidences of being an
ordinary serpent—if it do not seem angry nor
afraid of the inhabitants, but manifest an apparent purpose to remain—it is considered to
be the incarnation of some departed ancestor.
This advent of the spirit is supposed to be a
warning that some member of the family has
been guilty of an offence, and that, unless a
sacrifice be offered, a severe punishment, such as
sickness or death, will follow.[4]

The spirits are believed to send omens to the
living. Thus, speaking generally, if a wild
animal enter a kraal, which it is supposed it
would not do of its own accord, it would be
regarded as a messenger from the spirits to
remind the people that they had done something
wrong. (Ravenous beasts, which might have
come for prey, would not be viewed in the light
of omens; nor would antelopes and other small
animals which had run into the kraal while
being hunted.) Certain lizards visiting a kraal
would be regarded as omens; but it is remarkable
that many of the people put these reptiles in the
same class with serpents and look upon them,
not as mere messengers, but as incarnations of

the spirits. Domestic animals, doing anything remarkably contrary to their usual habits, would be deemed omens. If a calf were several times to lie down and sleep, while its mother was being milked; if a cow were repeatedly to produce two calves, or several cows were to produce dead ones; these would be ominous facts. If a dog or a sheep were to leap on a hut, it would be an omen. If a cow were to knock off the cover of a vessel containing heads of millet and eat them, she would be an omen; but not if she were to eat corn lying on the ground. If a calf were to enter a hut, it would not be regarded; but if a cow should attempt to do so, it would be ominous. If a sheep were to bleat while being slaughtered, it would be an omen and the flesh be thrown away. This omen appears to be deemed very dreadful. When it occurred at the kraal of one of Pande's chief councillors, the man was terribly frightened; and, on consulting the prophet, was told that it foreboded his death. Sacrifices were offered to avert the evil, Pande himself furnishing one; he appears however to have thought that the man was not fit to live, for he soon despatched a party of soldiers to kill him. The *in-duna* was fortunate enough to escape to Natal. Human beings may be omens —as a child born dead; a woman two days in parturition; a man burnt while sitting by the fire, unless he were asleep or drunk.

Sacrifices are offered to the spirits, (1) *to avert*

an evil, as in case of sickness, barrenness of women, serious accidents; when a serpent has visited a kraal, under the circumstances previously mentioned; when an omen has appeared. (In cases of sickness and barrenness, the seer or prophet is resorted to, and the sacrifice offered when he attributes the misfortune to the spirits. He is applied to when a serpent or omen has been seen). A soldier wounded in battle would only pray, if his hurt were slight; but if it were serious, he would vow a sacrifice on his return, naming perhaps the particular beast. If he were too weak, a comrade would invoke the spirits for him. If he were a "boy" and without cattle of his own, the beast would not be withheld on his return; and sometimes a father will chide a surviving son, if he have not vowed a sacrifice before his brother's death. On the other hand, if a "boy" were to vow an ox or a cow, not being in great danger, his father would not be pleased, though he would probably sacrifice a goat. (2.) Sacrifices to *procure a blessing* are offered after the building of a new kraal; when the army is setting out; by the seer or prophet to procure inspiration; after a burial, to secure the favour of the deceased. Mothers, when their sons are on an expedition, frequently vow a sacrifice, in the event of their returning safe; I suspect however that these vows are not always performed, for the prophet sometimes attributes sickness to their non-fulfilment, when the husband becomes angry at his wife's presumption. The natives employed by white men to hunt the elephant sometimes vow a sacrifice, when they are not successful. When Tshaka sent a mission to the Cape, he gave Lieut. King an ox to sacrifice. Pande has sacrificed to procure rain. (3.) *Thank-offerings* are made when a person has enjoyed a long prosperity; as for instance, if he have many children and no sickness in his kraal for some time. When Tshaka's mission returned from the Cape he sent an ox, to thank the spirit for Lieut. King's safe arrival. Sacrifices are offered when the Zulu army comes home from a successful expedition. Refugees from the Zulu-country sometimes testify their gratitude, for having been permitted to escape, by sacrificing the first beast they earn in Natal.

The animals offered are exclusively cattle and goats. The largest ox in a herd is specially reserved for sacrifice on important occasions; it is called the Ox of the Spirits, and is never sold except in case of extreme necessity.[5] The original idea of a sacrifice appears to have degenerated into that of a present of food; the only word to express it is *um-nikelo*, a gift (from *nikela* to give to); when the prophet prescribes a sacrifice, he directs the people to give the spirits flesh; when the spirits are addressed, they are invited to eat; beer and snuff are usually added; and, when a person has no animal to present, he offers these alone.

When an animal is to be sacrificed, it is brought into the cattle-fold, and there slain, by having an assagai plunged into its side. Just before or after its death the master of the kraal addresses the spirits. If the sacrifice be offered to avert an evil, he might speak to the following effect:

"Eat ye; here is your ox; I give it you. Eat, my father, my grandfather; all ye spirits of my ancestors, eat. Take care of me; take care of my children, take care of my wives; take care of all my people. Remove the sickness, and let my child recover. Give me plenty of children—many boys and a few girls. Give me abundance of food and cattle. Make right all my people."

If the sacrifice were a thank-offering for prosperity, he would, perhaps, after having called on the spirits, proceed thus:

"This kraal of yours is good; you have made it great. I see around me many children; you have given me them. You have given me many cattle. You have blessed me greatly. Every year I wish to be thus blessed. Make right everything at the kraal. I do not wish any omens to come. Grant that no one may be sick all the year."

When the animal has been skinned, it is cut into several portions, and the whole (including the skin, head, and blood collected in a vessel) placed in a hut, with beer and snuff. I have been told that a small fire is made, in the ordinary fire-place of the house, and a piece of fat (or flesh) burnt on it.[6] The contents of the paunch, or of some other internal part of the animal, are dashed against the inside of the roof of the hut, and scattered about the kraal. At night, young people alone sleep in the hut, without fire, the duty primarily falling upon the boys. Next day the beef is cooked in the usual way and eaten.

II.—The class of men to whom we have applied the name of SEERS or PROPHETS are by Europeans usually but improperly termed witch-doctors. They profess to enjoy the peculiar favour of the spirits, and to have received from them the gift of inspiration. If a person is sick, it is believed that the seer can tell whether the malady is owing to the anger of the spirits, and what must be done to propitiate them. If a serpent has come to a kraal, it is believed that he knows which of the owner's ancestors it is, and what offence has caused the visitation. It is supposed that he can tell why an omen has occurred. If an "evildoer" is secretly injuring another, it is not doubted that the prophet can point out the guilty individual. The knowledge which these men apparently possess is very great; and some persons have thought "that they are brought into contact with the devil, who by lying wonders and by superhuman manifestations helps them in their infernal work." It is not needful to resort to this explanation, as will appear when the manner in which they make their pretended revelations has been described.

When people consult a prophet, they do not tell him on what subject they wish to be enlightened. He is supposed to be acquainted with their thoughts, and they merely intimate that they wish to have the benefit of his knowledge. Probably he will "take time to consider," and not give his responses at once. Two young men, visiting him in consequence of their brother's illness, found the prophet squatting by his hut, and saluted him. He then invited them to sit down; and, retiring outside the kraal, squatted near the gate, to take snuff and meditate. This done to his satisfaction, he sends a boy to call the visitors into his presence, when they immediately join him and squat. The prophet asks for his "assagai"—a figurative expression for his fee, when the applicants reply that they have nothing to give at present—after awhile they will seek something to pay him with. "No," answers the prophet, not disposed to give credit, "you want to cheat me—everybody tries to do so now—why don't you give me two shillings?" They offer him a small assagai; but he is not satisfied with the weapon, and pointing to a larger one, says, "*that* is mine." The man who had brought this, excuses himself by saying that it does not belong to him; but the prophet persists and it is given. Having no hope of extorting a larger fee, the prophet says, "Beat and hear, my people." Each of the applicants snaps his fingers, and replies, "I hear." (The beating is sometimes, and perhaps more regularly, performed by beating the ground with sticks.) The prophet now pretends to have a vision, indistinct at first, but becoming eventually clearer, until he sees the actual thing which has occurred. This vision he professes to describe, as it appears to him. We may imagine him saying, for instance, "A cow is sick—no, I see a man—a man has been hurt." While he runs on in this way, the applicants reply to every assertion by beating, as at first, and saying, "I hear." They carefully abstain from saying whether he is right

or wrong, but when he approaches the truth, the
simple creatures testify their joy by beating and
replying with increased vigour.

The prophet's simulated vision is not a series of
guesses, in which he may possibly hit upon the
truth; but a systematic enumeration of particulars
in which he can scarcely miss it. Thus, he may
begin by saying that the thing, which the applicants wish to know, relates to some animal with
hair; and, going through each division of that
class, suggests whatever may be likely to occur to a
cow, a calf, a dog. If he find no indication that
the matter relates to one of this class, he takes
another, as human beings, and proceeds through it
in the same manner. It is obvious that a tolerably
clever practitioner may in this way discover from
the applicants whatever may have happened to them,
and send them away with a deep impression of
his prophetic abilities, especially if he have any previous knowledge of their circumstances. The following sketch will give the reader a general idea of
the prophet's manner of proceeding. A few particulars only, as being sufficient for illustration, are
given.

" Beat and hear, my people—[they snap their fingers and say
I hear]—attend, my people—[they beat and say *I hear*]—I
don't know what you want—you want to know something about
an animal with hair—a cow is sick—what's the matter with
her?—I see a wound on her side—no, I'm wrong—a cow is
lost—I see a cow in the bush. Nay, don't beat, my people—
I'm wrong—it's a dog—a dog has ascended a hut. Nay,
that's not it—I see now—beat vigorously—the thing relates to
people—somebody is ill—a man is ill—he is an old man. No—

I see a woman—she has been married a year—where is she? I'm wrong—I don't see yet. [Perhaps he takes snuff and rests awhile.] Beat and hear, my people—I see now—it's a boy—beat vigorously—he is sick—where is he sick?—let me see—there [placing his hand upon some part of his own person]—no—beat and attend, my people—I see now—THERE, [indicating the actual place.] Where is he?—not at his kraal —he is working with a white man. How has he been hurt? I see him going to the bush—he has gone to fetch wood—a piece of wood falls upon him—he is hurt—he cannot walk. I see water—what's the water for?—they are pouring it over him—he is fainting—he is very ill. The spirits are angry with him—his father is angry—he wants beef. The boy received a cow for his wages—it was a black cow—no, I see white— where is she white?—a little on the side. The spirit wants that cow—kill it—and the boy will recover."

In confirmation of the assertion that the people beat more vigorously as the prophet approaches the truth, an anecdote may be quoted from Mr. Isaacs. A man, who had joined the Europeans' settlement, alleged that he was suffering from the secret operations of an " evildoer;" and requested that they would send one of their own people to the prophet to be a witness of his accusation. Messrs. Fynn and Isaacs accompanied him to " watch the manœuvres and arts of these diviners." They met two, when beads were given them with the salutation, " We want your news." The prophets took the beads; and, after making a few indescribable gestures, disappeared for a short time, and then " returned with painted faces, not unlike that of a clown in a pantomime. They were, on their reappearance, accompanied by an aged female, who joined them in their chant or song to the spirit; and people were selected, to whom were given short sticks, with which they were to beat the ground in token of praise of everything these impostors uttered." One of them expatiated on the cause of the visitation; " but, finding that the people did not beat with their usual fervour, nor manifest any emotion or surprise, he retired. The other now made his debut, to perform his part, changing the subject. He mentioned what was current respecting the kraal of the monster Umsega. The idea of finding out the *um-takati*, or witch, so pleased the poor deluded natives, that they beat the ground with their sticks, and evinced their joy in the most extraordinary way; so much so that Umsega could not abstain from making some remark, which led the prophet to conclude they had touched the proper chord; and that the savage apprehended they would advert to matters not palatable, namely, that his wives had been cohabiting with his brother, and that this was the only sickness in his kraal. After some hours of such preposterous absurdities, these 'wise men from the East,' with profound gravity dismissed us, saying that the spirit would not impart anything on that day."

The explanation here given of the prophet's apparent knowledge has occurred to some of the natives. A party of visitors having come to a seer's kraal, during his absence, a young man who was present represented himself as the person for whom they were enquiring. They saluted him reverently, gave him a fee, heard his revelation,

and went away with the conviction that he was a
very good prophet.   Another young man was bold
enough to declare his belief that the prophets were
imposters, who coveted people's goods, and obtained
their knowledge by *seeking* it from those who consulted them.   This being denied he took an opportunity of personating a prophet, and dismissed the
visitors with a high opinion of his supernatural
wisdom.   He did not fail to boast of the feat and
triumph over the sceptics.   When the matter
reached his chief's ears, that personage was much
scandalized and reported it to the king.   Pande
did not take much notice of the subject—the young
man, he said, was a great rogue, and must not do
so "to-morrow."

It is not to be understood that the seer's knowledge is in all cases entirely obtained from the
people themselves.   It has been said that these
pretended prophets are always seeking for information relative to others; while, according
to Mr. Fynn, every member of the fraternity
has an assistant under the title of servant, who
generally receives a considerable share of his
master's fees, and is employed to collect information.   It may thus happen that the prophet
has some acquaintance with the circumstances of
his visitors and will not find it difficult to guess
what has induced them to consult him.

In the illustration before given the prophet was
supposed to ascribe the misfortune to the spirits.
If he attribute it to an "evildoer," he will have

to consult his own safety and make the revelation in a cautious manner. If the accused person were absent, he might, on hearing of the charge, escape and find an opportunity of revenging himself; if he were present, he might plunge an assagai into the heart of his squatting and defenceless accuser. The prophet, therefore, usually avoids any direct indication of the individual; and endeavours to make those who consult him the accusers, rather

than himself. When he does point out the "evildoer," it is sometimes done in the following manner. Sufficient people being assembled, and the suspected person among the number, he disposes them around him in a circle. To the shaggy ornaments of a Kafir's ordinary full dress he has probably added the skins of serpents; small inflated bladders are tied to his hair; in one hand he carries a short stick with a gnu's tail affixed to it, and in the other a trusty assagai. Thus equipped the prophet begins to dance, accompanying his movements with a song or chant; and, becoming gradually excited, he appears at length like a phrenzied being; "his eyes roll with infernal glare," tears run down his face, loud cries interrupt his chanting, and he seems as if an evil spirit really possessed him. The spectators, who believe that he is receiving inspiration, behold him with dismay; but their attention is turned from the prophet to themselves, when he proceeds to discover the culprit. Dancing towards several individuals in succession, he affects to examine them by means of his olfactory sense; and, when he has found the real or supposed offender, he touches him with the gnu's tail and immediately leaps over his head.

Sometimes the prophet pretends to discover poison concealed by an "evildoer" in a kraal, where its presence is supposed to be producing pernicious effects. The following is taken from Mr. Isaacs. Several persons being sick at one of his kraals, the people applied to a prophetess, who required a cow to sacrifice before she could discover the "evil-doer." She also sent a message to Isaacs, saying that she would convince him of the truth of all she uttered, notwithstanding his obstinacy, and giving him permission to be present when she dug from the huts the roots or medicine which were destroying his people. He gave the cow, and desired to be informed when the ceremony was about to commence. Two days afterwards, messengers arrived to say that the prophetess had refused his cow and required a larger one to be sent or the difference to be made up in calico. He gave the messengers about four yards of check, and was informed that she would be at the kraal next day, but wanted Maslamfu, one of his men. Isaacs objected to this, suspecting that she would be "cunning enough to elicit from him many things which might gain her credit with these ignorant and credulous people." When the prophetess reached the kraal, "she was surrounded by the people of the neighbourhood, who had come to behold the deed of divination and to hear the communications of the spirit. A sort of gloom hung on the features of every one: they all looked pensive, and were profoundly silent. Their countenances bore such evident marks of deep interest, that I could not help smiling at them, and at their solicitude to know the result of her 'smelling.' Messengers were passing to and from the various tribes, and a great number of people approached from the borders of the river Umlass, who were announced to be the tribes of the Fynns, accompanied by the chiefs of the different kraals under our command. Forerunners, announcing the advance of the prophetess, were numerous, and soon returned to report the eagerness of the people for her arrival, until we began to manifest some impatience, and grew wearied from suspense and delay of the ceremony. At length, however, the sun beginning to decline from his meridian splendour, and the evening creeping imperceptibly upon us, I sent to request that the pythoness would hasten her steps, and not keep us any longer waiting. She sent to inform us, that the spirit would not permit her to move on unless something more was given to her. Her demand was soon complied with by the chiefs sending her some beads which they procured from the people belonging to the kraal, who contributed more or less according to their means. The prophetess now made her entry into the place appointed for the ceremony, followed by forty native men belonging to Ogle and Cane. They were all armed with shields and spears, and marched in procession with great solemnity, until they arrived at the lower end of the kraal, where they halted in line, resting on the ground their shields, which nearly covered their bodies, and having their spears in their right hands. This had such a hostile appearance, that I was induced to stop the sibyl, until I made some inquiry into the cause for such an extraordinary movement; but I found it was customary for her to be attended in this way, upon all solemn occasions. Her person, also, did not less attract my attention than the hostile attitudes

and habiliments of her guards. Her head was
partly shaved, as is the custom of the natives.
Her hair was thick, and seemed besmeared with fat
and charcoal. One eyelid was painted red, the
other black; and her nose was rendered more
ornamental than nature had designed it, by being
also blackened by the same preparation. She was
attended by the wife of my captain, (who is a
descendant of white people,) her husband, and my
man Maslamfu, which was directly in opposition to
my strict injunctions; however, I did not inquire
the cause of his breach of my orders, not wishing
to impede the ceremony. By this time the woman
had taken her stick or wand, with a black cow's tail
tied to the end, which she flourished about with
infinite solemnity, frequently approaching within a
short distance of the faces of the spectators.

"Having made several advances towards the gate,
she suddenly stopped, and demanded more beads
before she could commence. A dispute now arose
between my people and those of Ogle, when many
illiberal hints were thrown out by the latter, which
annoyed us much. Had it been at any other period,
I should most certainly have interfered: but the
prophetess, seeing every one deeply interested in
the result of her occult art, wished to impose a
further demand on the people before she would
enter the kraal; I, therefore, took no notice of their
conduct. My captain now offered her his blanket,
which she refused. I gave her some beads, which
I borrowed from the mistress of the place, who
would have given all she possessed rather than the

prophetess should refuse to "smell" the "evildoer."
The pythoness soon renewed her gestures, and displayed such agility as she entered the gate, as
astounded every one; she danced from one side of
the place to the other, and sang in a language
which had no meaning, or was incomprehensible
to the natives; and her party joined in chorus.
She would frequently break off, and make some
attempts to smell, as if disturbed in her olfactory
senses by something disagreeable. She then affected
to smell several huts, and other such absurd and
ridiculous tricks, occasionally drawing back to make
the credulous and superstitious natives believe she
had discovered by her sense of smelling something
pernicious, which caused the sickness so prevalent
in the neighbourhood. After raising the expectations of the people to a state almost bordering on
phrenzy, she addressed me, and said, that it would
be offending the spirit to attempt digging up the
pernicious roots which were destroying the kraal,
unless I gave another cow. I remonstrated against
such an imposition; but, finding all arguments
useless, I consented, on condition that she would
perform the ceremony to my satisfaction, without
any further demands. After several severe expos-
tulations with my people respecting her enormous
charges, she addressed the eager and ignorant assembly, and said, ' You see that I have come here
to serve the kraal and not you, as all belonging
to the kraal, except the children, are 'evildoers;'
this day, before the sun sets, will decide your fate.'
Then, turning towards me, ' As for you, do you

doubt the charms that the spirit has given to me? You are cunning, and it is I that have made you so; I have brought you forward, and caused you to know all and everything; this day you will know more, as I intend to lay all doubts aside, and satisfy you as to my abilities and power.' At this address, delivered in an energetic tone, and without any faltering or hesitation, our natives were nearly paralysed. They sat in silent amazement, without apparently having the power to move a muscle of their bodies. An occasional glance at me involuntarily escaped from them, to see if I was affected by such absurdities. The enchantress frequently called for snuff, which she applied to her olfactory organ with more than usual eagerness, and which, I observed, was invariably handed to her by my man Maslamfu, who appeared a sort of secondary performer in the spectacle. After using it in quantities far from moderate, for streams issued from her eyes in consequence, she elevated her voice, as if she had received additional eloquence from its properties and power."

She now appointed a man to dig up the medicine. He was a huge muscular fellow, and approached his mistress with a trembling step. Desiring him not to be alarmed, and having put an assagai and broken pot into his hands, she " chewed a root, and then very unceremoniously caught him by the head, and ejected the contents of her mouth into his ear, and on the left side of his face and neck; turned his head, and bespattered the other side of his face in a similar manner, as well as both his arms. By this bedaubing he was made invulnerable to the effects of the pernicious roots. The man changed countenance, and appeared more firm; when she desired Umlambale to turn his face from her, and was going to pull off her petticoat to convince the people that she had nothing about her in the shape of roots, as a deception; but the willing and believing natives forbade her. Proceeding to the outer kraal, she pointed out three huts, which, after smelling them a little, she ordered to be unroofed, and cleared of every article within. This done, she ordered the man to put some ashes in the pot, and enter the hut for the purpose of digging up the roots. I was going into the hut that I might be able to watch more minutely the manœuvres of this wholesale impostor ; but, in a tone quite pathetic, she pressed me to remain outside, saying she was afraid to enter the hut, and related several instances of people having been struck dead by the effects of roots buried by the ' evildoers.' All this was confirmed by innumerable voices around me, which only added to my eagerness to enter the hut. However, my people begged that I would not, and, as the prophetess had refused to ' smell,' I was compelled to desist, and submit to their entreaties to stand outside with the Messrs. Fynn, and look through the parted sticks of the hut. The prophetess now presented the fellow with a stone, standing herself about three yards from the hut, and with her wand pointing to the upper part of it, where the man, as directed, beat the floor with the stone, dug up a little of the earth, and put a handful into the pot. In the same manner, he took a little earth also from above the fire-place. She next proceeded to another hut, and operated as before; and so on to the third. In the interim the natives were consulting each other, whether she had found the roots or not; most of them said that the roots were put into the pot with the handfuls of earth, but both Messrs. Fynn and myself were confident no roots had been dug. After the prophetess had in vain searched the three huts, she suddenly turned, and walked quickly out of the kraal, followed by her operative man, with the pot full of earth, her husband and Maslamfu, who were the whole time at her elbows, and proceeded to Mattantany's garden, where she threw a spear, and desired the man to dig on the spot on which her weapon had fallen; still no roots were found. Being now outdone, and closely followed by us, and finding all her efforts to elude our vigilance vain, for we examined into all her tricks with the most persevering scrutiny, she suddenly turned round, and in a quick pace proceeded to the kraal, where she very sagaciously called for her snuff-box. Her husband ran to her and presented one. This attracted my notice, as Maslamfu had hitherto performed the office of snuff-box bearer, and I conjectured that, instead of snuff in the box, the husband had presented her with roots. I did not fail in my prediction; for, as she proceeded to the upper part of the kraal she took the spear from the man appointed to dig, and dug herself in front of the hut, where the people had been sick, took some earth and added to that in the pot, then proceeded as quickly as possible to the calf-kraal, where she dug about two inches deep, and applied two fingers of her left hand to scrape a little earth out, at the same time holding the roots with the other two fingers; then, in a second closed her hand, mixing the roots with the earth, and putting them into the pot, saying to the man, 'There are the things you have been looking for.' This was performed in so bungling a manner, that I could not give this impostor any credit for her skill and adroitness. So little dexterity was displayed, that even my poor credulous and panic-stricken natives at once discovered the imposition. The principal senator, Soputa, became enraged, took the four roots that had recently been sewed in dirty leather, and said, 'These roots have not been dug from the ground.' I desired him to be silent, as I wished to see her 'smell' the 'evildoer.' Putting the roots into my pocket, I followed her to the gate of the kraal, where she took the pot of earth, turned it on the ground, and with great precaution took a little stick, gently turning the earth over with a view of showing the roots, which, alas! she could not find; I now took them from my pocket.

"Soputa, excited beyond control, asked her how she could think of practising such impositions, and thus deceiving the natives and swindling them out of their means. This was followed by a general murmur of disapprobation, and a confusion of tongues, so that I could not obtain a hearing. After silencing them, however, we missed the prophetess and her attendants, who had made their escape during the uproar which her impositions had excited."

In pointing out an evildoer, the prophet appears to be guided, as in other matters, by the suspicions of the people, and by the knowledge which he or his assistant may have gained in their habitual scrutiny of everything falling under their observation. The following extract is from Mr. Fynn's evidence: "Any native using a poisonous preparation is naturally very cautious in doing so; his cautious movements are noticed by his neighbours, and create suspicion in their minds. This is much strengthened if he is observed to rove alone at night . . . On sickness or death prevailing in any locality, a person whose actions had previously raised suspicions which had spread through the neighbourhood, is now suspected of being the guilty cause of such a calamity. The fearful rumours produced by these suspicions are eagerly sought for by the assistant of the prophet; thus the latter, having obtained a knowledge of them, is often prepared to give such proofs of his (supposed) supernatural discernment, when the matter is referred to him, as to leave no doubt of his great professional ability. Thus, it will be seen that it does not necessarily follow, as Europeans generally believe, that the prophet is in all cases wrong in pointing out the criminal.   As the result of many year's close observation, I am inclined to estimate the proportion of really guilty persons as about one-third of the total number who are accused by the prophets as *aba-takati,* or evildoers."

It seems to follow, from what has been already said, that if a man wish to accuse an innocent person and cause him to be put to death, as an " evildoer," he may succeed without engaging the prophet in a direct conspiracy. Several cows produced dead calves at the kraal of a wealthy individual; and about the same time a girl, going after nightfall from one hut to another, was startled to observe a man not many steps from her. On learning this, the people made a general search of the kraal, obtaining a precarious light by blowing on half-burnt sticks brought from the fire; but discovered nothing, except a hole through the outer fence.   Next morning, the owner traced, or professed to trace, the footsteps of a man from this hole to another of his kraals, where he immediately took up a temporary residence. The second night after his arrival, a dog barked loudly and rushed over the fence. Hearing it, the master called the people out of their houses, and found a dependant, named Sangatu, absent from the muster. Enquiring at the hut of the latter, he was told by the man's wife that her husband was sick. The master expressed surprise, observing that he was well two days ago; but the woman repeated her statement, and added that he had eaten nothing all day. If the master had chosen to enter, he might have ascertained whether his servant was in the house; but he withdrew without doing so. In a short time the dog returned and the people retired.

On the following day, as the master was sitting by a fire outside the gate, he observed Sangatu approaching, and referred to what had taken place the night before. The dependant replied that he was returning from the river, and that he was indeed very sick. He was then ordered to fetch another servant, and accompany him to a prophet, who lived at the distance of three days' journey. Sangatu, however, pleaded his illness, and was allowed to remain behind. When the other servant reached his destination, he found the prophet at home; and, having given him a fee, proceeded, with his companions, to "beat and hear." Suddenly the seer stopped in his pretended revelation; and, returning the "assagai," said that there was an "evildoer" at the kraal, whose name he would tell to none but the master. The latter refused to go, but sent his principal dependant or *in-duna*, whom he now obliged Sangatu to accompany. The prophet received them with tears; and he wept again on saying: "There is an 'evildoer' at the kraal—a girl sees him there at night—a dog tries to catch him—(I see one now present who does not beat vigorously)—when the people assemble near the gate, one is wanting—his wife says he is sick—(why don't you beat vigorously?") The last remark was addressed to Sangatu, who, doubtless, felt that he was doomed, and betrayed his sickness of heart in the feeble use of his fingers. He confessed that his wife had said that her husband was ill; but protested that the statement was true and that he was no "evildoer." The prophet dismissed them.

As they left the seer's, Sangatu declared that he would go to another prophet; but the chief servant allayed his fears, by pretending to believe him innocent, and enlarging on the fact that the prophet had not pronounced him guilty. Having reached home, he was still further deceived when he heard his treacherous fellow-dependant say to his master that the seer knew nothing and had told them only falsehoods. This was said before the people; but afterwards the chief servant gave to his master, in private, an exact account of what had taken place. Lumbo (for it was he) now communicated with his brother, the king's *in-duna*, and obtained through him an order for Sangatu's death. A party of soldiers arrived to execute the sentence; but Lumbo, fearing that their continued presence would excite suspicion in the victim's mind, dismissed them to the bush. He then invited the people of the kraal to drink beer in his own hut; and, while they were thus occupied, the warriors arrived from the bush. Lumbo addressed them as strangers, and asked what they wanted. They replied that they had been sent to fetch some of his brother's cattle. The master took them into his house, to join the carousers. In a short time he withdrew; and, calling one of the visitors after him, directed that the deed should not be done inside. He then, under the pretence of teaching them one of his brother's dances, summoned the whole party into the *isi-baya*, where the unsuspecting Sangatu was immediately seized and slain. The deceased left several girls, of whom Lumbo married four, killed one because she refused to become his wife, and sold another. Sangatu's cattle were divided by the master and his brother.

In some cases, the prophet is bribed to accuse an individual. Two rich men, who had built their kraals in proximity to each other, did not live in harmony. Umpisi loved quietness; but the other was arrogant and quarrelsome, and cultivated a desirable piece of land, to which custom gave his neighbour a prior claim. Umpisi having remonstrated, insult was added to injury; and, though the more wealthy of the two, he was stigmatised as a poor man. He sought another spot for his garden. The *self-eater* (to *eat one's self* is a native idiom, signifying to be proud and overbearing) sacrificed to the spirits; but did not invite Umpisi to the feast. The latter took no notice of the slight; but invited him, as usual, to his next banquet; nor was the self-eater too proud to accept the invitation. Afterwards, the haughty man had another feast, to which Umpisi was not asked; but this made no difference in the conduct of the latter, who again invited and again entertained his neighbour. He would have sent him even another invitation, but his son refused to carry it—he could not see why his father should act like a poor man, and invite a person who never invited him. The self-eater was chagrined; and, having received a message that his cattle had been trespassing among Umpisi's crops, returned a very insolent answer, commanding the latter to leave his vicinity. Umpisi rejoined that the country belonged to the chief and not to him, who had been but lately adopted into the tribe.

The self-eater endeavoured to obtain revenge by attempting to influence the chief; but that personage would not listen to his suggestions, and dismissed him with the scornful assurance that the fact of his son's being an officer of the king was a matter of small importance. The proud man now visited a prophet, whom he addressed mysteriously: "A certain person is my enemy; by and bye he will purchase poison; he is a rich man, and dwells near me." The prophet asked whether he wished somebody to die. "Yes, if any one will cause him to die, I will give him a cow." The prophet was indignant and said that his visitor's conversation was very ugly—he was a prophet and not an "evildoer." The self-eater deprecated his wrath—he did not wish him to administer poison to the man—it would be enough to accuse his neighbour of being an *um-takati*. The prophet replied that it would be useless to do so—nobody would believe it—besides, he was unable to utter a lie. Not discouraged by so virtuous a declaration, the self-eater repeated his offer of a cow, and departed.

Five days afterwards, his son being ill, the self-eater took one of Umpisi's dependants with him,

and paid a second visit to the seer. When the
latter asked for his fee, the visitor replied, " If you
tell me the truth I shall give you a cow; not an
assagai." The prophet was content, and made a
satisfactory revelation : " Your son is ill—an ' evildoer' scattered poison during the night near the
door—next morning the boy went out of the hut
and inhaled the poison—I see the ' evildoer '—he
is a rich man—he lives near you—you drink the
same stream—[the dependant asks for the name]—
he is called Nukwa [a woman's word for *impisi*]
—after a while he will kill you. Address the
spirits—give them meat and send me the cow."
This being communicated to the chief, he would
not believe the accusation; and, directing the
self-eater to accompany him, went to another
prophet. That individual ascribed the child's sickness to the spirits, who were angry because his
father had, on a previous occasion, sacrificed a
small beast instead of a large ox. The malicious
man told the prophet that his statement could not
be true—the child, he argued, was very ill, whereas
his ancestors never inflicted extreme sickness. The
chief, who did not doubt the prophet, told his
follower to sacrifice the ox; and as he threatened,
in case of refusal, to acquaint Umpisi with the
accusation, his wish was complied with. The
child recovered.

The self-eater made another attempt. Telling
the chief that many omens had come to his kraal,
he wished him to believe that they had been caused
by an " evildoer." The chief attributed them to

his ancestors; but was willing to consult a prophet. The self-eater conducted him to the bribed seer, who said that the omens had been occasioned by the evil arts of Umpisi; but he was still sceptical and told the complainant to offer sacrifice. The self-eater was not to be thus disappointed. His son now informed one of Pande's councillors that an "evildoer" was killing his father, and that the chief would not bring the circumstance to the king's knowledge. When the matter was reported to Pande, he enquired how many cattle the "evildoer" possessed; and, having asked whether a prophet had been consulted, told the self-eater's son to take some of the Nodwenge regiment and kill the *um-takati*. The victim having been despatched, his herd was driven to the Great Place.

After the order for this murder had been given, Pande sent for the chief, and asked whether he thought the accused was really an "evildoer." The chief denied that he was, and related the history of the case. Pande expressed great sorrow, and declared his belief that the prophet had been bribed —many he said, were. To ascertain the truth, he ordered the chief to visit the suspected seer, and tell him that the conspiracy had been discovered—that the king was very angry—and that his only chance of escaping punishment was to make a full confession. The expedient succeeded, and the prophet confessed his crime. He did not however escape punishment; being deprived of his cattle, and forbidden to practise again. The "self-eater" and his family, with one exception, were put to death.[8]

The seer's office, which may be filled by a female, is hereditary. It is, however (to quote the words of Mr. Fynn) "a principle understood throughout every tribe of Kafir-land that none of the children of a prophet can succeed their parent in that profession. It is believed that the requisite discernment and power are denied to them, but may frequently appear in their descendants of the second generation." Symptoms supposed to indicate an individual's coming inspiration are mental depression, a disposition to retire from his accustomed society, severe fits of an epileptic nature,[9] extraordinary and numerous dreams.[10] These last relate to "all sorts of wonderful things; but especially to wild beasts, as lions, tigers, wolves, and serpents." The neophyte talks about his marvellous visions, and "commences running, shrieking, plunging into water, and performing wonderful feats, until his friends say he is mad; and he speaks and acts like one under the influence of a supernatural being." He then catches live snakes (probably harmless ones) and hangs them about his neck. Thus arrayed, he goes to a prophet; and, presenting him with a goat, seeks to be instructed in the mysteries of the profession. Having remained with him some time, he visits a seer of greater reputation, by whom his preparation is completed.

The following narrative of a seer's preparation

relates to the father of one of my own servants.
Some of the particulars may be peculiar to his
tribe, and some due to the caprice of the individual. A married man (whose mother was the
daughter of a prophet) had manifested the symptoms of inspiration when a youth; but his father,
not willing to slaughter his cattle as custom would
have required, employed a seer of reputation to
check the growing *charge*.[11] The dispossession was
not, however, permanent; and, when the youth
became a man, the inspiration returned. He professed to have constantly recurring dreams about
lions, leopards, elephants, boa-constrictors, and all
manner of wild beasts; he dreamed about the
Zulu-country, and (strangest thing of all) that he
had a vehement desire to return t o it. After a while
he became very sick; his wives, thinking he was
dying, poured cold water over his prostrate person;
and the chief, whose *in-duna* he was, sent a messenger to the prophet. The latter declared that
the man was becoming inspired, and directed the
chief to supply an ox for sacrifice. This was disagreeable, but that personage did not dare to
refuse, and the animal was sent: he contrived however to delay the sacrifice; and prudently ordered
that, if the patient died in the meantime, the ox
should be returned. Having begun to recover his
strength, our growing prophet cried and raved like
a delirious being, suffering no one to enter his hut,
except two of his younger children—a girl and a
boy. Many of the tribe came to see him, but he
did not permit them to approach his person, and
impatiently motioned them away.

In a few days he rushed out of his hut, tore away through the fence, ran like a maniac across the grass, and disappeared in the bush. The two children went after him; and the boy (his sister having tired) eventually discovered him on the sea-shore. Before the child could approach, the real or affected madman disappeared again, and was seen no more for two or three days. He then returned home, a strange and frightful spectacle; sickness and fasting had reduced him almost to a skeleton; his eyes glared and stood out from his shrunken face; the ring had been torn from his head, which he had covered with long shaggy grass; while, to complete the hideous picture, a living serpent was twisted round his neck. Having entered the kraal, where his wives were in tears and all the inmates in sorrow, he saluted them with a wild howl to this effect: " People call me mad— I know they say I am mad; that is nothing; the spirits are influencing me—the spirits of Majolo of Unhlovu, and of my father."

After this a sort of dance took place, in which he sung or chanted: " I thought I was dreaming while I was asleep; but, to my surprise, I was not asleep." The women (previously instructed) broke forth into a shrill chorus, referring to his departure from home, his visit to the sea, and his wandering from river to river; while the men did their part by singing two or three unmeaning syllables. The dance and the accompanying chants were several times repeated, the chief actor conducting himself consistently with his previous behaviour.

His dreams continued; and the people were told that he had seen a boa-constrictor in a vision, and could point out the spot where it was to be found. They accompanied him; and, when he had indicated the place, they dug and discovered two of the reptiles. He endeavoured to seize one, but the people held him back, and his son struck the animal with sufficient force to disable but not to kill it. He was then allowed to take the serpent, which he placed round his neck, and the party returned home. Subsequently having (as he alleged) dreamed about a leopard, the people accompanied him and found it. The beast was slain, and carried in triumph to the kraal.

When our growing prophet returned home after his absence at the sea, be began to slaughter his cattle, according to custom, and continued doing so at intervals until the whole were consumed. Some of them were offered in sacrifice. As the general rule, when there is beef at a kraal, the neighbours assemble to eat it; but, when an embryo-seer slays his cattle, those who wish to eat must previously give him something. If however the chief were to give him a cow, the people of the tribe would be free to go. In this case the chief had not done so; and the visitors were obliged to buy their entertainment—one man giving a knife, another a shilling. An individual, who was unable or unwilling to pay, having ventured to present himself with empty hands, our neophyte was exceedingly wroth; and, seizing a stick, gave the intruder a significant hint, which the latter was not slow to comprehend.

During the consumption of his cattle, the neophyte disappeared again for two days. When it was finished he went to a prophet, with whom he resided two moons—his children taking him food; and afterwards, to receive further instruction, visited another seer. He was then considered qualified to practise.

A prophet of reputation possesses very great influence. The people reverence him not only because he is believed to enjoy the peculiar favour of the spirits; but because he possesses the tremendous power of charging a person with so called "witchcraft." An individual of this order visited a rich man belonging to his tribe, and stated that the spirit of a deceased chief had sent him to demand an ox. The master of the kraal possessed a full share of native cupidity; and, as an inhabitant of Natal, had no reason to fear the legal consequences of the prophet's accusation: yet he complied with the demand and gave the impostor one of his best bullocks. "There is abundant proof that throughout all the Kafir tribes, when living in their purely native condition, the prophets are regarded with feelings of fear and awe."[12]

Makanna, who led the attack on Graham's Town, in 1818, seems to have been one of this class. He was in the habit of visiting the British headquarters at that place, and "evinced an insatiable curiosity and an acute intellect on such subjects as fell under his observation. With the military officers he talked of war, or of such of the mechanical arts

as fell under his notice; but his great delight was
to converse with the chaplain, to elicit information
in regard to the doctrines of Christianity; and to
puzzle him with metaphysical subtleties or mystical
ravings." Combining the knowledge thus acquired
with native superstitions and his own wild fancies,
"he framed a sort of extravagant religious medley,
and, like another Mohammed, boldly announced
himself as a prophet and teacher inspired from
Heaven. He endeavoured to throw around his
obscure origin a cloud of religious mystery, and
called himself the brother of Christ. In his usual
demeanour, he assumed a reserved, solemn and
abstracted air, and kept himself aloof from observation; but in addressing the people, who flocked
in multitudes to hear him, he appeared to pour
forth his soul in a flow of affecting and impetuous
eloquence." He inculcated a stricter morality,
and upbraided the most powerful chiefs with their
vices. Speaking of Scripture-history, he adduced
in proof of the universal deluge, the existence of
sea-shells on the tops of the neighbouring mountains. "By degrees he gained a complete control
over all the principal chiefs, with the exception
of Gaika, who feared and hated him. He was
consulted on every matter of consequence, received
numerous gifts, collected a large body of retainers,
and was acknowledged as a warrior-chief as well
as a prophet. His ulterior objects were never
fully developed; but it seems not improbable that
he contemplated raising himself to the sovereignty
as well as to the priesthood of his nation; and pro-

posed to himself the patriotic task (for, though a religious impostor, he certainly was not destitute of noble aspirations) to elevate by degrees his barbarous countrymen, both politically and intellectually, nearer to a level with the Europeans "

The confederate chiefs, who in 1818 turned their arms against Gaika, though seeking to revenge their own wrongs, acted at the same time under the prophet's direction— it being one of Makanna's objects to humble, if not to crush, that chieftain, who was the great obstacle to his aggrandisement. Gaika having been defeated, the Colonial Government thought it necessary to interfere in his behalf,[13] and sent a powerful military force into the country. When the soldiers had returned, the Kafirs began to pour themselves into the colony, eager for plunder and revenge ; but Makanna, not satisfied with mere marauding incursions, endeavoured to " concentrate the energies of his countrymen, and bring them to attempt a decisive blow; and this he at length effected. By his spirit-rousing eloquence, his pretended revelations from Heaven, and his confident predictions of complete success, provided they implicitly followed his counsels, he persuaded the great majority of the Amakosa clans (including some of Hinza's captains) to unite their forces for a simultaneous attack on Graham's Town, the head-quarters of the British troops. He told them that he was sent by Uhlanga, the great Spirit, to avenge their wrongs ; that he had power to call up from the grave the spirits of their ancestors to assist them in battle against the English, whom they should drive before they stopped across the Zwartkops river and into the ocean; 'and then,' said the prophet, 'we will sit down and eat honey.'"

MAKANNA'S GATHERING.

WAKE! Amakósa, wake!
  And aim yourselves for war.
As coming winds the forest shake,
  I hear a sound from far:
It is not thunder in the sky,
  Nor lion's roar upon the hill,
But the voice of HIM who sits on high,
  And bids me speak his will!
He bids me call you forth,
  Bold sons of Káhabee,
To sweep the White Men from the earth,
  And drive them to the sea:
The sea, which heaved them up at first,
  For Amakósa's curse and bane,
Howls for the progeny she nurst,
  To swallow them again.
      *   *   *   *
Then come, ye Chieftains bold,
  With war-plumes waving high;
Come, every warrior young and old,
  With club and assagai.
Remember how the spoiler's host
  Did through our land like locusts range!
Your herds, your wives, your comrades lost—
  Remember—and revenge!
Fling your broad shields away—
  Bootless against such foes;
But hand to hand we'll fight to-day,
  And with their bayonets close.
Grasp each man short his stabbing spear—
  And, when to battle's edge we come,
Rush on their ranks in full career,
  And to their hearts strike home!

Wake ! Amakósa, wake !
  And muster for the war :
'The wizard-wolves from Keisi's brake,
  The vultures from afar,
Are gathering at UHLANGA's call,
  And follow fast our westward way—
For well they know, ere evening-fall,
  They shall have glorious prey !   *Pringle.*

Having called out the warriors of the several tribes, Makanna and Dushani the son of Islambi (the nominal commander) "mustered their army in the forests of the Great Fish River, and found themselves at the head of between nine and ten thousand men. They then sent (in conformity with a custom held in repute among Kafir heroes) a message of defiance to Colonel Willshire, the British Commandant, announcing that *they would breakfast with him next morning*. At the first break of dawn the warriors were arrayed for battle on the mountains near Graham's Town ; and, before they were led on to the assault, were addressed by Makanna in an animating speech, in which he is said to have assured them of supernatural aid in the conflict with the English, which would turn the hailstorm of their fire-arms into water. . . The English were completely astonished when they appeared soon after sun rise marching rapidly over the heights which environ Graham's Town ; for Colonel Willshire had so entirely disregarded the message sent him, considering it a mere bravado, that he had taken no precautions whatever, and was himself very nearly captured by the enemy as he was taking a morning ride with some of his officers."

"All was now bustle in the little garrison (which consisted of only about three hundred and fifty European troops and a small corps of disciplined Hottentots); the place had no regular defence, and the few field-pieces which it possessed were not quite in readiness. The Kafirs rushed on to the assault with their wild war-cries. They were gallantly encountered by the troops, who poured upon them, as they advanced in dense disorderly masses, a destructive fire of musketry, every shot of which was deadly, while their showers of assagais fell short or ineffective. Still however they advanced courageously, the chiefs cheering them on, almost to the muzzles of the British guns; and many of the foremost warriors were seen breaking short their last assagai, to render it a stabbing weapon, in order to rush in upon the troops, according to Makanna's direction, and decide the battle in close combat. This was very different from their usual mode of bush-fighting, but the suggestion of it evinces Makanna's judgment; for, if promptly and boldly acted upon, it could not have failed of success."

"At this critical moment, and while other columns of the Kafir army were pushing on to assail the place in flank and rear, the old Hottentot Captain Boezak, who happened that instant to arrive at Graham's Town with a party of his men, rushed intrepidly forward to meet the enemy. To old Boezak most of the Kafir chiefs and captains were personally known; and he was also familiar with their fierce appearance and furious shouts.

Singling out the boldest of those who, now in
advance, were encouraging their men to the final
onset, Boezak and his followers, buffalo-hunters
from Theopolis and among the best marksmen in
the colony, levelled in a few seconds a number
of the most distinguished chiefs and warriors.
Their onset was for a moment checked. The
British troops cheered, and renewed with alacrity
their firing. At the same time, the field-pieces,
now brought to bear upon the thickest of the
enemy, opened a most destructive fire of grape-
shot. Some of the warriors rushed madly forward
and hurled their spears at the artillerymen; but
it was in vain. The front ranks were mown
down like grass; those behind recoiled; a wild
panic and irretrievable rout ensued. Makanna,
after vainly attempting to rally them, accompanied
their flight. They were pursued but a short way;
for the handful of cavalry durst not follow them
into the broken ravines where they precipitated
their flight. The slaughter was great for so
brief a conflict. About one thousand four hundred
Kafir warriors strewed the field of battle; and
many more perished of their wounds before they
reached their own country." Makanna afterwards
surrendered to the British authorities and was im-
prisoned on Robben Island.[14]

Previous to the last Kafir war, Sandilli had
endeavoured to prevail on the chiefs, under British
rule, to rise against the white man. Pato refused;
while others, who approved the plan, thought the

time unfavourable for its execution. It was now reported—the son of Gaika probably knew whence the rumour had gone forth—that a child with two heads had been born; that it had spoken immediately after birth, and foretold the overthrow of the English. Public attention was also attracted by Umlanjeni, a young prophet of the Gaika tribe, who rendered himself notorious by standing up to the chin in a pool of water, for several hours, without food. (The fact that he subsequently refused to receive anything from his devotees, has been thought to show that he was merely a tool in the hands of Sandilli and his confederates.) Umlanjeni's influence quickly grew, and the principal chiefs were prevailed on to consult the great prophet, and leave the question of peace or war to his decision. They asked him what they were to do—the English had their land and were treating them like dogs—they were drying up the country with the sun—if left alone they would starve them to death. The seer pronounced that war was in the land, and directed his visitors to divide themselves into two parties—those with guns, and those with assagais. The latter were to lie flat on the ground, while the gun-party, representing the English, fired; they were then to spring up and rush quickly on their foes before the latter could reload. In this manner the Kafirs were to fight the troops. When asked what the warriors were to eat, he produced the skins of two sheep and one goat, and undertook to provide those animals during the war. He appointed Macomo and Umhala to the chief command; and directed that the signal for commencing hostilities should be an attempt which, he predicted, the English would make to seize him. Kreli, the paramount chief of the Amaxosa, and Umtirara, a chief of the Tambukies, are said to have visited him.

People were sent to recal the natives living in the colony. "A toil-worn messenger would arrive at a location of native huts, during the night; and before dawn the indwellers had disappeared with their moveable effects; whilst the courier passed on to warn others of his fellow-countrymen, or gave over the *word* to a comrade, by which means it was passed on from hut to hut and farm to farm." Many, who possessed cattle, abandoned them; "others had wages due, but they cared not to stop for money; a great and powerful magnet was drawing them towards the country of their chiefs." Some of these servants returned to advise their employers to "flee as fast and as far as they could."

At length, "in spite of the reluctance of the authorities to believe in any hostile intentions on the part of the enemy," the truth of the suspicions entertained in the colony "became so apparent, that intelligence of the unsettled state of affairs and an expected movement was despatched to Sir Harry Smith at Cape Town. He suddenly appeared on the spot and immediately commenced personal enquiries." The Hlambies affected submission; and the governor expressed himself satisfied with their loyalty. Sandilli feared to go to

King William's Town according to command, and was displaced by proclamation; but many of his people assembled to hear the deposal explained, and approved the governor's act. The councillors acknowledged that Sandilli owed everything to Smith, and must bear the consequences of his disobedience; while a few days later his mother declared, at a joint meeting of Gaikas and Hlambies, that he was no longer fit to rule. About the same time Botman, a Gaika chief, voluntarily surrendered some stolen cattle—a device which Sandilli himself had employed three or four months before. The governor was completely deceived, and left the frontier with the conviction that there was nothing to justify alarm. The following account of one of the meetings which he held, will show how artfully the Kafirs dissembled:—

VENA, a councillor, asked if he might speak; when the governor replied that he might say what he pleased, so that he did not ask forgiveness for Sandilli. VENA: "We will say nothing on that subject. The governor knows best how to treat Sandilli, who is but a child, and does not attend to his councillors."

TSHALA thanked the governor for the ground given him; and said that Sandilli was afraid to come, lest the governor should take him, and treat him as he was treated before. The GOVERNOR remarked that he must have been doing something wrong. TSHALA: "Sandilli must bear his own disgrace. We are all children of the government. We thank you much."

JONAS, Botman's son, thanked for his father. Botman was only a sickly old woman; he was paralyzed on one side. The governor was next to God over them. He was here to see they had their rights. They would bring all their cases to him, who never tired to hear them. He thanked very much for Botman, who only wished for peace. All old men lived on corn and milk, and they had now the means of doing so quietly. He thanked the governor for giving them Brownlee (the British Commissioner) who always looked well to their interests.

GOUIGAMA : " We thank our father for giving us peace, and allowing us to sleep in quiet. You are our god." GOVERNOR : " No ! there is but one God." GOUIGAMA : " You are our helper and protector."

VICA thanked. They were the governor's dogs, and would do as he wished. They were afraid of him.

VENA asked if the governor would be angry if he spoke freely. GOVERNOR : " No, but you must not ask forgiveness for Sandilli." VENA thanked the governor for having spared Sandilli's life.

TSHALA thanked for the treatment of Sandilli. Anything they had to say should come through Brownlee, who was a quiet and good man. GOVERNOR : " If he were not, I would remove him ; that is my principle ; that is the reason why I have removed Sandilli."

GENYAMA : " You are the person we are to look to, to put things right.

JAN TZATZOE thanked the governor for his word ; and said that, though there had been rumours of war, one man could not make war ; however great he might be, he could not do it without the assistance of his tribe. He thanked the governor for having spared Sandilli's life.

It was not long after the governor's departure that Umlanjeni directed the people to prepare themselves for the strife by ordering them to *slay and eat.* " Feasting became the order of the day ; frantic dances formed the interlude ; and a species of intoxication was thus produced which ripened the youth for mischief. Such a sudden engorgement of animal food stimulates them very powerfully, and they are ready for any desperate deed." Houses were now " broken open, chiefly for guns and amunition; bands of Kafirs were seen in the Chumie; assagais and *veldtschoens* were being manufactured in every direction; and all Kafirland was in a state of ominous ferment." The governor (in consequence of information forwarded by a Commission he had appointed) again visited the frontier, within less than a month from the time of his leaving it. Having marched his troops to the Amatola Mountains, that he might overawe the Gaikas without employing force, he held a meeting of that tribe at Fort Cox. More than three thousand people were present. Sir Harry addressed them respecting the conduct of Sandilli, for whose apprehension a large reward was offered; he expressed himself determined to preserve order; and spoke of his ability to bring ships full of soldiers to the Buffalo mouth. Upon this, Umhala asked very significantly whether he had any ships *that could sail up the Amatola Mountains.* At this meeting, Sandilli's mother was appointed regent. The "announcement was received with a shout; and with the re-echo of that shout her authority ceased." A few days after, a patrol of five hundred and eighty strong, were ordered to the Keiskamma Hoek, "where Sandilli was supposed to be concealed, in the expectation that he would surrender or fly, as the governor was led to believe. They marched from Fort Cox on the twenty-fourth of December, with orders to molest no one; and were treated in the most friendly manner by the Kafirs until they had reached a narrow rocky gorge of the Keiskamma, where they could only proceed in

single file, when a fire was suddenly opened on the
column of infantry, after the Kafir-Police and Cape
Mounted Rifles had been suffered to pass. The
fire was most resolutely maintained for some time,
and the ground was so well chosen for the attack,
that the troops could not dislodge the Kafirs, until
they had suffered considerable loss, the mounted
police and Cape corps being unavailable." Twelve
of the British were killed, and nine wounded.
The Kafir-Police had doubtless led the military into
this ambuscade. Next day three hundred and
sixty-five of that body deserted, taking their equip-
ments and amunition, as well as a knowledge of
our military manœuvres acquired in a long course of
training. The governor now proclaimed martial
law. Umlanjeni survived the war, and died shortly
afterwards in Kreli's country. Some said that he
was poisoned.[15]

Since the termination of the war, efforts have
been made to produce a renewal of the strife.
Some of the prophets (with the apparent design of
obliging the people to plunder the colonists) directed them to kill their cattle and abstain from
agriculture; they also predicted that the Russians
would invade the colony and sweep away the
English. Hundreds obeyed the command; but,
when the time fixed for the Muscovite invasion had
expired, the prophets lost their credit. After this
arose Umhlakaza to foretel the coming of a great
change; a resurrection of men and cattle was
about to take place—enemies and strangers were to

be swept as by a whirlwind from the earth, and the country now possessed by the white man was to revert to its original occupants. This consummation was contingent on the previous destruction by the people of their cattle, goats, and corn. Kreli's subjects listened with eagerness to the prophet, and killed their cattle in large numbers; many of the Hlambies did the same; Sandilli said to the British Commissioner that, if he sinned in disobeying Umhlakaza, it would be a sin of ignorance, which he hoped God would not severely punish. The prophet's connexion with Kreli, the acknowledged head of all the Amaxosa tribes, added much to his influence.

About the beginning of 1857, a great meeting was held at Butterworth, in Kreli's country. Six thousand persons—many of them reduced to skin and bone by privation—assembled on foot and horseback, to hear the prophet's instructions. Kreli was present but "not in a very comfortable mood. The wild extravagances of the prophet, who had been stimulated and protected by him, had become so gross as well as mischievous that even the most credulous of his dupes began to have misgivings on the subject and to call in question his claim to their further credence. This feeling led to a sharp cross examination of the chief by the assembled Kafirs; and he found it extremely difficult to parry the many hits made at him." The prophet, who did not condescend to appear, sent "a word" to the assembly, saying that some of the chiefs (one being mentioned by name) had not fulfilled his orders; but, when directed to kill their cattle, had hesitated, and asked why they should do it. This stubborn and rebellious conduct, he declared, had grieved the risen spirits and induced them to return to their graves. "He also said that if the full moon rose blood-red, the Kafirs must meet again at Butterworth, as it would be symbolical of the spirits having returned to their wonted good humour; but should the full moon not appear thus, they must re-assemble at the new moon." Kreli attempted to commit suicide while returning home, and his followers were obliged to disarm him.

The following extract is from the King William's Town Gazette of February 7th. "Cattle-killing is still carried on by the natives in British Kaffraria, though, calculating from the number of hides recently brought into King William's Town, not to any great extent. If the Kafirs desired to slaughter zealously, we question whether they are now in a position so to do, as, even within a short distance of this town, there are to our certain knowledge several kraals that have killed almost every head of cattle they possessed. At locations a short distance from the town, men may be seen tightly girthed-in to still the pangs of hunger. These, by doing a little work here and there, seem to get only sufficient to keep body and soul together; and the inference therefore is that those who live more inland, where they have not these slight advantages (inestimable though to men in their condition) are in a still more deplorable state. . . . . Though the sufferings of some must be most acute, they bear them with a stoicism worthy of Cato himself. The prophet's influence, too, in the midst of all this, continues unimpaired, and leads them daily to the performance of innumerable silly actions. The last decree issued by him is that all the huts must be newly thatched; otherwise, should a drop of rain penetrate into any one, the inmates will at once become defunct. In obedience to these instructions, many Kafirs are now re-thatching their huts, and, in several instances that have been brought to our notice, the work has been already completed, and the huts rendered perfectly water-tight."

Another great meeting was held at the prophet's residence about Feb. 8 (that day being full moon). " Kreli, with about eighteen followers, consisting of his head men and representatives of the frontier chiefs, and about four or five thousand warriors, were present. The latter, not having exactly ful-filled the orders of the prophet, were afraid to go very near to the place, in case anything should happen to them for not having killed all their cattle; they remained, therefore, about half a mile distant, while Kreli and the great men drew near. After a long consultation the chief returned, but those who saw him observed a change in his counte-nance—a change that betokened disappointment and chagrin. He, however, told the assembled throng that he had seen some wonderful things, and heard men talk under the ground. He then delivered the prophet's orders, which were that they were to kill everything, with the exception

of a cow and goat, and that eight days were to be
given them to do this, to be counted from the day
after the great chief got home; that the cattle and
people would rise, perhaps on the eighth day, but
certainly on the ninth; that the sign would be that
the sun would not rise until half-past eight, and
then it would turn red and go back, when darkness would follow; or otherwise a very heavy
storm, with thunder and lightning, and darkness,
would warn them that the prophecies were about to
be fulfilled. The assembled throng dispersed, and
went to their homes to fulfil these orders, and
they did it in right earnest. Cattle in thousands
were killed, and goats without number. You have
heard that hitherto Kreli and his people held back
the largest portion of their cattle; but now, it is
said, no deception was practised, and they killed
with right good will. At some of the trading
stations of Butterworth hides came in so fast that
they could not be purchased; while thousands,
killed higher up in the country, were not brought
to any market. The eighth day at length arrived,
but alas! no predictions were fulfiled; and at last
the ninth and final day came. On this day no
Kafirs were moving about until nearly ten o'clock.
They watched the sun from six o'clock until half-
past nine, but without result. Many of them then
visited Butterworth, but 'how are the mighty
fallen!' There is the expression of disappointment
upon their countenances, and they look down.
Thus is an end put to their hopes, and starvation
and misery are now staring them in the face.

During the eight days they also threw away most of their corn. . . . A Kafir has just told a person, he knows of fully one hundred children who have died from starvation, including one of his own."[16]

III.—RAIN-MAKERS work in secret and little is known of their proceedings. They are said to be visited by a serpent, which lies on their medicine. The profession is hereditary; and it is not unlikely that they possess some weather-wisdom, the result of their ancestors' observation, by means of which they are able to choose a promising season for the exercise of their vocation. A European asked a rain-maker to give him a proof of his power : a liberal fee was offered, but the artist declined; the fee was increased, and again increased, with the same result—the doctor excused himself by saying that the process required time and could not be begun there and then. "Not until the new moon," suggested the European.

There had been no rain for five moons; the pasturage was burned up, and the corn-plants were pale with thirst. Pande offered abundance of sacrifices, but he addressed his ancestors in vain; Tshaka and Jama gave no heed to his prayers, and the hearts of the people were sad. They were not older than their fathers, and did not grow more than was wanted for the year. The pits were nearly empty; and the mothers wept when they thought the cows were becoming dry. Famine was placing his eyes on the nation. The lean ones expected death; they who were fat hoped that they might see "the bow of the queen" in a more propitious season.[17]

Pande now despatched two men to a rain-maker.
The latter demanded their business, and was told
that the king desired him to " work the sky." He
replied that the king had said, on a previous occasion, that he did not know how to do so; and wondered, therefore, that he should be again applied
to. He then enquired for his cattle; but the
messengers had not brought any, and could only
say that he must speak to the king about his fee.
This was a step which he declined to take—the
king, he observed, would kill him. Having entertained his visitors with beer, he directed them to
depart early in the morning, and cautioned them to
travel quickly, lest the rain, filling the rivers,
should stop them. They were also told not to sleep
in a hut on the road; if they did, the rain would
cease at the spot, and not reach Nodwenge. They
had not travelled many miles, when it began to
thunder, and a copious shower confirmed their
belief in the doctor's ability; the rain however did
not continue, and the evening was fine. They
begged a brand, and slept in the bush. There
was rain also next day; and, when they reached
the Great Place, they found the people in better
spirits. The king would not, however, give the
rain-maker any credit for what had taken place,
but attributed it to Tshaka and Dingana.

Still he was not without faith in the doctor, and
sent for him to Nodwenge; but, at the same time,
he summoned a female practitioner of great repute.
The man was exceedingly indignant when he heard
that the king had attributed the rain to his ances-

tors; and, if he had dared to do so, would have disobeyed the summons. The woman promised rain at once, while the man said that there could be none till next day; she was therefore told to "work" immediately. A black sheep having been produced, an incision was made near the shoulder, and the gall taken out. Part of this she rubbed over her own person—part she drank—part was mixed with medicine. A portion of the medicine also was rubbed on her person—the remainder being placed on a stick, which was then fixed in the fence of a calves' pen. She now harangued the clouds. When the sheep was to be cooked, the fire was kindled by means of flame obtained new from fire-sticks: ordinarily, a brand would have been procured from one of the huts. Some additional ceremonies were performed by the woman about midnight.

No rain fell; a circumstance which she attributed to an "evildoer," though Pande thought that it was due to her old age. (She had been famous in Tshaka's time.) However, the prophet was consulted and some people were in consequence slain. She received a fee of ten cows and went home. When the man afterwards failed to produce rain, he ascribed it to an *um-takati*; but Pande would not kill people for him, who had failed twice before; he was sent home as a deceiver. Rain fell in a few days. Pande has had rain-makers from Natal and the Amaswazi-country.

IV.—The following practices, respecting animal

food, prevail in the Zulu-country. *Fish*, Crocodiles, *Serpents*, *Monkeys*, Hyenas, Zebras, the
Rhinoceros, Gnu, Hartebeest, are not eaten. The
Eland also is abstained from by the Zulus. Several
birds—as the *Duck*, *the Paauw*, *Domestic Fowls*—
Birds' *Eggs*—and *Porcupines* are eaten by none
except young persons and old. The Zulu-warriors
abstain from the flesh of *Wild Pigs*, Elephants,
and Hippopotami; though the Amatefula tribes
do not reject them. I was told, however, by an
old Tetwa man, that his people did not originally
eat those animals; which, he said, came into general
use among them, as food, when Tshaka had taken
away their cattle.[18]

It is said of the Amaxosa Kafirs that "if they
should appropriate the produce of land torn up by
the elephant, or if a young elephant should be
taken alive or should stray into a field, they believe
that the elephant will come and destroy the person
or persons to whom it belongs. Before they attack
an elephant, they shout to it and ask pardon for
the intended slaughter, professing great submission
to his person and stating the necessity of their
having his tusks to enable them to procure beads,
and supply their wants. When they kill one, they
deposit a few of the articles they have obtained for
the ivory, with the end of his trunk in the ground,"
thus expecting to avert some danger that would
otherwise befal them.[19]

The practice of drinking gall was mentioned in
connexion with the Feast of First Fruits. The
Amaxosa also "drink the gall of the ox, stating

that it makes them fierce." The notorious Matuana drank the gall of thirty chiefs, whose people he had destroyed, in the belief that it would render him strong. It is customary, among the Amampondo, for the chief, on his accession, "to be washed in the blood of a near relative, generally a brother, who is put to death on the occasion, and his skull used as a receptacle for his blood." When Faku, the present chief, succeeded to power, his brother Gwingi, who would have been the sacrifice, escaped to a neighbouring tribe. Diligent search was made for the fugitive, who endured many hardships in avoiding his merciless pursuers. Mr. Tainton, reasoning with the chief on his barbarous design, enquired how his father, his grandfather, and his great-grandfather had died. The chief confessed that they had been slain. The missionary reminded Faku that they had been washed in blood to protect them against wounds; and prevailed on him to forego his barbarous purpose, and permit Gwingi to return in peace. In the Zulu-country, when a lion has been killed, a portion of the animal is mixed with medicine to be taken by the king.[20]

To drive away thunder and lightning, medicine is burned, and sometimes put on the hut. A hoe is placed outside the door, while assagais are thrust through the roof. If a person is struck by lightning, the whole kraal fast and do not even drink water until the mediciner has performed his office. He does this by administering medicine to them—by placing it on the huts and near the gate—and by carrying it to the neighbouring hills.

In one case the fast continued four days, though, when the doctor came, he said that the people might have been allowed to drink water. If an ox or cow were killed, the flesh would not be eaten. It is believed that lightning may be caused by an "evildoer." Dingana, thinking that the crowing of the cocks occasioned it, ordered them all to be destroyed. The Amaxosa "conceive thunder to proceed from the Deity; and, if a person is killed by lightning, they say that Uhlanga has been among them. On such occasions they sometimes remove from the spot, and offer a heifer or an ox in sacrifice."

Heaps of stones occur in the Kafir-country, from the Frontier tribes to the Zulus. "I lived in a place near the Keiskamma, where I observed a great heap of stones, and that every one who passed by threw a stone or a handful of grass to it. The Kafir captain who lived in the same place, declared that he himself was ignorant of the reason of this custom. The Hottentots throw stones upon the graves of their people; but this was not a grave."[21] The Bishop of Cape Town passed a heap of stones on the top of a mountain in the Amampondo-country, and was told by Mr. Fynn that it was "customary for every traveller to add one to the heap, that it might have a favourable influence on his journey, and enable him to arrive at some kraal while the pot is yet boiling." I have heard substantially the same account given of the heaps in the Zulu-country.

Among the Frontier tribes, when a man is going

on a doubtful journey, he knots a few blades of grass together, that it may be propitious.[22]   In Natal and the Zulu-country, the natives, when crossing a river inhabited by crocodiles, chew some of the excrements of the animals and spatter it over their person, in the belief that it will protect them from reptiles.

CHAPTER VII.—SOCIAL INSTITUTIONS.

I.—PROPER NAMES among the Kafirs, are two-fold. The one, called *i-gama*, is given to a child soon after birth, and usually refers to some circumstance connected with that event or happening about the same time. If, for example, the mother were very sick, or the father had gone to the great Festival of First Fruits, the child might be named from that fact. The *i-gama* is formed from any description of word, by prefixing *u*; or, when the word begins with a vowel, by changing that vowel into *u*. If a hyena *(impisi)* were heard near the kraal about the time of birth, the child would perhaps be called *u-Mpisi*, unless *u-Huhu* were preferred—the root of the latter name being an imitation of the animal's cry. In one or two instances, when a child has been born on Sunday, it has received the name of *u-Sondo*. Sometimes the *i-gama* is formed by prefixing *uso*, abbreviated from *uyise*, his or her father, or *uno*, abbreviated from *unina*, his or her mother. The former is employed for boys' names; the latter for those of girls. Thus *Uso-mahashe*, "the father of horses," is the name of a chief in Natal; while *Uno-ntsimbi*, "the mother of iron" (from *intsimbi,* iron) might be given to a girl who happened to be born when her mother had just received a new garden hoe.[1]

The other name is called *isi-bonga*—a noun formed from *uku-bonga* to praise. This is an honorary name, borne in addition to the *i-gama,* and independently of it. A name of this description is usually given to a boy while young, and is employed whenever his parents have occasion to commend his juvenile merit. A second *isi-bonga* will signalize his first appearance at the Great Place; and, if he afterwards distinguish himself in war, his companions will acknowledge his bravery and reward his prowess by saluting him with a new *isi-bonga*. When Isaacs had been wounded in an expedition which Tshaka obliged him to join, and was being carried back to the Great Place, " the warriors," says he, " *bonga'd* or offered thanks to me, every one being surprised at the bravery of the white men; and I was honoured with the designation of Tambuza, or the brave warrior who was wounded at Ingoma." When he reached the king's residence, Tshaka saluted him by the same name, saying "I see you, Tambuza;" and by this title he was ever afterwards accosted.

Among the Amatefula tribes, a man is sometimes called by the name of his son, *uso* (for *uyise,* his father) being prefixed to it. A person having a son named Bambula, might therefore be designated *Uso-Bambula,* the father of Bambula. This usage, which is said to prevail among the Amalala and

Amaswazi, is also a Bechuana custom. Related to it is the practice of calling a man by the name of his father, no prefix or addition being made to it; and also by the name of a more remote ancestor.

It has been already stated that individuals affected by the custom of *uku-hlonipa*, may not pronounce each other's *i-gama*. They may use the *isi-bonga*, but the other name is sacred and must be avoided. A breach of this rule would give serious offence, and require to be atoned by a peace-offering. The restriction is not however confined to the custom of *uku-hlonipa*. A wife may not publicly pronounce the *i-gama* of her husband or any of his brothers; nor may she use the interdicted word in its ordinary sense. If her husband, for example, be called *u-Mpaka*, from *impaka*, a small feline animal, she must speak of that beast under some other appellation. Again, the chief's *i-gama* is withdrawn from the language of his people, and may not be used as an ordinary word. Thus, the present ruler of the Zulu-country being called *u-Mpande*, from *impande*, a root, his subjects avoid that term in their conversation and substitute *ingxabo*. (This usage is more strictly observed by the women than the other sex.) The same rule applies to the names of deceased chiefs: the Zulus still abstain from using the verb *enza* to make, *u-Menzi* having been the *i-gama* of Tshaka's father. The Dwandwes do not say *i-langa*, the sun, out of respect to *u-Langa*; while the Xnumayo, who had a chief called *u-Mayusi*, sub-

stitute *kagesa* for *alusa* (or *ayusa*) to herd cattle.
It seems also that the word which forms the
root of a tribal name is, or was, treated with the
same respect—a circumstance to be explained by
the fact that the tribe is named after its founder or
some subsequent chief.

It is easy to perceive that this usage respecting
the *i-gama*, has great influence on the language of
the people ; every tribe must have words peculiar
to itself, and the women a considerable vocabulary
of their own. Members, too, of one family may
not be able to use words employed by those of
another ; the women of this kraal may call a hyena
by its ordinary name ; those of the next may use
the common substitute ; while, in a third, this may
be unlawful, and some other invented to supply its
place.

In one sense, the *isi-bonga* may be considered
as a title of honour ; but, inasmuch as it is peculiar
to individuals and in reality a proper name, it does
not strictly answer to our notion of an honorary
title. The chief's titles have been already alluded
to. His principal officers are addressed by the title
um-gana ; which, like Esquire among ourselves, is
applied to many not strictly entitled to it. In
Pande's presence, it would be limited to its proper
use. It is the title ordinarily given to the English;
but sometimes a Kafir addresses you with the nearest
approach he can make to *Sir.* R being wholly
beyond his power to pronounce, he alters the word,
and calls you *Sa* or *Swi.* This, like the native

title, is applied to both sexes; and ladies, no less than their knights, are honoured with the salutation of *Swi*.

A Kafir does not apply titles of honour merely according to our own usage, and say only "Yes, *'myana*," or "No, *Swi*." Etiquette requires him, on some occasions, to pronounce them in a formal manner. When, for instance, a person visits the kraal of an important man, he proceeds to his hut, but without entering; and repeats the master's titles, or as many as he may think necessary. In the same way thanks are expressed—more or less abundantly, according to the value of the favour. For a present of snuff, a man might have the pleasure of hearing his *isi-bonga*—unless he happened to be rich, when he would most likely be addressed as *'Baba*, (my father,) or *'mgana*. A gift of beef would excite more enthusiasm, and elevate you at once to the rank of *in-kosi* or chief. In the Zulu-country it is usual, when thanking the king, to hold up the fore-finger of the right hand.

II.—SNUFF-TAKING is eminently a social usage. Almost every individual, male and female, practises it; and Kafirs seldom meet without indulging in a concert of snuffing. The most important person is expected to supply the material, but he must be *asked* to do so; for, "should you offer snuff before it is asked for, or even give it readily when asked for (the custom is to refuse it at first and then present it) they would look upon you suspiciously; and, if they should be taken ill, think you have poisoned them. Many have been thus suspected and killed."[2] The mode of asking differs, according to the quality of the person addressed. If he were poor, he would be solicited in plain literal language and requested to give snuff; but, if a rich man, he would have his generous instincts excited by a respectful innuendo, and it would be said to him: " What do you eat, Sir?" A rude man, who did not intend to give his snuff, answered that he eat food; but a polite man, who wished to reply in the negative, would say that he did not eat anything at present. When a man furnishes snuff for a party, he usually pours a large quantity into his left hand, and holds it for the others to take pinches as they may require, but without looking at them. If however he be rich and liberal, he first helps himself, and then tosses the box to his companions, that they may do the same. When a chief entertains his *ama-pakati*, the box is brought to him in a basket; he then shakes out a large quantity into the united hands of a servant, by whom it is carried round to the guests.

When a person takes snuff—especially if, being the entertainer, he is also stretching out his hand—he is comparatively defenceless. It may be owing to this circumstance that a man would be considered rude and ill-mannered, if he were to stand up while taking snuff with another: he would possess a decided advantage over him; and, if treacherously disposed, might easily overpower him. The cowardly agents of the Zulu despot have frequently made snuff-taking an auxiliary

in the destruction of their victims. Pande having
resolved to kill one of his officers, despatched a
messenger to summon him to the Great Place,
under the pretence that he was required to assist
in some war-ceremonies. The officer, who had
but lately returned from court, was not deceived;
he felt sure that the king wanted him for another
purpose, and that if he went to Nodwenge he
should never come home again. Having dismissed the messenger, with an assurance that he
would immediately follow, he called together his
wives and dependants, and held a family consultation as to what it would be advisable to do.
He expressed his conviction that he was a doomed
man, and the council could hardly doubt it; yet
they advised him to obey the king's summons—if
he did not he would certainly be slain, whereas
it was possible that Pande really wanted him for
the purpose alleged. He yielded and set forth,
having been particularly cautioned not to part
from his weapons by the way. Before he had
gone far, he was descried by a party of men,
whom Pande, rendered suspicious by delay, had
sent to kill him. When these monsters saw the
in-duna approaching, two of the party walked
forward along the path; while the rest, to prevent alarm, concealed themselves in the grass.
When the former came up to him, he was squatting on the ground, and helping his melancholy
cogitations with copious inhalations of snuff. One
of the messengers immediately began a conversation, and asked permission to partake. The *in-*

duna replied that he had no snuff; and, on being reminded that there was some in his hand, said it was a very small quantity and not worth acceptance. The request being repeated, he imprudently held his hand towards the stranger, who took up the snuff very slowly. Meanwhile his companion came forward, saying that he also wished to partake; but instead of doing so he snatched the councillor's weapons, which were lying near him, and in a few minutes the unfortunate man was dead.

III.—It has been previously mentioned that an ox is slaughtered at every wedding, and consumed by the company: invited guests alone join in the dances, but any one may help to consume the meat. Marriage-feasts are those which most frequently occur; but, generally speaking, a feast takes place wherever there is beef to eat. If, for instance, a man have sacrificed an ox to propitiate or thank the spirits, his neighbours assemble to devour it; if he have killed a beast to celebrate his daughter's espousal, it will be consumed in the same way. This custom has no doubt arisen from a want of acquaintance with the art of preserving meat.

Rich men usually require an invitation to a feast; but dependants and unmarried men go unasked. A party of "boys," having gone to a kraal where it was known that an ox had been slain, saluted the master respectfully. He addressed them in a surly tone, and said that he had no beef for "boys"—he did not choose to have "boys" coming to his kraal. The "boys" replied that they would like to know where the "man" was to whom he would give meat—they found *him* at every feast—his beef was nothing—he was a shabby fellow, and they would not touch it. Saying this, they left the kraal. Some time afterwards there was beef to eat at the " boys'" kraal, where the churl did not fail to appear. The "boys" had been watching for him, and immediately informed their father, who received his uninvited guest with an expression of surprise and referred to the treatment which his sons had received. The mean man denied that beef had been refused—the "boys," he said, came to see his daughters, and went away because he disapproved of their visit. Hearing this, the "boys" reminded him that, when they entered his kraal, they went direct to himself; and repeated his positive refusal to give them meat. Unable to support his falsehood, the shabby man now treated the matter as a joke, and said pleasantly that they ought not to have told their father; but the "boys" were not disposed to let him escape so easily, and read him a lecture on the impropriety of telling lies. Another churl was chagrined to see his kraal invaded by a number of married men. He had not the courage to ask what they wanted; yet, being determined that they should not eat his beef, he addressed their dogs as hungry thieves come to steal his beef; and, attacking the animals with a stick, maimed one and killed another. The owner of the latter having expressed displeasure, the man replied that he had not invited dogs to eat. The hint was intelligible, and his visitors answered that his beef was nothing—they would not eat it—they would go. *That*, he intimated, would be nothing.

When a Kafir is travelling, he generally finds entertainment among his own tribe. If he go beyond it and seek the hospitality of strangers, he will hardly succeed, unless his chief be known to them and enjoy a good reputation. They would give him permission to sleep in the young men's hut for the night, but would scarcely let him taste their food.[2]

Two "boys" were going to Nodwenge; and, about sunset, reached a kraal where they purposed remaining for the night. Being acquainted with a bachelor-relation of the owner's, they went to his hut, and asked for food. He called a girl, and told her to bring some curds for the travellers. The repast was set before them; but they had hardly begun to eat when the owner of the kraal, discovering what had been done, ordered her to fetch it away. With tears in her eyes (for her father had beaten her) she entered the hut, and snatched away the vessel; as the young man was following her in great wrath, the owner appeared, and, entering the hut, stormed furiously at his offending relative: "You rascal—this is not your kraal— it is mine—go and build a kraal for yourself, and then give people food." The young man, who was chastised as well as scolded, said that he would not endure such treatment—he was not a young boy to be beaten—he would become the dependant of some other person—he was beaten for giving food to the king's people. The infuriated man replied that he did not care whose people they were— they had not come to salute him as owner, and should not eat his food. Then, turning to the visitors, he told them to go, and began to beat the ground with his stick. They were not disposed to be silent—the country, they said, was not his— it belonged to the king. He did not care—they might go to the king—they should not stay in his kraal. The beating on the floor continued; the blows came nearer and nearer their feet; and they thought that it would be necessary to leave. Their friend, not liking to see his floor destroyed, entreated them to do so; and they now told the man that, but for his outrageous conduct, they would have gone before. Taking the hint, he left the hut and called them to follow. They crept after him, but the darkness of the night appalled them, and they refused to leave the kraal—they did not wish to be killed by the wild beasts. The man said that *he* should not be sorry to hear of such a consummation, and drove them out.

They were unable to find the path, and wandered among the grass. Hearing the howl of a hyena, they stooped down, and, looking along the surface of the ground, discovered two of the grizzled beasts within a few yards of them. This animal being fortunately a great coward, a little vigorous shouting, seconded by a missile or two, put the

enemy to flight; and our travellers proceeded.
Walking very fast and stumbling very often,
they came, at length, to a fence. They were
some minutes in doubt whether it belonged to a
kraal or a garden; but a well known sound
revealed the presence of cattle disturbed by the
noise they made, and assured them that they had
reached a human habitation. Shouting loudly,
they aroused the owner, who left his hut, armed
with an assagai; and instead of replying to their
question, "Where is the gate?" crept stealthily
about the kraal to reconnoitre. Not doubting
that they had been heard, the wanderers upbraided the people of the kraal with their want
of hospitality, and said that it was very wrong
not to open the gate. The man replied that it
was very wrong to disturb honest people at
night; and asked where they came from. "From
the kraal of an 'evildoer,' who has turned us out
in the dark." When told who the *um-takati* was,
he said: "Do you call him a *takati?* He acted
very improperly; but you must not call him a
takati. I shall tell him what you say." They
had no objection, they said, to his doing so.
The owner now admitted them, and indicated the
hut in which they were to sleep. When they
asked for food, he wished to know where they
thought it likely he could obtain it, all the women
being asleep; but they fared no better in the
morning, and departed very hungry.

Their host did not forget to tell his neighbour
that they had denounced him as an "evildoer."

The inhospitable man was wroth, and threatened the elder offender with a merciless beating. The latter, having heard of the menace through his bachelor-friend, took care not to show himself in the neighbourhood for a long time.

More than twelve months afterwards, he was sent from the Great Place with a message to a subject chief. The path leading him near the inhospitable kraal, he determined to revisit it. Presuming on his security as a royal messenger, he went to the principal hut and stooped down to enter. At that moment the owner was creeping out; and, as they came into contact, his head was slightly injured. He was more frightened however than hurt; for, seeing the unceremonious stranger, he imagined that a party of soldiers had been sent to kill him. Springing, with surprising agility, to his feet, he bounded towards the gate and was ready to run to the bush; but, not discovering the armed men his imagination had painted, he returned to question his unwelcome visitor.

" Where do you come from?"

" From Isangu."

" Where is the King?"

" At Isangu."

" Where are you going to?"

" To Mapite's."

" What are you taking to him?"

" Nothing. I am going to talk."

" What are you going to say?"

" I shall not tell you. It is the king's business."

" I should not divulge it."

" I am not silly. I shall not tell you."

" Has the king ordered you to tell Mapite to kill any one?"

" No."

The stranger was now recognized; but, instead of the beating that had been promised, he was regaled with the best food the kraal afforded.

IV.—Generally speaking, the Kafirs are a good humoured people, with a keen relish for AMUSEMENTS. Of these, gossip may claim to be considered one. The men, especially, having no serious occupation, spend much of their time in telling or hearing some new thing. Information thus travels very quickly. A European had shot a crocodile near his house; and, wishing to procure some of its fat, determined to boil a portion of the animal. No other vessel being at hand, he made use of the iron pot in which his native servants were accustomed to cook their food. He could not have done anything more calculated to shock their prejudices, crocodile's flesh being held in extreme abhorrence. Not one of them would have willingly touched the abominable thing; to find that their cooking-vessel had been polluted by it —this was " horrible, most horrible," and they immediately deserted the white *um-takati*. Being left without servants, he went to several kraals in search of others; but the story of the crocodile was known wherever he came, and he could find no one willing to engage with him. He determined therefore to make his enquiries at a greater distance, and reached a kraal where the people were willing to listen to him. He now ventured to hope that he had outstripped rumour itself, and that the fame of his unfortunate mistake would no longer interfere with his success. The owner seemed peculiarly friendly, promised to send him a boy, gave an unsolicited permission to beat the youth if he were disobedient, but requested that he might not be fed on—crocodile.

Jesting seldom displeases a Kafir, provided it be apparent that you are really in jest. Nor are practical jokes unknown. Some women, carrying maize for sale, went to a European's. Near the house was a newly-dug trench, which they were preparing to cross, when a native boy, a servant at the place, told them that his master required all Kafirs before they passed the trench, to kneel down and kiss the ground. This was said with a perfectly grave countenance, and the women would have obeyed the alleged injunction, if something had not occurred to reveal the jest. A more mischievous prank was played at the same farm and perhaps by the same urchin. Seeing an old woman carrying a pumpkin, a boy went towards her and shouted hastily that there was something on her head. The burden was too usual a thing to occur to her mind; she shrieked at the thought of some hideous object; and, with a start which dislodged the pumpkin, ran frantically forward, unconscious of the hearty laughter of her tormentor, who picked up the prize and cooked it.

The principal and most conspicuous amusements are dances and songs, the latter being chiefly accompaniments of the former. A Kafir-dance bears little resemblance to the English amusement of that name. The motion of the feet is altogether different: in some cases, they are alternately lifted, to descend with a stamp; sometimes the performers jump or leap up and down on each foot alternately; "sometimes a leaping stride is taken to each side;" on some occasions they "use a more violent gesture. Forming four deep, in open order, they make short runs to and fro, leaping, prancing, and crossing each other's paths, brandishing their sticks, and raising such a cloud of dust by the vehemency and rapidity of the exercise, that to a bystander it has all the effect of the wildest battle-scene of savage life, which it is doubtless intended to imitate." In some dances the performer carries only a stick in his right hand; in others he has a shield in his left hand, and a stick or an assagai in his right; but whatever he carries is kept in constant motion, while his lungs are occupied with the chant or song. The exertion required is very great, and the amusement a real labour. This description applies to the men; the women employ other gestures.

In wedding-dances (these being the most frequent) the performers are arranged in a semicircle (sometimes there are two such lines, one behind the other)—the people, men and women, facing inwards. The men bear a small shield in their left hand, and in their right a stick (by which must be understood not only a stick in the ordinary sense, but a long wooden spear sometimes substituted for it). Assagais are very properly interdicted by custom on these occasions, when the wrangling disputes which frequently occur might render them very dangerous. I once saw the rule infringed by a gigantic coxcomb, who brought a barbed assagai to a wedding. He belonged to the bride's party, who were engaged in dancing, when the bridegroom entered the *isi-baya* and careered before them in truly savage style. This was thought disrespectful to the dancers, and the giant stepped forward as their champion. He was very violent, flourished his assagai, and created no small disturbance. The bridegroon was equally excited; and blood might have been shed, but for the interference of wiser and more pacific persons. During or at the conclusion of the dance, the leader makes a speech. If he mentions one of his followers, the latter leaves the line and exhibits himself in front. If a powerful man, he runs forward, stamping the ground vigorously; but, if not able to make an imposing display of strength, he shows his agility by leaping up in the air and kicking his shield.[3]

The accompanying tunes will give the reader some idea of native music. He must imagine them sung in concert by a party of dancers. The sound of a war-song at the Zulu-court, where hundreds of voices are combined, has been described as overpowering. A song in praise of

Tshaka will be given in the next chapter. The following is the substance of a marriage-song.

> " We tell you to dig well.
> Come, girl of ours,
> Bring food and eat it ;
> Fetch fire-wood,
> And don't be lazy."

The subjoined lines are the translation of a hymn composed by one of the first fruits of Missionary labour among the Frontier Kafirs.

> " Thou art the great God—He who is in heaven.
> It is Thou, Thou shield of Truth.
> It is Thou, Thou Tower of Truth.
> It is Thou, Thou Bush of Truth.
> It is Thou, Thou who sittest in the highest.
> Thou art the Creator of life, Thou madest the regions above.
> The Creator who madest the heavens also.
> The Maker of the Stars and the Pleiades.
> The shooting stars declare it unto us.
> The Maker of the blind, of thine own will didst thou make
> The Trumpet speaks—for us it calls.   [them.
> Thou art the Hunter who hunts for souls.
> Thou art the Leader who goes before us.
> Thou art the great Mantle which covers us.
> Thou art He whose hands are with wounds.
> Thou art He whose feet are with wounds.
> Thou art He whose blood is a trickling stream—and why ?
> Thou art He whose blood was spilled for us.
> For this great price we call.
> For thine own place we call."[4]

The Kafirs have three musical instruments. One is a bow, with a small hollow calabash attached and a single string. The instrument is held as in the illustration, the string being struck with a small stick.

Another is a common reed, also shown in the illustration. The third is the leg bone of a sheep, goat, or antelope, from which sound is produced as children obtain it from a key.

T.GILKS.S^c

V.—The Frontier Kafirs look with great horror on persons subject to fits. A poor creature of this description having come to a missionary station, to escape the persecution of his friends, the native servants refused to eat out of the vessels he had used, and it was necessary to give him a separate house to sleep in. In the neighbourhood of Clarkbury, epileptics are cast over a precipice, or tied to a tree to be devoured by hyenas.[5] In the Zulu-country a girl of weak intellect was treated with great barbarity. Having been cruelly beaten,

she left the kraal with a bleeding head ; the neighbours were as hard-hearted as her relatives—no
one would even give her a morsel of food. At
length she reached a trader's wagon, where she
was received with kindness and soon satisfied her
hunger. When the men of the kraal saw the
white man they declared that they would kill her
—a threat which, he told me, they eventually
fulfilled.

Sick persons are sometimes exposed, both among
the Frontier Kafirs and those of Natal and the
Zulu-country. "Instances are not rare," says
Mr. Isaacs, "in which the dying are carried to
the bush and left to perish, rather than the living
should have to carry them away when dead."
Captain Gardiner mentions the case of a woman
who, as her end approached, was carried out into
the woods. I have heard of an instance in which
a dependant was thrown into a river before he
was quite dead. This barbarous custom arises
partly from the dread which the people have of
touching a corpse (when a man has done so, he
washes himself) and partly, I imagine, from the
circumstance that a sacrifice is deemed necessary to
cleanse from pollution a person who has "buried"
another.[6]

When a person is allowed to die at home, the
mourning-ceremonies begin as soon as he is deemed
past recovery.[7] If it be the master of a kraal
who is sick unto death, the people permit their
hair to grow, abstain from greasing and washing,

lay aside their ornaments, and wear the worst dress they have. Death having taken place, they add another sign of grief, and fast. Sometimes the women do not acquaint the children with their father's decease, until they have supplied them with a good meal.

It is said by Mr. Isaacs that " when a man dies, his body is dragged on the ground, by his wife or mother or nearest female relative, to the thicket or jungles; where, the first night after it is so deposited, it becomes a repast for wolves and other wild animals." I have been assured that this is not true of the Zulu-country, where only dependants and those executed by the king's orders are thus treated.

The owner of a kraal is buried within it, the grave being dug by his brother and one or two of his elder wives. They then carry or drag the body to the place, and deposit it in the hole in a sitting posture. The deceased's personal articles are buried with him—the assagais being broken or bent lest the ghost, during some midnight return to air, should do injury with them. The grave being filled, the eldest son stands upon it. The people now go to the stream and wash—the brother returning to sit outside the gate, and the wives retiring to the bush. The doctor having given medicine to the family (excepting sons' wives) and to the brother, the people are relieved from their fast, milk the cows, and cut their hair. The sextons, however, may not eat *ama-si* nor cut their hair, until they have taken medicine a second time. The eldest son furnishes a beast, which is slain to "wash" or cleanse them from their uncleanness. The brother receives another for his fee, and goes home. After some time, the wives leave the bush and cut their hair. The eldest son remains at home a considerable time; and afterwards offers a sacrifice to the deceased.[8]

I have not interrupted the description of these ceremonies to mention that friends and neighbours come to condole with the family. They assemble near the principal hut, and bewail the loss which the kraal has sustained. They express sympathy for the wives, who now have no one to direct them —old men know how to do so—young ones are ignorant and hasty. The son is lectured on the duties of his new position; he is exhorted not to beat any of his mothers, to be kind to the children of his father, and treat the dependants well. Tears are usually very much at the command of these people, but an abundant use of snuff augments the decent exhibition of sorrow.

The mourning for a chief does not materially differ from that above described. Formerly he was buried with his head above ground; but that practice is said to have been abandoned in the Zulu-country; oxen are slain and placed near his grave. When a chief has breathed his last, the *ama-pakati* are informed that he is sick and desires them to dance. They are then directed to remain all night, and it is not till next day that an *induna* announces his demise.[9]

Mourning-ceremonies, at the Zulu court, have been the occasion of great slaughter. That which took place on the death of Tshaka's mother is still spoken of with horror. The Zulu king was hunting elephants, sixty miles from his residence, when messengers came to say that she was seriously ill. The evening had arrived, but he ordered his men to march at once, and reached home about noon next day. Mr. Fynn, who had returned with him, was now requested to visit his mother. " I went," says he, "attended by an old chief, and found the hut filled with mourning women, and such clouds of smoke that I was obliged to bid them retire, to enable me to breathe within it. Her complaint was dysentery; and I reported at once to Tshaka that her case was hopeless, and that I did not expect she would live through the day. The regiments, which were then sitting in a semicircle around him, were ordered to their barracks; while Tshaka himself sat for about two hours in a contemplative mood, without a word escaping his lips, several of the elder chiefs sitting also before him. When the tidings were brought that she had expired, Tshaka immediately arose and entered his dwelling; and, having ordered the principal chiefs to put on their war-dresses, he in a few minutes appeared in his. As soon as the death was publicly announced, the women and all the men who were present, tore instantly from their persons every description of ornament. Tshaka now appeared before the hut in which the body lay, surrounded by his principal chiefs in their war-attire. For about twenty minutes he stood in a silent mournful attitude, with his head bowed upon his shield, on which I saw a few large tears fall. After two or three deep sighs, his feelings becoming ungovernable, he broke out into frantic yells, which fearfully contrasted with the silence that had hitherto prevailed. This signal was enough. The chiefs and people, to the number of about fifteen thousand, commenced the most dismal and horrid lamentations. . . The people from the neighbouring kraals, male and female, came pouring in, each body as they came in sight, at the distance of half-a-mile, joining to swell the terrible cry. Through the whole night it continued, none daring to take rest or refresh themselves with water; while, at short intervals, fresh bursts were heard as more distant regiments approached. The morning dawned, without any relaxation; and before noon the number had increased to about sixty thousand. The cries became now indescribably horrid. Hundreds were lying faint, from excessive fatigue and want of nourishment; while the carcases of forty oxen lay in a heap, which had been slaughtered as an offering to the guardian spirits of the tribe. At noon the whole force formed a circle, with Tshaka in their centre, and sang a war-song, which afforded them some relaxation during its continuance. At the close of it, Tshaka ordered several men to be executed on the spot; and the cries became, if possible, more violent than ever. No further orders were needed; but, as if bent on convincing their chief of their extreme grief, the multitude commenced a general massacre. Many of them received the blow of death while inflicting it on others, each taking the opportunity of revenging his injuries, real or imaginary. Those who could no more force tears from their eyes— those who were found near the river panting for water—were beaten to death by others who were mad with excitement. Toward the afternoon I calculated that not fewer than seven thousand people had fallen in this frightful indiscriminate massacre. The adjacent stream, to which many had fled exhausted to wet their parched tongues, became impassable from the number of dead corpses which lay on each side of it; while the kraal, in which the scene took place, was flowing with blood." Mr. Fynn stood unharmed contemplating the horrors around him, and thankful that he "had so far gained the respect of this tyrant as to hope for escape even from this horrible place of blood. While standing thus motionless, however, a regiment of young Zulus passed by me, when two of them with their uplifted knob-kirries rushed towards me, the leader demanding fiercely why I stood there without a tear. I made no reply, but gazed upon them sternly and steadily. They moved on, shouting vengeance." At sunset, Tshaka stopped the massacre, but the cries continued till ten A. M. on the following day, when the people were permitted to take some refreshment.

The ceremonies of Mnande's burial "were the subject of much deliberation between Tshaka and

his favourite councillors.   On the second day after
her death, the body was placed in a grave, in a
sitting posture, near the spot where she died."
Mr. Fynn, who was not permitted to see the
interment, was informed that ten of the best-
looking girls of the kraal were buried alive with
the deceased.   "All who were present at this
dreadful scene, to the number of twelve thousand,
drafted from the whole army, were formed into a
regiment, to guard the grave for the next twelve
months.   About fifteen thousand head of cattle
were set apart for their use, which were contributed by all the cattle-holders of the country,
as offerings to the spirits of the departed queen
and her ill-fated attendants."

The chiefs proposed that further sacrifices should
be made.   Gomana, whose name will be again met
with in Tshaka's history, recommended that "as
the great Female Elephant with Small Breasts—
the over-ruling Spirit of Vegetation—had died, and
as it was probable that the heavens and the earth
would unite in bewailing her death, the sacrifice
should be a great one: no cultivation should be
allowed during the following year; no milk should
be used, but as drawn from the cow it should be
all poured upon the earth; and all women who
should be found with child during the year, should
with their husbands, be put to death."   At the
close of Gomana's speech, "which was received
with acclamation, regiments of soldiers were dispersed throughout the country, who massacred
every one they could find that had not been present

at the general wailing." This slaughter is said
by Mr. Isaacs to have continued for a fortnight.
For three months Gomana's first two proposals
were strictly carried out; but at the end of that
time "these orders were *redeemed* by large offerings of oxen being made to Tshaka from all the
chiefs." The third proposal, however, "was strictly
enforced throughout the year, during which also
lamentations on a smaller scale took place from
time to time at Tshaka's residence."

At the end of the year Tshaka removed from
the Folosi, where his mother had died, to Tuguza,
a new residence he had constructed on the Umvoti.
Mr. Fynn met him near the Tugela; and, learning
that another lamentation was to take place at Tuguza, entreated that he would not allow any of
his people to be put to death. He was amused
to hear the white man pleading "for the life of
dogs," but he granted the request. " He now
advanced, with his chiefs, in their full war-dress.
Presently Tuguza, lying, as it were, in a basin,
came full in sight; and the outrunners, shouting
out the praises of Tshaka, announced his approach.
Upon this he began to sigh and sob loudly, pretending to falter and stumble in his steps, and
then commenced crying aloud. The whole of the
able-bodied population of the country, each regiment by itself, came in sight, as it were in a
moment, standing upon the edge of the hills which
surrounded Tuguza. They took up, as before,
the frantic cry of their chief; but now with the
general yelling was mingled the bellowing of about

a hundred thousand oxen, brought from the remotest parts of the country, expressly for this occasion. I stood at the distance of half-a-mile, near enough to see that no lives were sacrificed; and glad was I to find that at sunset the lamentations, which began late in the afternoon, were brought to an end, the regiments being ordered to rest, and to slaughter cattle for the evening meal. I retired to my hut; but to sleep was out of the question, from the bellowing of the oxen and the dinning sound of the multitude."

Next morning Tshaka was purified from his uncleanness. "Every cattle-owner had brought calves for this purpose, each of which was ripped open on its right side, the owner taking out the gall of the living animal, which then was left to die in its agonies, and not allowed to be eaten. Each regiment in succession then presented itself before Tshaka; and, as it passed in a circle round him, each individual, holding the gall-bladder in his hand, sprinkled the gall over him."

Gomana now made another speech. "The tribe had now lamented for a year the death of her, who had become a spirit and would continue to watch over Tshaka's welfare. But there were nations of men, inhabiting distant countries, who, because they had not yet been conquered, supposed that they never should be. This was plain from the fact of their not having come forward to lament the death of the Great Mother of Earth and Corn. And, as tears could not be forced from these distant nations, war should be made against them, and the cattle taken should be the tears shed upon her grave." The "war-dance was now performed; several droves of oxen were slaughtered; and Tshaka was finally washed with certain decoctions prepared by the native doctors. And thus this memorable lamentation ended; in which however I cannot help suspecting that reasons of state-policy had as much to do, as any feeling of regret for his dead mother; and that he wished his people to infer, if such a sacrifice was necessary upon the occasion of her departure, how frightfully terrific would be that required at his own !"[10]

T. GILKS. S?

CHAPTER VIII.—HISTORY OF TSHAKA.

I.—EARLY LIFE. II.—CONQUESTS. III.—POLICY. IV.—INTERCOURSE
WITH EUROPEANS. V.—REVERSES OF HIS ARMS. VI.—DEATH.

I.—TSHAKA—the Napoleon of South Africa and founder of the Zulu-dynasty—was born towards the end of the last century. His father, Senzangakona, was chief of the Zulus—a comparatively inconsiderable tribe living on the White Umfolosi. His mother, a daughter of Makedama, chief of the Amalanga, bore the prepossessing name of Mnande (Pleasant)—a name to which her character did not entitle her. She was wilful, obstinate, and uncontrollable; and in the end either absconded from her husband or was repudiated by him. Nor was the son more amiable than the mother. Those who are old enough to remember his early days, describe Tshaka as having been exceedingly mischievous and cruel; chastisement, of which he had no lack, failed to improve him; and he grew up a most perverse and incorrigible youth.

"Tetchy and wayward was his infancy;
    His school-days, frightful, desperate, wild and furious."

How long Tshaka remained with his father, I am unable to say; but, sooner or later, he found it necessary to withdraw from the tribe and seek refuge with Dingiswayo, chief of the Tetwas. Isaacs says, that his father had "resolved that he should

die, and began to plot his death . . . This he
desired to effect the more from another motive;
he well knew, from the fate of his progenitors, that
the children, when they came of age, were allowed
by the Zulus to dethrone their grey-headed fathers,
because they conceive that a young king is more
capable of commanding a nation than an old
one . . . Tshaka's precocity, shrewdness and
cunning, soon enabled him to learn the intention of
his father;" and he fled to the Tetwas. I have
been told that he went, in the first instance, to his
grandfather, Makedama; and that it was not until
his father had demanded him of that chief, that he
fled to Dingiswayo.

Dingiswayo is "reported to have been a man of
great sagacity and to have originated some parts
of the military system which Tshaka afterwards
brought to such perfection."[1] His conquests appear
to have been considerable; an old Umtetwa prophet mentioned no less than thirty chiefs who
acknowledged Dingiswayo's supremacy. The success of his arms has been partly attributed to the
presence of a white man, who appeared on horseback about 1810, among the astonished people.
"He came," say the natives (who treasure up the
memory of this apparition), "from the westward,
having passed through numerous tribes, inspiring
much terror from his extraordinary figure. His
hat was conceived to be a part of his head, which
he had the faculty of removing at pleasure. From
his shoes covering his toes, and his footstep leaving
no impression of them, it was imagined he was

devoid of those appendages. The singular weapon with which he was armed (a gun) vomiting out fire, smoke, and thunder, and the creature on which he was mounted (a horse)—an animal never before seen—caused additional dread; and he was generally shunned by the natives, as a being not of earth. Some kraals killed cattle on his approach as a peace-offering; and on returning to them they state they found, deposited upon the slaughtered beasts, beads and other trinkets. Others honoured him as a wizard, or a creature armed with celestial powers." Dingiswayo "took the traveller for some distance in his train," and (as before intimated) was assisted in his conquests" by the alarm of this awe-inspiring auxiliary." At the Tugela, "having attended Dingiswayo thus far, the stranger proceeded towards the sea; when entering the Quabi tribe, he was murdered by order of its chief Pagatwayo, who conceived him to be some unnatural animal. The tradition of the visit of this individual (of whom little more of a determinate nature beyond what has been related could be collected) is constantly referred to by the Natalese; and the following song, made by the Quabies upon Dingiswayo, is still sung upon festivals:—

> " Clatter, clatter, he is going,
> He goes with them.
> He is going,
> He goes with (a horse or) speed."[2]

It is said that, when Senzangakona discovered his son's retreat, he asked Dingiswayo to give him up. That chief was disposed to yield; but Gomana, his principal councillor, befriended the fugitive, and the messengers returned unsuccessful. Tshaka was committed to Gomana's especial guardianship. Isaacs says that he distinguished himself among the warriors, and was held by them in great esteem as a songster and a punster. He failed, however, to obtain the good will of the people generally— a circumstance which he did not forget.

While Tshaka was with the Tetwas, his father died (by poison, it is supposed) and was succeeded by his son Sikutshane. This displeased Dingiswayo, who is said to have previously requested Senzangakona to appoint Tshaka his heir. The old man naturally refused; but the other replied as a great chief might to a small one and declared that his protegé should govern the Zulus. When he heard of Senzangakona's demise, he sent Gomana, with a sufficient force, to remove Sikutshane and put Tshaka in his place. Having by this means acquired power, Tshaka destroyed his brother's principal men, and all who were supposed to disapprove of his accession.[3]

It is not likely that Dingiswayo would permit Tshaka to act independently; and we may regard the Zulus as being now subject to the Tetwas. It is said that a neighbouring chief, who had frequently fought with Senzangakona, treated Tshaka with great scorn, and insolently required Dingiswayo's " poor man" to become his tributary. A battle being the result, the scoffer was killed and his people submitted to Tshaka; but the surrendered cattle were claimed by Dingiswayo, though he allowed his favourite to retain a large portion.

Dingiswayo's death, which released Tshaka from his subjection, happened in the following manner. Switi, chief of the Dwandwes, attacked the chief of the Xnumayos and killed him. The deceased having married a daughter of Dingiswayo, the latter set out to avenge his death. On the march he captured some of the enemy's cattle; but, when he came to an engagement with Switi's soldiers, his followers were defeated. Dingiswayo was not in the battle, but at some distance with a few attendants. When one of these pointed out his flying men, he would not believe that *his* warriors could be defeated by those of Switi—the fugitives, he asserted, were not Tetwas—they were Dwandwes. Nor was he undeceived until he saw a party of the latter coming upon him from another direction. He was too fat or too dignified to run, and awaited the foe's advance. One of his attendants fled; but the others remained. The Dwandwes, having approached, danced around the captive in savage triumph, and required him to accompany them to Switi. He refused—he was a great chief—his army was very valiant—they could not take him. He now demanded his oxen, and a messenger went to Switi, who immediately sent ten as a nominal present to the prisoner. The latter ordered one to be slaughtered, but none of his followers were bold enough to obey the command; whereupon he redoubled his boastings, declaring that Switi would tremble to see him and order a dance in his honour. The captives were conducted to Switi's kraal; but, before they entered, a doctor sprinkled medicine about the central enclosure and on the huts, giving some also to the conqueror, who rubbed it on his face. Switi then entered the enclosure from the upper part, his soldiers being already assembled, and Dingiswayo standing near the gate. Medicine having been again used, the captive was ordered to approach his conqueror and sit down. After a dance by the exulting warriors, Switi's cattle were driven into the kraal and paraded before the fallen chieftain. The victor ordered food to be given to Dingiswayo, but the latter refused to accept it—he was a great chief—he would not eat the food of a dependant—let it be given to his wives and followers. Another dance having taken place, Switi danced round his prisoner, and leaped several times over his head, exclaiming: "See the great chief, how valiant he is! The dependant jumps over the great chief." Next morning the captives were again obliged to witness a dance, after which Switi addressed them—he intended to give them cattle and send them home —the attendants might go at once—the chief should follow. They replied that they did not wish to go without him, but Switi ordered them to leave immediately; and, cattle having been given them, they proceeded—to be killed outside the kraal. The conqueror struck Dingiswayo with a knob-kirrie on the temples. The blows were slight, but the club was poisoned (so my informant said) and the victim soon expired. Medicine, into which a portion of the deceased's head-ring had been put, was administered to the victor, who dipped his assagai into another boiling decoction, spat on the weapon, and held it towards the sun. This ceremony was repeated for several days afterwards. Dingiswayo was buried by a doctor, and several oxen slain. Of these, one was interred near the grave—the rest being placed in the bush. Dingiswayo's defeat has been abscribed to the fact that he was too impatient to wait for the assembling of his army (perhaps he despised his enemy) and marched with an insufficient force. Tshaka, who is said to have been summoned to join him, was unable to do so, owing to the hasty movements of the impetuous chieftain.[4]

II.—Tshaka could now act independently, and make war on his own account. After Dingiswayo's death, he attacked Pagatwayo, already mentioned as chief of the Quabies. The occasion of the attack was some contemptuous expression applied to him by the latter, and reported by a traitorous *in-duna*. Tshaka resolved to punish the insult; but wished first to strengthen himself by the use of superstition. It is believed that if a chief obtain anything connected with the person of another, it will give him power over the latter. The councillor was therefore sent back, and directed to obtain something belonging to his master. He had little difficulty in executing the commission; and sent to the Zulu chief a piece of Pagatwayo's dress, scrapings from his wooden pillow, and clay from his hut floor. With these materials and some roots, a great mediciner prepared a powerful potation;

which, when taken by Tshaka, rendered him stronger than the chief of the Quabies. Having expressed a doubt as to the efficacy of the medicine, I was answered, "Did not Tshaka conquer Pagatwayo?" Not being satisfied to strengthen himself, Tshaka resolved to weaken his enemy by having medicine scattered in the kraal of the latter. The servant, to whose lot it fell to perform this perilous task, was duly prepared by the doctor, that he might retain his presence of mind, if questioned, and not say that he had come from Tshaka. All being ready, Tshaka set out, and arrived before Pagatwayo's kraal at sunrise. The fat chief was ill, and not able to direct his *ama-pakati*—a circumstance which frightened them terribly. They attempted to withstand the assailants, but in vain; they were very weak, my informant said, and could not resist the Zulus. Pagatwayo was brought out of his hut, when the conqueror triumphed over him and he died. Tshaka sent messengers among the people, to say that he should not injure them, if they quietly submitted. He took all their cattle, but lent cows to those who acknowledged him as their master.[5]

On Dingiswayo's death, his brother, Mundiso, assumed the government of the Tetwas. He attempted to avenge Dingiswayo's death, but was defeated and fled. The enemy pursued and ravaged his country, when many of the people joined themselves to Tshaka. It was perhaps owing to this latter circumstance that the Dwandwes invaded the Zulu-territory. Tshaka did not venture to oppose them; but, taking refuge in the bush, remained there until the enemy retired. Switi, having sent his army with express orders to bring Tshaka, was not satisfied to see them return without him. He therefore ordered them to make a second irruption into Tshaka's small dominions. The Zulu chief again retreated; but at length, overcoming the fears of his people, he prevailed on them to resist an enemy who would evidently leave them no peace. The long crane's feather which he wore on his head having, by accident or design, dropped to the ground, an attendant, who would have picked it up, was struck violently and rated for a fool—could he not see that the feather was a sign of victory?— it had fallen to signify that the spirits would cause Switi to crouch at his feet. The trick succeeded; the spirits were immediately invoked; and the usual ceremonies performed to prepare the men for action. This done, Tshaka despatched his un-married warriors to plunder the enemy's unpro-tected country; and ordered the rest to attack the Dwandwe force, then near his retreat. A severe engagement ensued, in which the Zulus suffered a partial defeat; but they were eventually success-ful and routed the enemy with great slaughter. Meanwhile, the unmarried men had reached the Dwandwe-country, and were approaching Switi's residence. Supposing them to be his own troops, he did not doubt that they were returning victori-ous; but, while he expected them to go straight to himself, they turned aside and entered a neigh-bouring kraal. Presently a woman escaped; and,

running as fast as a wound in her shoulder would
permit, informed the astonished chief that the Zulus
had come. Switi and his people sought refuge in
the bush, where they are afterwards joined by the
remnant of his army. Having no hope of resisting
the victorious Zulus, the Dwandwes took possession
of another country.[6]

It is said that, when Mundiso assumed the
government of the Tetwas, Tshaka made an alliance
with him; but that he subsequently invited him to
a dance and killed him.[7] He then claimed the
allegiance of all Dingiswayo's people. Sotshangana
had, I think, already gone over the Maputa.
When the chief of the Amakoba submitted, Tshaka
enquired why his brother Manzini, who was at the
head of part of the tribe, did not follow his example.
Jogo did not know; he could not tell even where
his brother then resided. Afterwards, while Tshaka
was hunting, he discovered Manzini's large herd,
and sent him a message demanding food for his
followers. The demand having been refused once
and again, Tshaka attacked Manzini's kraal, and
killed him. The chief's son asserted that he had
always advised his father to submit, and was
allowed to retain the cows.

Somveya, Dingiswayo's son, subsequently incurred Tshaka's displeasure, and was summoned
to appear before him. He insisted, not very
prudently, on going immediately into Tshaka's
presence, on the ground that his father had fed
him. An *in-duna* prevented the breach of eti-

quette. When the tyrant came out, Somveya shed
tears and said: "Why do you wish to kill the
Tetwas? My father gave you food. He did not
kill you, nor give you up to your father." Tshaka
replied that the Tetwas were rascals—they gave him
cows with ugly horns, which kicked and jumped
when he attempted to milk them—Dingiswayo's
officers beat him and persecuted his sweet-hearts—
they called him by opprobrious names and said he
was a dependant—he disliked the Tetwas—he was
a great chief now—he did not, however, wish to
kill Somveya, and, giving him an ox, desired the
young chief to remain all night at the kraal. The
latter, who was old enough to penetrate Tshaka's
purpose, expressed a wish to sleep in another of
his master's establishments, and thus obtained an
excuse for leaving. He then made all haste home;
and, acquainting his people with their danger,
advised an immediate flight. A considerable number having approved of the plan, sacrifices were
offered; and the fugitives, with their cattle, hurried
towards the Maputa. The women and younger
girls were left to their fate. When the Tetwas
reached the river, Makazana's people ferried them
across—that chief exacting a girl and an ox for his
fare. The refugees then bent their course towards
the country occupied by Sotshangana, who was very
glad to see them—they must live with him and
become his people. Not choosing to be governed
by one who had been subject to his father, Somveya preferred to seek another site. When Tshaka
discovered that he had been outwitted, he sent

a detachment of soldiers to the Tetwa-country. These, finding that Somveya had fled, massacred the women left behind, and pursued the fugitives. Reaching the Maputa, they endeavoured to obtain from Makazana intelligence of their route; but without success—Makazana knew nothing about them—he had not seen Somveya. The soldiers having returned, Tshaka sent for the residue of the people, and killed the married men under the pretence that they were "evildoers." The "boys" were ordered to assume the head-ring—Milandela, a grandson of Dingiswayo, being appointed chief of the tribe.[8]

It was about 1820, that Tshaka's forces invaded the present colony of Natal. The country was full of people; but they could not resist the Zulu armies. Some tribes living near the Tugela were allowed to remain as tributaries; but the rest of the district was nearly depopulated. Multitudes were slain, or taken captive; others fled to a distance or sought refuge in the bush. Nor did the Amampondo escape. They had the advantage however of occupying a country "particularly well adapted for defence: hence in two attacks made upon it by the Zulu army" (one being subsequent to this period) "although Faku lost many thousand cattle, he held his territory." In consequence of his favourable situation, Faku became an important chief. "He was not originally greater, nor had he a force superior to many of his neighbours, until the remnants of tribes despoiled and scattered by

Tshaka sought an asylum with him: other tribes, dreading the great Zulu chief although unmolested by him, attached themselves to Faku." Mr. Fynn, who arrived in Natal in 1824, did not find a single tribe (with the exception of about thirty natives near the Bluff) from within a few miles of the Umzimvubu to the Tongati—a distance of two hundred and thirty miles: "there were neither kraals, huts, cattle, nor corn. Occasionally I saw a few stragglers—mere living skeletons—obtaining a precarious subsistance on roots and shellfish."

The following account of the resistance made by the Amatuli is from the evidence of an American Missionary:—"Before the country of Natal was invaded by the Zulus it was densely populated from the Umgeni to the Umkomazi, and inland, some twelve or fifteen miles at least, by one large and powerful nation. Their great chief was Untaba, son of Uyebu, who was son of Umtshatwa. Untaba lived not far from New Germany, which place is still known to the natives by the name of Kwentaba, in honour of that chief. Under Untaba there were several subordinate chiefs who ruled over particular tribes and separate sections of the country included in the above limits. (Thus from the Umkomazi to the Ilovo the people were under Usojuba, son of Umatshoka. From the Ilovo to the Amanzimtote they were under Uashu; and from thence to the Umlazi, under Umcwane. From the Umlazi along the Bluff to the Bay the people were under Amabone or Umante, father of Umnini; and from the Bay to the Umgeni and inland Utusi was chief.) All these, however, were for a time at least, subject to the great king Untaba . . . On the arrival of the Zulu invader, at one time at least, they gave battle and resisted bravely. They not only stood their ground, but pressed hard upon the forces of the assailant. Says Ujodile, one of our authorities for this sketch, speaking of the approach of the Amazulu, 'That day I remember well. I was then a young man. The Amatuli all collected upon a plain this, east, side of the Umkomazi. The Zulus came up in the afternoon, we gave them battle and drove them back to the Umzimbazi, leaving the dead strewn in heaps by the way. With this right hand of mine I slew many. When the sun was down we returned, took our cattle and fled, well knowing that the Amazulu would come again in greater numbers.' Some, perhaps many, were slain in battle. Many others, however, escaped death by taking refuge in the bush and rocks which skirt the coast from the Bay to the southwest. Among them was the present chief of the tribe, Umnini. There concealed, between the Bluff and the sea, they lived upon herbs and roots, and such insects and animals as could be obtained from land or water, till their country had rest from war and it was safe for them to emerge from their hiding places."[9]

After the arrival of the Europeans, Sikonyana, son of Switi, appeared with a large force, to reclaim the country of his fathers. Tshaka seems to have been afraid of the Dwandwe chief, for we find him sending an order to the Europeans to bring their boat to the Tugela, then swollen, "to enable him to cross, for the purpose of paying a visit to our habitations." The jolly-boat was immediately repaired and carried to that river. When the natives saw it launched and veer with its head to the stream, their astonishment was excessive—they were "now older than their forefathers, who had never seen the great river crossed when it was in wrath." Having moored the boat to a large stone, Messrs. Fynn and Isaacs proceeded to a neighbouring kraal, to await the despot's arrival. In the evening messengers came to say that Tshaka had, for the present, given up his intention; but desired them to proceed at once to his residence. When they reached one of his kraals, the *in-duna*, who had charge of it, " arrived (says Isaacs) from the king, to prepare his regiment for immediate service. He informed us that the enemy (Inconyarner), with whom they were at war, had encamped within a day's march of the royal residence; that their force was large; and that he saw four vessels standing to the westward. He gave us a cow for our use, and some milk. We now began to guess the cause of Tshaka's sending for us and for the boat, and experienced some little difficulty in determining how to act. To advance would in all probability, we thought, bring us into contact with the force of the enemy with whom Tshaka was at ·war. To retreat would incense him, and remove the high opinion he entertained of European bravery; we therefore resolved on proceeding to his capital." After their arrival, they were told that Tshaka intended to meet the enemy at the full moon. Some days later, as they were sitting in his presence, they "observed a large quantity of small white flowers, blown from the shrubs in the vicinity, floating in the air, covering the whole space of the kraal, and 'light as thistle-down moving,' which were carried off by the first ripple of breeze that sprang up. The king asked us the cause of this; when, we being at a loss for a plausible reason, he observed that it was a sign the enemy had retreated from his position. While we were communicating with him, messengers arrived to announce the fact, and that they had encamped two days' march nearer the confines of their own country. Tshaka immediately gave orders for his warriors to hold themselves in readiness for an immediate attack." The two following days, "the king amused himself by dancing with his people, and superintending the driving of his cattle to the rivers—the latter being a favourite occupation." On the third day, "three regiments of 'boys' arrived to be reviewed. There appeared to be nearly six thousand, all having black shields. The respective corps were distinguished by the shape and ornament of their caps. One regiment had them in the shape of Malay hats, with a peak on the crown about six inches high, and a bunch of feathers at the top. Another wore a turban made of otter-skin, having a crane's feather or two on each side; and the third wore small bunches of

feathers over the whole head, made fast by means
of small ties. Thus accoutred and distinguished,
they entered the gate, ran up the kraal, halted in
front of the palace, and saluted the king. One
boy stepped in front and made a long harangue.
When the orator had concluded, the whole of his
comrades first shouted, and then commenced running over the kraal, trying to excel each other in
feats of agility, regardless of order, regularity, or
discipline. After this exhibition, which lasted
three hours, a regiment of men arrived with white
shields, having on them one or two black spots in
the centre; they saluted Tshaka, then retired to
put away their shields, and assembled again in one
body to dance.

"They formed a half circle; the men in the centre
and the boys at the two extremities. The king
placed himself in the middle of the space within the
circle, and about one thousand five hundred girls
stood opposite to the men three deep, in a straight
line, and with great regularity. His majesty then
commenced dancing, the warriors followed, and the
girls kept time by singing, clapping their hands,
and raising their bodies on their toes. The strange
attitudes of the men exceeded anything I had seen
before. The king was remarkable for his un-
equalled activity, and the surprising muscular
powers he exhibited. He was decorated with a
profusion of green and yellow glass beads. The
girls had their share of ornaments; in addition too
they had each of them four brass bangles round
their necks, which kept them in an erect posture,

and rendered them as immoveable as the neck of
a statue. This ceremony was performed with
considerable regularity, from the king giving, as
it were, the time for every motion. Wherever
he cast his eye, there was the greatest effort
made; and nothing could exceed the exertion of
the whole until sunset, when Tshaka, accompanied by his girls, retired within the palace,
and the warriors to their respective huts. Many,
however, first went to the river and performed
their evening ablutions." Next morning Tshaka
was again among his warriors, and commanded
the *izin-duna* to point out those who had displayed
cowardice in the previous war. He was assured
that every coward had been slain. After this
statement a pause ensued, during which the Europeans obtained permission to return home. Subsequently messengers arrived at Port Natal, "from
the king to request all the white people to proceed
with their fire-arms immediately, to accompany him
to war, as he had resolved on attacking Isse-
konyarna at his encampment." Others came to
say that they need not go till the full moon; and
others to request that the tent might be taken to
Tshaka. When Isaacs, who superintended the
delivery of that article, had reached the Zulu-
country, he found that the king had "recently
ordered one of his best regiments, with their wives
and families, to be massacred for supposed cowardice. They had been defeated in battle, although
they fought with great bravery, having been overpowered by superior troops and greater numbers,

and compelled to retreat." Having seen the tent
erected, Tshaka was much pleased and thought that
the sight of it would strike his enemy with dismay,
and give him an easy victory.

Though Tshaka had required all the Europeans
to go with him, he was ultimately prevailed on
to be content with the company of Messrs. Farewell
and Fynn. He set out with a force of thirty
thousand men, and marched ten days before he
reached the enemy. For the first three days, they
journeyed through a rather mountainous country;
and for the three next, over a wide plain, which
did not afford them even fire-wood; they were
obliged to broil their beef with green grass. The
last portion of the journey was through a country
of rocky precipices, "partly inhabited by a small
tribe of murderers; who, from want rather than
otherwise, make human sacrifices for food." The
Dwandwes were strongly posted on the top of a
high rock; where, with their families and cattle,
they awaited the enemy's attack. When the Zulus
attempted to scale the hill, stones were showered
upon them from above, and the assailants fell back.
Ultimately however the hill was carried, and the
Dwandwes routed with great slaughter. Sikonyana and a few followers alone escaped.[10]

Previously to this expedition, Tshaka had carried
his arms beyond the Maputa, and subdued the
tribes near Delagoa Bay. His ravages are said
to have extended as far even as Inhambane. The
following song was composed (I have been told by
himself) in celebration of his conquests.

" Thou hast finished, finished the nations.
　Where will you go out to battle now ?
　　Hey ! where will you go out to battle now ?
　Thou hast conquered kings.
　　Where are you going to battle now ?
　Thou hast finished, finished the nations.
　Where are you going to battle now ?
　　Hurrah ! Hurrah ! Hurrah !
　Where are you going to battle now ?"[11]

III.—Tshaka possessed a most surprising influence over his subjects. The majority were of conquered tribes, and could not therefore have any hereditary respect for him; yet the people submitted to his unnatural institutions, and rendered implicit obedience to his commands; the father would execute the sentence of death on his child; and the son " become the inhuman mutilator of his own mother." They were ready, at his bidding, to undertake the most perilous task; and a man has been known even to thank him while the executioners were beating him to death.[12]

It is interesting to consider how he maintained his influence. Isaacs says that he was liberal in distributing the spoils of war among his soldiers; while those who did the work of executioners had a good share of the property of the deceased. The warriors were also well fed, and the people diverted by amusements. These means, however, would have been very inefficacious, if used alone: he employed two others, which operated with greater force, namely Superstition and Severity.

It has been previously stated that, in the normal

condition of the people, the chief's authority depends much on the seer's influence. Tshaka did not attempt to govern without that support; but he contrived to unite the two offices in his own person, and persuade the people that he was himself inspired. The following is an example of the manner in which he produced this impression.

Having arisen unusually early, Tshaka ordered a large number of black and white oxen to be slaughtered. As these belonged to his favourite herd, the people naturally concluded that something of great importance was about to be transacted. The warriors were summoned and directed to join in a grand dance, which was prolonged to a late hour of the night. At its conclusion, Tshaka asserted that Umbia, a noted chief of his father's time, had appeared to him the preceding night, and stated that Senzangakona was very angry with the Zulus, because they were losing their reputation, and had ceased to be more cunning than their neighbours. The spirit added that the nation, which was becoming too large, required constant employment; and that there were many enemies to conquer before they could be merry. Umbia also said that he and all the people who had died, were very comfortable under ground, having plenty of cattle and fine girls, but no enemies to disturb their enjoyment. Tshaka ordered cattle to be slaughtered at all his kraals, in honour of the dream; the descendants of Umbia were created great men; the name of that chief resounded through the country; and all his good deeds were talked of.

While these things were taking place, an old man belonging to one of the subjugated tribes disappeared; nor could any information be obtained respecting him, except from his wife, who said that a lion had entered their hut in the night and carried him away. A report of the affair was made to Tshaka, who received it in the presence of his warriors, with apparent unconcern. After some months the man was forgotten; when he suddenly reappeared before Tshaka and the soldiers. He was dressed in a peculiar manner; his head-ring had been removed, and the hair suffered to grow long; he looked like a being not of earth. Some enquiries having been made as to whence he came, he rose and said that he had been to the spirits, who, after he had remained with them three moons, had directed him to go to the Great Chief and say that they were making merry, and would soon pick out all the "evildoers," that the Zulus also might be merry. "I am," said he, "the son of Fetehlu, of the Amacele, who was taken away by the lion and dragged to his den, where I sank into the earth. The lion went with me and treated me as a mother would treat her child, until I came to some red earth. The lion left me there. In wandering about, I walked upon earth that trembled and gave way; I then fell into a deeper abyss, and was rendered insensible by the fall. Recovering, I found myself in a fine country inhabited by the spirits. I saw all the old people who had been killed in war, and those who had died at home. They are much smaller than we. They have plenty of cattle, but all very small. The girls are handsome. Umbia is a great chief, and enjoys himself very much; he is also a great doctor. He strolls about at night, no one knows whither; but he always says that he goes to visit his relations."

Tshaka affected to be indignant at the speaker's audacity, and denounced him as a liar and an "evildoer." The people remembered the king's dream, and did not know what to think. Their doubts were relieved when some prophets had been summoned to *smell* the man, and decide whether he were really a messenger from Umbia. The seers decided that he was what he professed to be; and said that, because some of the people did not believe the king's dreams, the spirits had sent the lion to fetch the man that he might return and corroborate them.[13]

The barbarous severity with which he acted, contributed to establish Tshaka's authority. Death was inflicted for all important offences, and sometimes for the most trifling. Isaacs says that, to prevent intercession, he never gave his reason for ordering an execution until it was too late to recal the sentence. The order, generally given by pointing with his finger or by a nod, was promptly obeyed by any who were present. The following instance is from the writer just quoted. Tshaka, having come out in the morning to perform his toilet, summoned Isaacs into his presence. Three "boys" approached, carrying vessels of water, which they bore with extended arms over their heads. "One held a broad black dish before him, while another poured in water for his majesty to wash, and a third stood ready with a further supply in case of need, holding it in the position before described without daring to put it down." While performing his ablutions, which extended from head to foot, Tshaka conversed with the people near him. The washing being done, an attendant presented a basket at arm's length. The vessel contained a sort of red paste, which Tshaka rubbed over his person until it had disappeared. Another attendant then advanced with a greasy substance which, applied in the same manner, gave his majesty a fine glossy appearance. At this moment a body of about three hundred men approached; and, saluting the king, sat down. Tshaka, having uttered one or two words, some of the warriors arose and seized three of the people, who made no resistance. The king was silent; but "from some sign he gave the executioners, they took the criminals, laying one hand on the crown and the other on the chin; and, by a sudden wrench, appeared to dislocate the head." The victims were then dragged to the bush, blows being at the same time inflicted, and were left for the wild beasts and vultures to devour. Having ordered his warriors to withdraw, he retired into his palace.

Innocent people were frequently accused of some crime and killed. When any of his concubines —he had no wife—became pregnant, they were immediately taken away, and an imaginary crime alleged as a reason for putting them to death.

Sometimes he practised wholesale massacres. Rising early one morning, he told the people that he was going to choose a new site for a kraal. The intended victims were then sent out to survey the neighbourhood and report a fitting spot. When they had gone he sat down near the path; and, desiring his attendants not to divulge what he should say, asserted that he had been much disturbed by a painful dream; in which he saw that several "boys" had been holding forbidden conversation with his concubines. He expressed his determination to punish the offenders, and the people applauded his resolve: "Father, kill them; they are not fit to live." Finding his design approved, he proceeded to say that Umbia had visited him several times respecting this offence; which (the spirit said) had been frequently committed during his absence from the kraal—he had no doubt that some were committing it at that very moment, for why had they remained behind? —"look at the white man; he is a *man*; he knows that it is improper to stop in the kraal when I am away." While this was being said, two or three men left the crowd and went towards the kraal. Isaacs did not think that they had any criminal purpose in view; but they were immediately slain. Tshaka now rose and walked forward, the people following at the distance of about twenty yards and bending to the ground every time he stopped. Sitting down again, he said: "Let me see if there be a *man* among you. How are we to secure the people in the kraal?"

Some proposed to surround it. "Well, how will you manage it? Will they not see you and many of them escape?" The people being at a loss what to recommend or perhaps really wishing them to escape, he directed that, when they approached the kraal, a few should run to each side of it, the rest following shortly after; and then, while those within were unsuspectingly looking on, all were to unite and surround it. A party was ordered to remain with Tshaka, both to prevent suspicion and that they might be employed in taking the people out of the huts. His plan having been heard with applause, the tyrant entered the kraal. At first he beat his old mother because she had not taken proper care of his girls. He then worked himself into so violent a rage that Isaacs, knowing his want of discrimination when excited, judged it prudent to withdraw.

The victims, including those who had been sent to examine the neighbourhood and several girls, were now brought from the huts, to the number of about one hundred and seventy. Having summoned the men who had surrounded the kraal, Tshaka told them that his heart was sore, and that he had been beating his mother because she had neglected to look after his girls. He then selected several fine lads and ordered their own brothers to twist their necks: this done, they were dragged away and beaten with sticks until life was extinct. The rest were butchered indiscriminately. When the warriors had returned, Tshaka said: "You see that we have killed a number of

' evildoers.' I shall now consult Umbia and find out the remainder." Then, having directed oxen to be slain as a thanksgiving to the spirits, he added: "To-morrow I shall kill all those who have offended during my reign. There will then be nothing wanted to make you and me happy." He arose, and went into his palace. Next day droves of hyenas were howling immediately around the kraal.[14]

IV.—In 1823 Lieutenant Farewell and Mr. Alexander Thompson chartered the brig "Salisbury," to explore the coast N.E. of the Cape Colony. Having landed at St. Lucia and attempted to trade with Tshaka's subjects, they returned, putting into Natal Bay for provisions. When Lieutenant Farewell reached the Cape, " he was of opinion that favourable openings for commerce presented themselves at Natal, and induced about twenty persons to join him in his favourite scheme of founding a new colony." Mr. H. F. Fynn, with some others, proceeded by land, and reached Natal early in 1824. He then set his companions to erect temporary buildings on the present market-square of Durban, and proceeded to Tshaka's country. On his return, he found that Farewell and others had arrived by sea. In the following year, the party were joined by Lieutenant King and Mr. Isaacs, who were unfortunately shipwrecked while attempting to enter the bay. The latter individual says, that " the place selected by Mr. Farewell for his residence had a singular appearance, from the peculiar construction of the several edifices. His house was not unlike an ordinary barn made of wattle, and plastered with clay, without windows, and with only one door composed of reeds. It had a thatched roof, but otherwise was not remarkable either for the elegance of its structure, or the capacity of its interior. The house of Cane was contiguous to that of Mr. Farewell, and about twenty yards from it, while that of Ogle was at a similar distance, and had the appearance of the roof of a house placed designedly on the ground, the gable end of which being left open served as a door. Opposite Mr. Farewell's house was a native hut, in the shape of a bee-hive, about twenty-one feet in circumference, and six feet high, built of small sticks and supported by a pole in the centre. It was thatched with grass, and had an apperture about eighteen inches square, through which the owner crept into his mansion, when he was disposed to enjoy the sweets of repose." A triangular fortress, to enclose two hundred square yards and a permanent habitation, was in progress. The ditch was being dug, and palisadoes were being planted, A mud fort had " been commenced, at each angle, designed to mount three twelve-pound carronades, which were lying there dismounted." In the neighbourhood of the ditch, " was a cattle-pound, partly finished; and at the distance of two hundred yards, a native kraal in a similar state, enclosing an elevated space of ground, of about as many yards in circumference."

A square piece of land had been enclosed for cultivation, but nothing had been planted except mustard and cress, and some maize.

When Mr. Fynn first attempted to communicate with Tshaka, he was well treated but ordered to return. The king then sent an *in-duna* to scrutinize the strangers; and, having heard a favourable report, permitted them to visit him. They were received "with an air of surprize and amazement, but with a civility which they had little contemplated." This was attributed to the influence of a Frontier Kafir then with Tshaka. Having been arrested in the act of stealing cattle, "Jacob" had been put on board the "Salisbury" to be conveyed to Cape Town. The voyage being rough and long, he suffered much from the inclemency of the weather—a circumstance which induced the commander, Lieutenant King, to remove his irons, and give him clothes with an occasional allowance of grog. After reaching the Cape, he was tried and transported to Robben Island. When Captain Owen was engaged in his survey, Jacob became his interpreter, and made a voyage to Delagoa Bay. The vessel then returned to Algoa Bay, and he was about to be sent back to his own country; but, before his release, the "Salisbury" (chartered by Messrs. Farewell and Thompson, as before mentioned,) put into the port. Seeing his old friend, Lieutenant King, Jacob agreed to accompany him as interpreter, "as did also his companion 'Fire,' who had been transported at the same time and for a similar act."

The vessel having reached St. Lucia, Jacob distinguished himself as an expert swimmer, saving his own life and that of Mr. Farewell. When the party had landed, one of them struck Jacob; who in consequence refused to return on board and absconded. Taking an inland direction he reached Tshaka's residence; and, being regarded as a spy, narrowly escaped death. For some time he lived in apprehension, but ultimately rose to great importance.

Jacob was shrewd enough to discover that, notwithstanding his despotism, Tshaka lived in constant fear of assassination. He therefore told him, among other stories of the white people, how the king was guarded by sentinels; and added that he had been made a sentinel on board the king's ship and had kept watch during the night at the captain's door. The latter, he said, gave this reason for choosing him—namely, that being a stranger he would be vigilant, as his life depended on that of the person he was appointed to guard. To confirm this, he asked what would now become of himself, but for Tshaka's protection —would not the people destroy him on suspicion of his being a spy?

Influenced by Jacob's plausible talk, Tshaka raised a party of sentinels and placed them under his command, at the same time taking him by the ear and saying: "Remember, if anything happens to me, my people will kill you for being in my favour; your prospects depend on my safety." Cattle and wives were given him. Tshaka listened with interest to Jacob's account of the white people, and frequently summoned him to his hut, when his ordinary attendants had retired. More cattle and more wives were given to the chief of the sentinels, who gradually "acquired considerable influence in the government." Jacob's narratives, mingled doubtless with many fictions, had excited in Tshaka's mind "no ordinary anxiety and solicitude to see" a race of whom he had previously known nothing. The arrival of the Europeans in 1824, was therefore "conceived to be a good omen." The king had now an opportunity of gratifying his curiosity, while Jacob appears to have recommended them to his "consideration and respect."

Jacob's importance increased after the settlement of the Europeans at Natal; for, in addition to his former office, he became the king's interpreter in all his interviews with the white people. When Lieutenant King arrived, he went to Natal to greet his benefactor. "It is not easy," says Isaacs, "to describe the joy he evinced on seeing us; and the care and anxiety he displayed on hearing of our being shipwrecked. He sought to aid us in every way, sent us a bullock for food, offered to Lieutenant King a quantity of ivory, and accosted him as his father and protector, compelling his wives as well as his people to do the same."

Having succeeded in opening a communication with Tshaka, Mr. Fynn proceeded southward to

visit the Amampondo, who lived on the Umzimvubu. He returned soon after the arrival of
Isaacs, who says that he "had been trading with
the natives and had collected a great quantity of
ivory. For eight months he had separated himself
from his solitary companion, Mr. Farewell, and
had associated solely with the people with whom
he sojourned. We sat to hear him detail his
adventures—the many vicissitudes he had endured,
and the obstacles with which he had contended,
not only in having been often without food and
ignorant where to seek it, but in daily terror of
being destroyed by wild animals or massacred by
the savage natives. . . . He was highly beloved
by the natives, who looked up to him with more
than ordinary veneration, for he had been often in-
strumental in saving their lives; and, in moments of
pain and sickness, had administered to their relief.
About a hundred had attached themselves to him."
These were some of the people who, at the time of
Tshaka's invasion, took refuge in the bush. Others
were subsequently collected (including refugees
from the Zulu-country) until a considerable native
population had settled itself under the protection
and chieftainship of the English.[15]

Messrs. Fynn, King, and Isaacs being at
Tshaka's kraal, he summoned them into his presence, and dismissed all his attendants. He then
invited them into his hut—an honour never before
conferred—and stared at them in silence. After a
few moments, he thanked Lieutenant King for some

medicines he had sent; and regaled the party with a basket of boiled beef and a pot of beer. Having thrust his head through the doorway to see whether any listeners were near, he said "that he should like to cross the water to see King George; but feared that he should not receive a welcome. He would therefore send a chief under the charge of Lieutenant King, as soon as the vessel should be finished. He further said that he would send two elephant's teeth as a present to King George, to show that he desired to be on terms of amity with him. He wished also that Lieutenant King would procure more medicines for him, and particularly some stuff for turning white hairs black, as he had heard from Mr. Farewell that it was to be got on the other side of the water, and he wanted it much for his aged mother. He appeared more than ordinarily anxious to obtain this latter preparation; and promised to reward Lieutenant King with abundance of ivory and droves of cattle, provided he should return with it." (Mr. Farewell had told Tshaka of some specific possessed by white men, possibly Rowland's Macassar, which would remove all indications of age. The king was now beginning to fear the approach of gray hairs; to procure the means of eradicating which, was probably his principal object in sending the mission.) He begged that they would not betray his confidence, but keep his project a profound secret. They promised to do so, at the same time intimating that they might not be able to obtain the specific he required. He proposed to detain Isaacs, as a hostage for the safe return of the chief; and, presenting the party with some cattle, gave them permission to go home. Shortly afterwards his mother died, and the horrible massacres previously mentioned took place. Referring again to his design, he said to Isaacs: "I am like a wolf on a flat, that is at a loss for a place to hide his head in. The Zulus have killed all my principal people and my mother. I will go to the other side of the water to see King George."

When the vessel (built partly out of the wreck) had been launched, Mr. Fynn visited the king to arrange the business of the mission. A chief named Sotobe was appointed to represent Tshaka, but he was associated with Mr. King, to whom was confided the entire management of the embassy. Another chief, of less importance, " was to accompany them, but to return, on their arrival at the first port, with tidings of their reception, of the friendship shown them, and likewise the terms existing between the English and the frontier tribes, with whom Tshaka designed going to war. (He had however promised to delay it, until this chief returned with the Cape government's opinion of the step he was about to take.) Jacob was appointed interpreter, though he could not speak much English and but little Dutch. It was agreed that Sotobe should take two wives, and Jacob one; and that Mr. King should furnish them with three of his native boys as servants. The object of the mission was particularly detailed to Lieutenant King by Tshaka himself, when he created him chief of Tuguza, and promised him great advantages if he brought his people safely back." Isaacs being unwell, Fynn generously consented to remain as the hostage.

The schooner sailed April 30th, 1828, and after a short voyage anchored in Algoa Bay. Lieutenant King wrote to the Colonial authorities, and was directed to have the chiefs entertained at the expense of Government, "until an opportunity should occur for conveying them to Cape Town. At the same time strict injunctions were given that they should not be permitted to approach Graham's Town nor view the frontier." While the party were expecting to go to Cape Town, Major Cloete visited the Zulus, telling Isaacs that he had been directed by the Governor to ascertain the object of the mission. The following is the conversation between the Major and Sotobe, as given by Isaacs, who acted as interpreter.

"Can Tshaka write, or make any characters whereby to show that he sent the chiefs on their mission, and to show his authority?" "No. He cannot write or make characters." "How is Sotobe to be known as a chief, and how is he distinguished as such?" "By the bunch of red feathers; and there is no one allowed to wear them but the king, and two or three of his principal chiefs." "Did you come by your own free will and consent?" "We were sent by our king to show his friendly disposition towards the governor and the white people; also to ask for medicines." &c. "What authority have you from your king to show that you are sent by him?" "We have nothing. We were sent with Lieutenant King." "Have you no sign, or token, or feather, or tiger's tail, or tooth, to show that you were sent by Tshaka?" "We generally send cattle, but as the vessel could not take them, Tshaka has sent an ivory tusk." "Will Sotobe go to Cape Town with me?"

"No; we have been here so long, that we are quite tired, and we wish to go back to our king." "What was your motive for coming here, if you did not intend to see the governor?" "We have heard that our king is near the colony [Tshaka had sent his army towards the Kei, after the departure of the mission] and we want to return, as we understand that the governor will protect the neighbouring tribes, and our king was not aware of it before our leaving Natal. We also hear that Lieutenant King is going to meet Tshaka, and we cannot leave him; we were sent with him, and we know no other person. We look upon him as our father and protector. Unbosom Boser [the inferior chief] ought to have returned long ago, and then I could have gone to see the governor, as my king wished me to do." "Provided Unbosom Boser returns from hence, will Sotobe go and see the governor?" "As Lieutenant King is absent, we cannot say anything about it; we will not leave him, as he is sent with us, and he is one of our mission." "How is it possible that Lieutenant King can go to Cape Town with you, and back to Tshaka with Unbosom Boser?" "I do not care who goes back with Unbosom Boser, so long as Lieutenant King remains with me; I am particularly entrusted to his care." "What did you consider Lieutenant King to be? did you consider him as a chief; a person authorized by government to act for them, or as agent for them?" "We look upon Lieutenant King as a subject of King George's, and a Chief, as he is our principal at Natal and always had the command of the people [?]." "If you were to return without seeing the governor, would you not be punished by Tshaka?" "No. We have been here so long without getting any intelligence from the governor, that we now wish to go away on our return and inform the king that we have heard the white people will protect the neighbouring tribes."

The Major had subsequent interviews with the chiefs, at one of which Isaacs was present.

"You must now decide whether you will return with Unbosom Boser, when the vessel is ready, or go on with me to the governor? Mind Jacob (addressing the interpreter) I mean you to go with me." "I have no objection to go with you, but I cannot leave Lieutenant King, he is sent with us on this mission; our king has put every confidence in him, and we consider ourselves under his particular care." "Ask him, if he expects that Lieutenant King will return with him to his country, after seeing the governor, and if he looks to Lieutenant King to send him back?" "I cannot think of leaving Lieutenant King, but if you or any other person have a desire to accompany us, with him, we should not object to it, as our king would always be glad to see any white man in his country." "How is it that you differ so? yesterday you said you would all return; to-day you want to go on with Lieutenant King to the governor, and to return your wife with Unbosom Boser?" "Yesterday I was very unhappy, and much depressed about my wife. She is very ill, I wish her to return with Unbosom Boser, but she will not. My reason for saying that we would all return was, because you told us yesterday that you had been near Gaika's, and saw we could not get back by land, and that the vessel we came in could not go back from this place without a written order from the governor; and your repeated questions made me unhappy." "If you like you can all go back from hence with Lieutenant King, as you have refused to go to the governor with me?" "We do not refuse to go with you to the governor; we say that we cannot go without Lieutenant King, as our king has made him a chief, and he is our principal on this mission; he knows the road, we do not (meaning that Tshaka, their king, had confided to Lieutenant King the whole charge of their mission) and cannot proceed without him." "Tell him Jacob (the interpreter) that I know the road, and that I am sent expressly to take him away." "Your path is from the governor here, and our path with Lieutenant King is from Tshaka to the governor." "I am a chief under the governor, and when the governor heard that you were in his country, he sent me expressly to bring you to him; he knows nothing of Lieutenant King, he is not a chief, neither is he a person authorized by the governor to act for him; if you like to go to the governor with me alone, you can." "Lieutenant King is a chief in our country, and sent by Tshaka to communicate with the governor, and we cannot go with any other but him; if we were to leave him what would our king think?" "What is it that makes you adhere so much to

Lieutenant King, do you always expect him to be with you?" " Because our king has sent us with him, he is kind to us, and our king has given him every information respecting this mission, and trusts to him, as we are unacquainted with your ways." " If Sotobe will go on with me to the governor, I will find a large present to send on to his king by Unbosom Boser. If you will not go on with me, you can go back to your country when the vessel is ready, together with Unbosom Boser." " How is it that you are constantly asking us questions? We have told you all that we have to say, and that we wish to see the governor. You make us quite unhappy talking to us so repeatedly about one thing; and I now begin to think that you suspect us to be spies, and that we are a people come to steal your cattle, and will not allow us to go back again." Lieutenant King having entered the room, the Major became silent. This led Sotobe to regard the latter as an intruder who was afraid to speak before King, and induced him to say in an angry tone: " Why do you come here alone, why do you come here in the absence of Lieutenant King, who is our principal on this mission? he knows all about Tshaka, and he is a white man and knows your ways, and you know we do not; it is to him you ought to apply for information respecting the object of our visit here, and he is competent to satisfy you."

Having understood that they were to return, the party made preparations for the voyage; but were surprised by the arrival of H.M.S. " Helicon," which had been sent to take the chiefs to Natal. She also brought them a present, and carried one for Tshaka. Sotobe and his companions were elated at the prospect of going home; but refused to embark unless King or Isaacs accompanied them. The former therefore went on board the Helicon, while the latter followed in the schooner.

Soon after the mission had left Natal, Tshaka

marched his army to Mr. Fynn's kraal on the Umzimkulu. Retaining one regiment for his own protection, he sent the remainder forward " to the Amampondo, with directions to extend their operations, and sweep the whole of the Kafir tribes, until they should reach the borders of the colony." The Amampondo fled to their fastnesses; and the Zulus passed on towards the Kei. Tshaka had ordered his soldiers to sit on their shields if they saw the white people; and, if attacked by the latter, to retreat. Mr. Fynn prevailed on him to recal the army and await the result of his mission.

When the Frontier tribes heard that the " Fecani," or marauders, were approaching, they besought the Colonial Government to protect them. A force was ordered to be sent to their assistance, but the preparations occupied so much time that the Zulu army—always, says Mr. Fynn, rapid in its movements—had returned before the European troops took the field. The British commander entered Kafir-land unaware of the enemy's retreat; and the chiefs, instead of undeceiving him, held a council " to decide in what manner the force should be employed." The Amangwane—one of the tribes disturbed by Tshaka's earlier wars—were now settled near the sources of the Umtata, under Matuana. For many years that chief had been a roving plunderer, but had located his tribe on its present site with the professed intention of living peaceably with his neighbours. These, having no confidence in his professions, determined to make use of the Colonial force to effect his destruction.

"The troops were led to his position under the belief that Matuana's people were the marauders against whom they had been sent. In a few hours the tribe was destroyed, the Frontier Kafirs taking their part in the engagement by killing the women and children. The greater part of the cattle then captured were distributed among the native allies; and many of the Amangwane, who were taken prisoners, soon afterwards became the servants of the colonists." After the lapse of several months the Cape Government discovered its mistake.[16]

When the mission had returned to Natal, it was found necessary, for the convenience of carriage, to open the case in which the presents sent to Tshaka were packed. The assortment was curious, consisting of some sheets of copper, medicines, knives, trinkets, and a piece of scarlet broad-cloth—the only article of any considerable value. "We had them laid out," says Isaacs, "to the best advantage, first taking the precaution of having Sotobe and Jacob present; when they gave it as their opinion that the present was a paltry one, considering that it came from so great a nation as the English and was intended for so powerful a monarch as Tshaka. However as I thought that the king knew nothing of the value of the medicines, I enhanced their worth as much as I could; and, to add to the whole, Lieutenant King sent a valuable looking-glass, which cost one hundred and twenty rix dollars; a quantity of beads; and a variety of little trifles. In the evening, Unbosomboser and a native boy were despatched, to announce our return." Three days afterwards they came back with two oxen to be sacrificed for the recovery of Mr. King—he was dying—and that his sickness might be transferred to Sotobe, who had offended his master by tarrying at the Bay. The messengers brought him positive orders to proceed at once, with some of the Europeans, that Tshaka might hear what communication had been sent. In the evening other messengers came, repeating the previous orders, and saying that Lieutenant King's illness *ought* to have taken hold of Sotobe. They also asked for medicines; which were given. (Tshaka's chief anxiety was doubtless the hair-dye.)

Isaacs and the chiefs, having set forth towards Tuguza, were met by one of the last messengers. To the white man he would not say a word; to Sotobe he was abundantly communicative—he was going to Lieutenant King to ascertain why Sotobe had been detained—Tshaka was in an unusual rage and had dashed the bottle of medicine to the ground—Sotobe was to go at once and not wait for the paltry present—the king would not accept it. The chiefs were alarmed; and, to save themselves, agreed to forget their differences and attribute all blame to the Europeans. Isaacs discovered this from his native servant, who had overheard their conversation; but determined to proceed. The plot having been agreed on, and their parts rehearsed during the evening, the two chiefs were unusually complaisant and communicative. When Isaacs enquired of Sotobe what he intended to say on seeing Tshaka, the treacherous chief replied that he should depend for pardon solely on the influence of the white people. They reached Tuguza at sunset and found the king, with about two hundred warriors, sitting outside the kraal. He beheld them with indifference and the presents with contempt. Isaacs was silent. Sotobe spoke as follows:

"You mountain, you lion, you tiger, you that are black. There is none equal to you. You sent us to the other side of the water. We have been, and who has crossed the great water but ourselves? Did our fathers know anything of the white people? No. We know much more than they did, and there is no king equal in power to you. Has any other black king sent people to cross the great water as you have done? We have been to a small town, and seen an officer who annoyed us by asking numerous questions; and we know not whether he looked upon us as friends or foes. Our long absence has been a source of misery to us; and, what is still worse, our king is angry with us; and why? Because we have delayed attending to the presents, and because Lieutenant King is sick, whom we did not like to leave in his present state."

Tshaka talked to his warriors during the delivery of this speech. When it was ended, he asked Isaacs where the present was, though it had been placed before him, and what had become of the large box sent by the Governor. When the reason for unpacking it had been explained, he enquired of Sotobe whether he had seen it opened. The chief replied that Mr. Fynn had desired him to sit outside the hut, and that the contents had been handed out for his inspection. Tshaka said to the people: "You see these rascals" (Sotobe and his retinue) "have not attended to my interests. They

have been deceiving me." He tried to induce
Isaacs to accuse Sotobe; and then remarked: " It
is all that fellow, Fynn's fault. He has been insti-
gating Lieutenant King to open the chest. He
is like a monkey. He wants to peep into everything." Isaacs having been directed to point out
those articles which had come from the Governor
and those added by King, Tshaka said: " Lieutenant
King's present is more valuable than that of the
Governor. What a pity it is that he is sick! I
think they have given him poison on the other
side of the water." The mirror attracted Tshaka's
notice and astonished his warriors. It also made
him curious about the other presents; which, when
it was nearly dark, Isaacs was directed to bring
into the *isi-gohlo*. The latter availed himself of
the opportunity to refer to the mission, and stated
that the Governor particularly requested him not
to make war on those tribes who were under British
protection. Tshaka said that the white people had
no control over the blacks, and did not know how
to command them—those whom they " took under
their shield" were daily committing depredations
on his tributaries—he should attack them whenever he pleased. He now spoke of the medicine-
chest; and, when it had been opened, desired Isaacs
to see whether any one were coming. He took
out an ornamented case of lancets, which he doubtless supposed to contain the great medicine; and,
not thinking that he was observed, concealed it
under the mat he sat upon. The other articles
were exhibited and their use explained; but they

did not answer his expectation and he replied
sulkily. The first package was bark, which, he
was told, was useful in debility. He answered:
" I am strong enough. Do you think we are such
weak things as you?" Respecting some ointment
he said with a savage grin : " Do you think we
are such scabby fellows as you?" Some spirits
of lavender were praised as beneficial in cases of
depression, when he asked: " Do you think we
ever need anything to exhilarate us, or that we
are ever dull?" The box being emptied, he
changed his tone and enquiried gently for the
medicine he wanted: "These," he said, "are of
no use to my subjects. They are not troubled
with the disorders you mention. The best medicine for them is beef. When they cannot eat, they
are of no use to me. The medicine I want is the
stuff for the hair." Finding that this had not
been brought, he turned over on the mat and fell
asleep. Isaacs went to his hut.

Next morning Tshaka renewed his enquiry about
the medicine, and remarked that Lieutenant King
had probably reserved it to bring himself. Isaacs
detailed the events connected with the embassy ;
but the king had received Sotobe's account, and
paid no attention to the narrative. He observed,
however, that he had been told that Lieutenant
King had spent all his time with the women, and
left the business of the mission to Isaacs. He
abused the former, and threatened to kill the latter.
He said that he would send John Cane to discover
whether any of the presents had been stolen, and

to procure what had not been obtained. Isaacs, who vainly demanded that Sotobe and Jacob should be confronted with him, expected no less than death. The king's rage, which was mainly owing to his disappointment with regard to the "stuff for the hair," had been increased by the statements of Sotobe and Jacob, who had told him that the English were a small people, whom he might conquer with a single regiment; and that King George was only the name of a mountain. For three days Isaacs was abused and often threatened with immediate death. At last he told the merciless monarch that, though, as a single individual, he could not resist him; yet, as a British subject, his death would be certainly avenged. Tshaka laughed, and said: "The little white man is a spirited fellow. He does not fear death." Having, after this, frequently failed to obtain permission to return home, Isaacs took the liberty of departing without leave.

Soon afterwards Lieutenant King died, his illness, it is said, having been "greatly aggravated by many circumstances of disappointment and chagrin which had arisen out of their visit to Algoa Bay, and by the preplexities and difficulties which arose in connexion with the return to Tshaka of the two chiefs whom they had taken with them." A messenger having announced his death, the king expressed great sorrow, and said that he should now regard Isaacs as chief of the Europeans. Fynn and Isaacs went to Tuguza, at his desire, to give an account of King's death and his property. Tshaka was persuaded, and nothing could remove the impression, that some black person, either at Natal or Algoa Bay, had administered poison to the deceased. He "said that he had mourned for his death, and regretted exceedingly having spoken warmly to him and abused him; but that he was irritated at not receiving the medicine, and the mission not having succeeded to his wishes." He assured them that he had sent to recal John Cane, and would send them to the Cape "to negociate a friendly alliance and obtain such articles as he wanted. To this however we objected (though much in want of ivory to pay us for our past services) as Sotobe and his suite had not been confronted with us." After some further talk, Tshaka said that he could not give them food, because they had neglected to bring a calf that he might wash himself from grief for his deceased friend. Gomana was directed to furnish them with one, and they performed the ceremony next morning at the customary hour. Tshaka was washing, when "our servant," says Isaacs, "cut the calf between the middle ribs, took the caul from the liver, then let the poor wounded animal run, to be devoured by the wild beasts in the neighbourhood or by the vultures in the rocks. We went towards Tshaka, Mr. Fynn carrying the caul. He desired us to pass it to each other, and sprinkle it round the king and my companions in succession; after which a pot of roots was handed for the same ceremony; and then a stick was presented, on which Tshaka spat and said: 'I look upon the deceased as one of my family, and had he been a brother of my own mother, I could not have felt the loss more. I must therefore forbid you to moan again, as it will affect me seriously. I wish all his people well, and will be a friend to his black people, of whom I know he was very fond.' We now left him." Two oxen were presently sent them—one as a sacrifice, and the other for their own use.

Tshaka soon renewed his proposal to send another mission to the Cape, and offered Isaacs a kraal of cattle to conduct it, promising also to send soldiers to hunt elephants for him. He likewise, in consideration of his presents and past services, gave him a large tract of country (which included the Bay of Natal) and the exclusive right of trading with his subjects. A memorandum of the gift having been written, Tshaka affixed his mark to it. The interpreter did the same; but, as he made a larger cross than his master's, the latter asked in a stern tone how a common man's name could be bigger than a king's. He then took back the paper; and, having "scribbled and made marks all over the blank part," said (pointing to his egregious signature): "There! any one can see that is a king's name, because it is a large one. King George will see that it is King Tshaka's name."

He now desired his visitors to return home—he had a great deal to say to them, but his heart would not let his tongue speak as he could wish, so recently after the death of his friend—he would send for them again. At their departure he remarked : "If you all return to your native land, I have this consolation that a white man and a chief lived a long time in my country without molestation from myself and my people, and that he died a natural death. That will ever be a source of satisfaction to me."

V.—About a year before the departure of the mission to King George, Tshaka's army had made an unsuccessful attack on a tribe living on the upper part of the Black Folosi. Having taken refuge in a rocky fastness, that people had resisted the Zulu force for three months and destroyed a regiment of Tshaka's best warriors. He therefore required the Europeans to proceed to the assistance of his soldiers and employ their fire-arms against the enemy. The white men were at this time placed in a very critical position, and felt that they had no alternative but to obey. "To go to war with such innocent people," says Isaacs, "was painful; it was, however, not a measure of choice but one of necessity; and we were led to hope that, instead of any protracted contention, we might be able to parley with them and bring them to terms." When Isaacs and the party that accompanied him were about to proceed, Tshaka directed them to kill every individual of the tribe. They remonstrated against the slaughter of women and children, who could do him no harm; but in vain—the women, he said, would bear children to become his enemies—it was not his custom to give quarter—he commanded them to kill all.

Having reached the Zulu encampment—a kraal, apparently—they found the chiefs afraid to attack the enemy; but unwilling that the white men, by the use of their muskets, should achieve a victory which would contrast with their own want of success, and provoke the rage of their implacable king. After three days' inactivity, the Europeans saw the enemy's cattle, and rushed from the kraal to take them. The chiefs followed and begged that the attack might be delayed till next day; but, while they were talking with Isaacs, his companions had obtained possession of the herd. The Zulus now came up, to the number of about five thousand, and were duly prepared for action by the doctors. The enemy appearing in small detachments on some rocks which crowned the summit of a hill, Isaacs and his party ascended the slope. In front of them were about fifty men, whom they defeated. The report of their guns, reverberating from the rocks, terrified both the enemy and the Zulus. The latter, who had retired to the distance of a mile, " were observed all lying on the ground, with their faces under and their shields on their backs, having an idea that in this position the balls would not touch them." Seeing them fall, the enemy concluded that they were dead; and, attributing it to the report of the fire-arms, fled precipitately. A large body of them, however, were rallied, and advanced against the Europeans. "My party," says Isaacs, "for a moment felt some doubt. On perceiving it I rushed forward and got on the top of a rock. One of the enemy came out to meet me, and at a short distance threw his spear with astonishing force, which I evaded by stooping. I levelled at him and shot him dead. My party also fired, and wounded some others, when the whole ran off in great disorder and trepidation." The Europeans now " advanced along the side of the rocks to dislodge some few who had halted to oppose us again; they had got behind the bushes and large trees, and hurled stones at us with prodigious force—the women and children aiding them with extraordinary alacrity. I received a contusion on my shoulder, and our interpreter had his foot injured. Advancing a little farther, we reached some huts, which we burnt, and killed their dogs; this we did to induce them to surrender without further bloodshed. We continued on their track, encountering occasionally their missiles, which did us no injury, until we arrived at the place where their cattle usually stood; from hence, like the women and children, they had dispersed in all directions, there being occasionally three or four only to be seen at a time. The position of the enemy was of a triangular form—one portion of it protected by rocks, and the other by a swamp; the former were almost inaccessible, and the latter was difficult to get through. The whole, besides, was greatly sheltered by trees and bushes."

A chief having come forth from the thicket to view the assailants, said to his warriors: " Come out, come boldly. What are you afraid of? They are only a handful." Thus encouraged, a thousand men now appeared in front of the bush. Both parties paused a moment; when the chief, running in advance of his followers, rushed towards a Hottentot who had accompanied the Europeans. Not having sufficient confidence in his own skill, Isaacs "allowed the chief to approach Michael, while I aimed at one of the main body, thinking that if I missed him I might hit another. The Hottentot's piece missed fire at first, but at last went off and shot the chief as he was preparing to throw his spear. Just as I had pulled my trigger, and saw the man fall and another remove his shield, I felt something strike me behind. I took no notice, thinking it was a stone, but loaded my musket again; on putting my hand however behind, I perceived it to be bloody, and a stream running down my leg. Turning my head I could see the handle of a spear which had entered my back. John Cane tried to extract it, but could not; Jacob and four others tried successively; I, therefore, concluded that it was one of their barbed harpoons. I retired a short time in consequence, when my native servant, by introducing his finger into the wound, managed to get it out. All this time I felt no pain, but walked to a small stream at a short distance, and washed myself, when I found that the wound made by the spear had lacerated my flesh a good deal. I now was more anxious than before to renew the attack, but felt myself getting weak from loss of blood; I therefore descended the hill, and got to the position where a regiment of Zulu boys had been stationed. I requested some of them to conduct me to the kraal, as I had to go along the side of the bush where the enemy had small parties, but they refused to lend me the least assistance. I took a stick and began to beat them, and levelled my peice at them, but not with the intention of firing, at which they all ran off in great confusion. My party now came up, the enemy having retreated, and we proceeded towards the camp in a body; but I had not gone far before I was compelled to drop, and my wound being extremely stiff and painful, I was obliged to be carried on the backs of my boys." He reached the kraal at sunset and during the night endured excruciating pain.

Next day his comrades advanced a second time against the enemy, and were followed by the Zulus. The former arranged themselves for attack in front of the forest, but found that the enemy was not there. The young warriors becoming suddenly courageous, rushed forward without orders; "the chiefs followed, overtook them, and beat them back; and, while they were engaged in debating on the subject of their conduct, three people from the enemy made their appearance, unarmed, on a conspicuous part of the mountain," and announced the willingness of the tribe to submit—they did not understand the medicine which they supposed the white men to employ—they could not contend with people who spat fire from their mouths. The chiefs required them to give up their cattle and become tributary to the conqueror—terms which were at once complied with. It was now dis- covered that the enemy " were in strange consternation respecting their dead and wounded. Not being able to discover the cause of death," they concluded that the spirits of their forefathers were angry and had employed a supernatural agency to punish them.

When Tshaka had recalled his forces from the neighbourhood of the Kei, he despatched them against Sotshangana. Having reached the enemy's country, after some skirmishes with other tribes, the Zulus approached Sotshangana's kraals. They had seen no token of alarm, and anticipated an easy victory. Arrangements were made for an attack before sunrise; and, the night being dark, the warriors slept without apprehension. Their confidence was premature. A traitorous *in-duna*, having feigned indisposition when the army set forth, had proceeded by a nearer route and acquainted Sotshangana with his danger. That chief, suspecting treachery, received the information with doubt and secured his visitor. He then sent out spies, who returned with an ample confirmation of the *in-duna's* statement. The good faith of the latter being thus established, Sotshangana entrusted him with a military command, and confided in his advice. The Zulus, though closely watched, were permitted to advance without opposition; and, while sleeping in fancied security, were attacked at the dead of night. They were obliged to retreat, one regiment being nearly destroyed; but, having recovered from their surprise, they soon rallied and dispersed the enemy.

Sotshangana's people rallied in turn; and the Zulus, weakened by want of food, found it necessary to retire. They attempted to redeem their want of success by attacking weaker tribes; but these managed to secure their cattle in the bush, and punished the marauders by setting fire to their own corn-fields. The Zulus were reduced to the necessity of eating their shields (made of hide) and the sinews with which their assagais were bound. Having reached Makazana's country, they were supplied with food: but famine and sickness had made frightful havoc among them; for, while five thousand were slain by the enemy, three times that number fell victims to fatigue, hunger, and disease.[17]

VI.—When the shattered remains of his army returned, Tshaka was dead. It is said that after its departure his brothers, Dingane and Umhlangani, were visited by Makabäi and Mama, two sisters of the deceased Mnande. Believing that Tshaka had caused her death, they instigated the brothers to avenge it. "The blood of your mother," they said, "cries for vengeance. The tiger who hath drunk it, is thirsting for your own. Go then and kill him, before he can throw himself upon you. The troops will be thankful to you, if you do. You may be certain that, on their return, they will look to you to become their leaders." The brothers answered, " *You have spoken* "—a short sentence which implied much.[18]

Whether this be true or not, it is certain that

Dingane and Umhlangani agreed to destroy Tshaka;
and I have myself heard that a very fat woman,
with a name not essentially different from Makabäi,
was connected with the plot. Bopa, the king's
principal domestic, was induced to join it. The
conspirators, who probably knew that it would be
impossible to introduce poison into the king's food,
determined that he should be assassinated. Having
armed himself with an unshafted assagai, Bopa
approached Tshaka as he sat with two or three
councillors witnessing the return of his herds.
The traitor spoke rudely to the councillors, bade
them to cease pestering the king with their falsehoods, and attempted to drive them away. Astonished and alarmed at his presumption, they
endeavoured to secure Bopa; but, while they were
so occupied, the two brothers stole behind the king
and stabbed him in the back. Throwing aside his
blanket, Tshaka attempted to escape; but he was
pursued by the conspirators, and stabbed by Bopa.
Having fallen to the ground, "he besought them
to let him live that he might be their servant. To
this, however, no heed was given. They soon
speared him to death; and then left, to execute a
similar deed" on the councillors, who had attempted
to fly. These being slain, the assassins returned
to Tshaka's corpse and danced round it with savage
joy. Captain Gardiner states that the "two unnatural brothers are said to have drunk, on the
spot, the gall of the chief they had conspired to
assassinate."

The greater part of the people fled from the

kraal; but Sotobe and a few others seized their weapons to avenge the fallen chief. The conspirators stood on their defence and addressed them: "Do you not know that it is the sons of Senzangakona who have killed Tshaka for his base and barbarous conduct, and to preserve the nation of the Zulus, the sons of our fathers, that you may live in peace and enjoy 'your homes and your families; to put an end to the long and ceaseless wars, and mourning for that old woman Mnande, for whom so many have been put to a cruel death." Thus saying, they entered the palace, while Sotobe withdrew to his kraal.

CHAPTER IX.—TSHAKA'S SUCCESSORS.

I.—BOTH Dingan and Umhlangani claimed the
chieftainship; but the one contrived to get rid of
the other; and, when Umgwati, an illegitimate
son of Mnande, manifested a disposition to dispute
Dingan's claim, Bopa attacked his kraal and killed
him. The army are said, on their return, to have
been indignant at Tshaka's murder; but Dingan
promised them peace and relaxed the severe rule
relating to the compulsory celibacy of the warriors.
He killed most of the important men connected
with his predecessor, but made Sotobe principal
chief on the Natal side of the Tugela. In 1829,
he was living at Nobamba, and remarked to the
traveller, Green, that he should not fail to do right
by doing the reverse of Tshaka's acts.[1]

It is asserted that, when the army returned from
beyond the Maputa, Umhlaka, the commander,
made an attack on thé royal kraal and captured
some thousands of cattle. With these and part
of the troops, he "made off to the East of the
Malutis, where he settled and still remains."[2]

Qnetu, one of Tshaka's principal captains, refused

to acknowledge Dingan and fled to the southward with five thousand followers and much cattle. Having been refused permission to settle in Faku's territories, he became the implacable enemy of the Amampondo, who succeeded however in defeating him near the Umzimvubu, where the greater part of his people were either assagai'd or drowned. The remnant were attacked by Ncapai, who thus got possession of the herds taken from the Zulu-country. To recover these Dingan (having failed to defeat Qnetu) sent an army against Ncapai. That chief retreated; and the Zulus, in following him, endured much fatigue and hunger. Reaching a cold country, where many of the soldiers died, the principal officers pretended that the spirit of Tshaka had appeared to them all in one night and demanded what they were doing so far from home, since they had slain him to enjoy peace and tranquillity—Dingan, said the spirit, had sworn that he would lay down the spear and shield and go to war no more. Subsequently Tshaka reappeared and warned them that, if they went on, the Zulus would surely perish. Trusting that these inventions would be believed by Dingan, they directed the army to return.[3]

Umzilikazi was another who retired from Dingan. He went over the Draakensberg and attacked the Bechuana tribes. "Those who resisted and would not stoop to be his dogs, he butchered. He trained the captured youth in his own tactics, so that the majority of his army were foreigners." When visited by Mr. Moffat, in 1830, he was living on

the Elephants' River; but afterwards he moved
westward and fixed his residence on the Marikua.
An army sent by Dingan attacked him while
building a large kraal; some of his people were
killed, others fled, and the Zulus drove away many
of his cattle. At the Marikua, he came into contact with the Emigrant Boers. Some of these were
moving up the Vaal River, when an advanced
party was suddenly attacked by Umzilikazi's people,
"and twenty-eight of their number barbarously
murdered." Of another party, "some twenty-five
men and women were also massacred, and their
wagons and properties destroyed and plundered;
but a few of their party fortunately escaped to
warn the numerous little parties, who were still
scattered about those vast plains, of their impending
danger. They had scarcely collected themselves
in a *laager* of about fifty wagons, when they were
attacked by the whole" of Umzilikazi's army.
Though the latter were finally repulsed, they swept
away six thousand head of cattle and upwards of
forty thousand sheep. The intelligence of these
disasters having reached them, "the numerous and
powerful clans, who had remained peaceably con-
centrated about Thaba, 'Nchu, resolved to take
ample revenge and recover the cattle stolen from
their countrymen; and, a party of two hundred
warriors, headed by Gerrit Maritz, crossed the
Vaal River, and making a flank movement across
his western boundaries, attacked one of Umzilikazi's principal military towns named Mosega;
where they killed several hundreds of his principal

warriors, and recovered about seven thousand head of cattle," together with the wagons which had been taken after the attacks made on the small parties. Umzilikazi fled to the North, and is now residing beyond the Limpopo.

The following is Mr. Moffat's description of his first interview with this imitator of the renowned Tshaka. "We proceeded directly to the town, and on riding into the centre of a large fold, which was capable of holding ten thousand head of cattle, we were rather taken by surprise to find it lined by eight hundred warriors, besides two hundred who were concealed on each side of the entrance, as if in ambush. We were beckoned to dismount, which we did, holding our horses' bridles in our hands. The warriors at the gate instantly rushed in with hideous yells, and leaping from the earth with a kind of kilt around their bodies, hanging like loose tails, and their large shields, frightened our horses. They then joined the circle, falling into rank with as much order as if they had been accustomed to European tactics. Here we stood surrounded by warriors, whose kilts were of ape skins, and their legs and arms adorned with the hair and tails of oxen, their shields reaching to their chins, and their heads adorned with feathers.

"Although in the centre of a town, all was silent as the midnight hour, while the men were motionless as statues. Eyes only were seen to move, and there was a rich display of fine white teeth. After some minutes of profound silence, which was only interrupted by the breathing of our horses, the war

song burst forth. There was harmony, it is true,
and they beat time with their feet, producing a
sound like hollow thunder; but some parts of it
was music befitting the nether regions, especially
when they imitated the groanings of the dying on
the field of battle, and the yells and hissings of the
conquerors. Another simultaneous pause ensued,
and still we wondered what was intended, till out
marched the monarch from behind the lines, followed by a number of men bearing baskets and
bowls of food. He came up to us and, having been
instructed in our mode of salutation, gave each a
clumsy but hearty shake of the hand. He then
politely turned to the food, which was placed at
our feet, and invited us to partake. By this time
the wagons were seen in the distance, and having
intimated our wish to be directed to a place where
we might encamp in the outskirts of the town, he
accompanied us, keeping fast hold of my right arm,
though not in the most graceful manner, yet with
perfect familiarity. 'The land is before you; you
are come to your son. You must sleep where you
please.' When the 'moving houses,' as the wagons
were called, drew near, he took a firmer grasp of
my arm, and looked on them with unutterable surprise; and this man, the terror of thousands, drew
back with fear, as one in doubt as to whether they
were not living creatures. When the oxen were
unyoked, he approached the wagon with the utmost
caution, still holding me by one hand, and placing
the other on his mouth indicating his surprise.
He looked at them very intently, particularly the

wheels, and when told of how many pieces of wood each wheel was composed, his wonder was increased. After examining all very closely, one mystery yet remained, how the large band of iron surrounding the felloes of the wheel came to be in one piece without either end or joint. Umbate, my friend and fellow-traveller, whose visit to our station had made him much wiser than his master, took hold of my right hand, and related what he had seen. 'My eyes,' he said, 'saw that very hand,' pointing to mine, 'cut these bars of iron, take a piece off one end, and then join them as you now see them.' A minute inspection ensued to discover the welded part. 'Does he give medicine to the iron?' was the monarch's enquiry. 'No,' said Umbate, 'nothing is used but fire, a hammer, and a chisel.' Moselekatse then returned to the town, where the warriors were still standing as he left them, who received him with immense bursts of applause."[4]

The following poem, composed in Dingan's praise, will show how grossly the Zulus flattered their despot.[5]

THE PRAISES OF DINGAN.

There is a bird hovering.
It hovers above Bulawalo.
This bird devours the other birds;
It has devoured the Sagacious One of Bulawalo.[6]
The lustral waters have been drunk in silence;
They have been drunk by Mama and Makhabäi.[7]
The bird has perched at Nobamba, in the cattle fold.
   Liberator! thou hast shown thyself to this people;

Thou hast delivered from oppression the virgins,
The women, the men, and the children.
Thou art a king who crushest the heads of the other
    kings.
Thou passest over mountains inaccessible to thy prede-
    cessors.
Thou findest a defile from which there is no egress.
There thou makest roads; yes, roads.
Thou takest away the herds from the banks of the
    Tugela.
And the herds of the Babanankos, a people skilled in
    the forging of iron.
Thou art indeed a green [vigorous] adventurer!
Thou art the pillar which supports the house of Mnande.
Before thee the true men of the nations faint in their
    heart.
The true men of the nations faint away.
    Bird of the morning! give in secret thy commands
To thy soldiers; to the veteran and to the more youthful.
They will go, before the dawn of day,
To ravage every place whithersoever thou may'st com-
    mand them
To carry desolation.
Of night we know nothing!
    Formerly we used to say of him,—He is a man of
    no importance.
We did not know thee!
But now we know thee;
For thou hast cast a spell on the Tshakas.[8]
    Author of our tranquillity!
Thou givest us flesh and marrow;
We are no longer lank and lean.
Of old the hostile nations disturbed our repose;
They did it as do the *mazeze* [fleas].
To-day they trouble us not,
For thou hast caught and crushed them.
Thou makest all the world to keep silence.
Thou hast silenced even the troops;
Thy troops always obey thee:

Thou sayest and they go;
Thou sayest and they go again.
   All have respect for a king whom no one can approach
     unto.
When the king eats there remains with him no one but
     Ceyelele;
For Ceyelele has his confidence.
The king speaks not to Pande,
Nor to his other brothers.
   Thou art the purple dawn of the morning.
Thou art beautiful as an isle in the Umzinyati.
Thou puttest nations to silence,
As thou wouldst silence thy cooks.
Thou art the salvation of thy subjects.
Thou art not the man to rest at ease in thy palace!
Thou delightest in the military expedition!
Out then; flocks have been seen
Going up from the sea shore.
Pursue these herds and seize them.
The ox of the Zulu is his assagai.
Father of praise, give an ox,
The ox of thy troops.
New troops have arrived,
Who stand before their king
To receive from him their food.
Thou art indebted to no one for what thy belly de-
     vours,
But thou fillest all bellies,
O conqueror of kings!
   Thou, the only one issuing commands,
Issuest orders even to thy seniors.
Thou art not young, for thou art powerful.
If some head of cattle have gone astray,
The herdsmen fear to come and inform thee.
Matshetshe, that chief of the herdsmen, trembled
When the black heifer disappeared.
He pulled up the supports of his cabin,
And went to plant them far from thy wrath.
   Noble sovereign, reign over the subjects of Mnande,

Of the land of Buza.
Thou art a vulture, thou hast pounced upon Busako.
Thou art he who abaseth all other men.
   In the race, by thy agility, thou causest to pant
The lungs of the Basutos.
Dost thou not say to them, Ha! ha!
When they speak they tell lies.
They are beasts of the fields from all lands.
If they slaughter an ox, the cutting up
Begins with the shoulder;
They cut first the shoulder, then the leg,
And the other flesh remains there;
A pretty spectacle it is!
These gross Basutos are numerous!
Multitudes of petty tribes,
Which know not whence they have come,
A host of beasts of the field from all countries.
   Thou hast the whole nation under thee.
Thou art Tshaka; thou causest to tremble all people.
Thou thunderest like the musket.
At the fearful noise which thou makest
The inhabitants of the towns take to flight.
Thou art the great shade of the Zulu,
And thence thou expandest and reachest to all countries.
Thou puttest out of breath thy soldiers.
Thou art like the door of a house;
If it close itself upon an adversary
He must perish.
So it happeneth to those whom thou shuttest up,
Even amongst thine own people.
   Thy granaries are larger than those of Kokobane.
Thou art sagacious as the elephant,
Thou stabbest the other elephants:
Thou hast stabbed the elephant of Tebethlango [*i. e.*
   Tshaka].
   Thou slaughterest the nations as thou slaughterest
   a lamb.
Thou hast slain a great number of them,
Who no more dared to make a noise

Than the dumb sheep.
Hast not thou devoured Tshaka?
Hast not thou devoured Umhlangani?
The bitter herbs of expiation,
It is thyself who hast eaten them.
   Boko'khu'khus keep quiet.
You are indeed men of courage;
But we know one
More courageous still;
It is your conqueror.
Submit your soul, obey him.
Sleep a tranquil slumber.
All the horses of the nations are his.
All leaders belong to him.
Silence! Silence! obey him without a murmur;
Or else, murderer of men, do thou arouse thyself and slay.
   He who scattered the Mathlubis on the Umzinyati
Is no youthful warrior.
Do not fear
That he will ever want fat oxen
Wherewith to feast his concubines.
Do not fear
That he will ever permit any to take away his flocks.
Powerful conqueror,
Triumph over all the powers of the east.
Thou art violent; thou art cold
Like the wind which comes from the sea,
Thou causest to perish all the nations.
It is said that thou hast wrenched from the Tseles their
    herds,
And that thou hast delivered to the flames their habi-
    tations,
Forcing them to go and construct new ones elsewhere.
Thou hast subjected the tribes on the Folose,
And on the Folosane.
Ravager of provinces,
Deep abyss, which engulphest all;
Thou covetest all the riches of the tribes,
And thou hast gathered them together as into a pit.

Go, thou sagacious one, take away the cattle of the
 cunning.
Bird, king of the other birds, scream,
Since thou hast been placed at the head of the troops
Call Petlelele, thy faithful herald,
Give to him thy commands, and our chiefs, with speed,
Will run from all corners of the realm
To appear before thee at the appointed day.
Thou reignest here, thou reignest there ;
Thou reignest in all directions.

II.—Soon after Tshaka's death, Isaacs left Natal
with the vessel and effects of his deceased friend,
Lieutenant King. Mr. Farewell sailed with him to
Algoa Bay; and, accompanied by Messrs. Walker
and Thackaray, attempted to return by land.
Having reached Faku's place, he determined to
visit Qnetu, whom he had known at Natal. The
Amampondo chief would have dissuaded him; but
believing that the Quabies had much ivory to
barter, Farewell persisted. Qnetu received the
European party with apparent kindness; but, fearing probably that they might assist Dingan against
him, wished them not to proceed. This request
was denied, and Qnetu's countenance altered.
Though his two companions were alarmed, Farewell was unwilling to think that the chief would
venture to kill them; and they retired. A little
before day-break, a party of men surrounded their
tent, silently cut the strings, and assagai'd the
inmates. Their native servants, who slept in a
hut hard by, were attacked; and of seven only
three escaped. The barbarians then went to plunder the wagons, which had been left at a short

distance. " On seeing them advance, the people in charge (both English and Hottentots) immediately fled into the woods, so that there was no further obstacle in the way." The booty was rich; for, besides the oxen, ten or twelve horses, and some guns, the ruffians obtained several thousand pounds of beads—a treasure, in their eyes, of great value.

Isaacs, having been absent about a year, returned to Natal, and determined to remain.[9] After this, Dingan sent Cane on another mission to the Cape; where, however, the authorities refused to receive it.[10] Cane then sold the ivory which had been taken as a present to the Governor, and purchased goods for Dingan with the proceeds. Having returned to Natal he sent these forward to the king, but himself imprudently remained behind. The messengers were directed to say that he was detained by the illness of one of his companions; but, the day after he had been told this, the king learned that Cane was hunting elephants. Dingan was incensed, not only at Cane's want of respect, but because his conduct seemed to confirm a malicious report made to him by Jacob.

On the death of Tshaka, Jacob was deprived of his position as chief of the sentinels, and retired to his kraal. When Cane went to the Cape, he was appointed to accompany him. This was done at Cane's request; and, as Jacob did not like the journey, he ever afterwards cherished feelings of revenge towards that individual. Having returned he reported to Dingan that he had met a Frontier

Kafir who wished to find a home with the Zulus, it being impossible to live near the white men. These people (Jacob's informant said) came at first and took part of the Kafirs' land; they then increased and drove the natives further back, and had frequently taken more land from them as well as cattle; their next step was to build houses (mission-stations) to subdue the people by "witchcraft." Of these, he said, there was already one at every tribe; and, as the prophets had predicted would be the case, some chiefs had died in consequence. Jacob added that at Graham's Town the soldiers had frequently asked whether the roads in the Zulu-country were good for horses, and whether the people had many cattle. He had heard, he said, that a few white people intended to come first and obtain land; and, when they had built a fort, others would follow and subdue the Zulus. He stated also, that after they had left Graham's Town, Cane had told him that some people were coming soon, and that Major Somerset was about to visit Dingan. He concluded by insinuating that Cane had stopped behind to guide them.

Isaacs endeavoured to convince Dingan that Jacob had fabricated a story to be revenged on Cane; who, he said, would be certain to come when he heard that the king was angry. "I do not want to see him again," Dingan replied; "I wish you very much to drive him away." Subsequently he said: "If I knew that a white army was coming, I would distribute the people, and tell them to separate in all directions; and, for my part, I would take only five men and go where you would never find me; and then what would you do for food? Besides, I would poison our waters." Dingan had already said that a regiment had been ordered to proceed to Cane's and take away his cattle; and when Isaacs was leaving, Tambuza, a principal *in-duna*, said to him: " It is the wish of the son of Senzangakona that I should impress you with the friendship he bears to the white people; and how he wishes to renew and cultivate that friendship. He trusts, therefore, you will not be displeased with him if he sends to take away John Cane's cattle, as that person has irritated the king and compelled him to do what he is sorry for. We are the conquerors of the blacks, but know nothing of the system of fighting of the white people, and are afraid to learn. You have been in our country ever since the first war with the Amampondo, and we have never molested you in any way, but have always esteemed you as friends." Isaacs having replied that Cane would doubtless defend his property, the *in-duna* remarked: " Losing people on such an occasion is usual and to be expected, and the chance as much in our favour as Cane's."

When Isaacs returned to the Bay, he found that Cane's residence (near the site of the present Horticultural Gardens) had been destroyed. The first thing which attracted his notice were a few sheets of an encyclopedia scattered along the path. " The kraal had been burnt for fuel; the cat had been speared and skinned; the ducks were scattered lifeless about the place;" even the growing corn had been levelled. As he was going away, a terrified dog made its appearance, crouched at the visitors' feet, and seemed to supplicate their protection. Cane had fled before the arrival of the army, together with Mr. Fynn. Isaacs went on board a vessel which had just arrived, while his companion, William Fynn, departed in search of his brother. In a short time the fugitives returned to the Bay, and Dingan assured the Europeans that Cane alone had cause to fear. Mr. Fynn, having visited the king, undertook to disprove Jacob's statements, and was referred to the principal *izin-duna*. A council was therefore held; and the officers, after hearing both parties, declared themselves satisfied with Mr. Fynn's explanation. He did not, however, think them sincere, but felt convinced that they believed all that Jacob had said. "The execrable villain," says Isaacs, "had poisoned the mind of the king and his chiefs, to be revenged on Cane, and would make every effort to excite the wrath of Dingan against the Europeans, fearing an exposure by them, when his fate would be sealed."

Isaacs left in the vessel; Fynn took his people to the Umzimvubu; and Cane went into the bush. But subsequently Dingan, believing that he had been deceived, induced Cane to leave his retreat; Jacob was put to death, and Mr. Fynn returned.[11]

III.—In 1837, Pieter Retief visited Dingan;

and, on behalf of the Emigrant Farmers, requested a formal cession of the present colony of Natal. Dingan promised the territory on condition that the boers first recovered from Sikonyela (residing near the sources of the Caledon) a number of cattle which had been stolen from him by that chief. Retief accepted the condition; and, having obtained the cattle, returned with seventy Dutchmen and about thirty young Hottentots and servants, to Dingan's residence. The king was pleased to see the cattle; and, for two days, entertained his visitors with a series of war-dances. A formal grant having been written, he affixed his mark, and next morning Retief prepared to depart. Dingan invited the Dutchmen to enter his kraal for the purpose of taking leave, but desired them to comply with the usage of his court and not bring their weapons. Being unsuspicious, they piled these outside the gate; and, having directed their servants to saddle the horses, went in. The king, surrounded, as usual, by warriors, talked to Retief and his principal companions in a very friendly manner, and ordered some bowls of native beer to be set before them. While they were engaged in drinking, the warriors rushed upon them from all sides, exclaiming *Bambani abatakati*, seize the "evildoers." The Dutchmen drew their knives and made a determined defence, killing some and wounding more; but it was impossible to resist the assault of thousands, and one after another they were disabled and carried away to be slain.[11]

Relying on Dingan's promise to Retief, a con-

siderable body of Emigrants had descended the
mountain, and were now spread over the basin of
the Upper Tugela. Immediately after the massacre
at Umkungunghlovu, Dingan despatched ten regiments to exterminate these hapless people. The
army divided itself into several detachments, which
fell at day-break on the most advanced parties of
the emigrants, near the present town of Weenen
("Weeping"), its name being derived from the
events of that terrible morning. Other parties
were surprised and murdered; "but from one or
two wagons a solitary young man escaped, who,
hastening to the parties whom he knew to be
in the rear, at length succeeded in spreading
the alarm." Some *laagers* or encampments were
hastily formed, and preparations made for resistance. None of these *laagers* were forced; and at
a large one on the Bushman's River, a fight took
place which continued the whole day. The Farmers'
amunition was nearly expended, when "their last
shot from a three-pounder, which had been rigged
to the back of one of their wagons, struck down
some of the leading Zulu chiefs and forced them
to a precipitate retreat." When the survivors were
able to visit the stations of the advanced parties,
"a scene of horror and misery was unfolded which
no pen can describe. All the wagons had been
demolished, the iron parts wrenched from them,
and by their ruins lay the mangled corpses of
men, women, and children, thrown on heaps and
abandoned to the beasts of prey. Amongst these
heaps, at the Blue Krantz River, they found

literally amongst the dead corpses, the bodies of two young females, about ten or twelve years of age, which appeared to show some signs of vitality. The one was pierced with nineteen and the other with twenty-one stabs of the assagai." They lived nevertheless; and, though perfect cripples, grew up to womanhood. The number of persons murdered is said to have been six hundred.[12]

Hearing of their countrymen's misfortune, other parties hastened to join them, and four hundred fighting men set forward, under the command of Uys and Potgieter, to punish Dingan for his perfidy. The expedition proved unsuccessful; Uys, with some others, was killed, and the Boers returned to their *laagers*. While Uys and his people were occupying Dingan's attention, the English settlers proceeded with their natives against the kraals of Sotobe and another *in-duna*, situate between the Mooi River and Tugela. The followers of Cane and Ogle (who were the most considerable leaders) quarrelled about the right of precedence; and, having no other means of settling the dispute, resorted to their clubs. The battle, in which fifty were disabled from continuing the journey, appears to have resulted in favour of Cane's people. Ogle's men threatened to revenge themselves, nor was it long before they had the opportunity of so doing. Having reached their destination, the expedition found the kraals undefended (the men being absent with the army) and carried off six thousand cattle, besides a considerable number of women and children. " On the return of the settlers, the booty was divided amongst them, according to the proportion of people they had, each chief settling with his own followers."

After this successful foray, Mr. R. Biggar (whose brother had been slain in the massacre near the site of Weenen) returned from Graham's Town, and proposed a second expedition. When this had been agreed to by the leaders, some of the people were unwilling to go, while others were filled with extraordinary enthusiasm; the plunder obtained on the previous occasion had excited their cupidity, and old men barely able to walk could not be dissuaded from accompanying the more vigorous. The army, having crossed the Tugela, advanced towards a kraal situated on the side of a hill, and surrounded it before daylight. It being known that some of Dingan's warriors were here, volleys of musketry were directed against the huts, and aimed low that the balls might strike the sleepers. When these discovered their danger, they endeavoured to avoid it by taking hold of the sticks which formed the framework and suspending themselves from the roofs. The huts however sunk with the weight, and the assailants aimed higher. The inmates were killed and the kraal was set on fire. The movements of the invaders being well known to the Zulus, ten thousand warriors marched to repel them. The Natal army was drawn up near the burning kraal—those who had fire-arms being in front. When the first division of the enemy approached, it was received with a steady fire, checked and driven back. The first

division, however, "only retreated to make way for
others that advanced from different points, as the
formation of the hills permitted." "Cane sent
Ogle's Kafirs to attack the Zulus on the south-
west, whilst he with the main body of the Natal
army took the north-east. When Ogle's Kafirs
had dispersed these, they were to come round and
take the Zulus in flank." Instead of doing this,
they dispersed the enemy and fled, thus fulfilling
their threat to be revenged on Cane's people. The
Zulus, encouraged by their flight, closed in upon
the diminished forces of Natal. The struggle was
fierce, and the slaughter frightful. "The Zulus
lost thousands of their people; they were cut down
until they formed banks, over which those who
were advancing had to climb." So great was their
fury that the wounded who could manage to crawl
still endeavoured to stab their foes; and thus it
became necessary to shoot them a second time.
Cane, who was mounted, received an assagai in his
breast; another pierced him between the shoulders;
and, falling from his horse, he was quickly
despatched. Stubbs was stabbed by a boy, and
Biggar fell close by. Their leaders being dead,
the Natal Kafirs threw away their badges; and,
having exchanged their shields for those of Dingan's fallen warriors, fled towards the Tugela.
The Zulu officers, who knew the ground, so placed
their forces as to oblige the fugitives to run towards a part of the river where the descent was
over a precipice one hundred feet deep; and, to
destroy those who might survive the fall, sent a

division by known approaches into the stream. "Very few gained the opposite bank. It was here that Blankenberg was killed. Of the few who escaped, some swam, some dived, and some floated along feigning to be dead. One, Goba, crossed the river four times, and was saved at last." Of the white men and Hottentots, not a dozen survived this terrible engagement; while, out of the seven hundred and fifty Kafirs who had been mustered at Port Natal, only about two hundred returned (these being chiefly Ogle's people). "The few who escaped arrived at home singly, many of them having been pursued nearly to the Bay, and owing their deliverance to the shelter of the bush and the darkness of night." After a few weeks a Zulu army was sent to Port Natal, when the English "took refuge on the island in the middle of the Bay, where they remained by day, and at night went on board the 'Comet,' which was lying at anchor there at the time." The Zulus remained above a fortnight in the neighbourhood, destroyed everything destructible, and swept away all the cattle.[13]

The Dutchmen, disheartened by the result of their own attack on Dingan and by the fate of the English expedition, "gave up all hope of resuming hostilities for the present. They had been taught a lesson of prudence by the talent and daring displayed by the Zulu armies, and they accordingly kept a watchful eye upon their Northern Frontier, and sent messengers out in various direc-

tions imploring further accession to their numbers,
both from the Cape and the present [now late]
Sovereignty. Many parties, upon hearing of their
distressed state, came to join them ; but this at the
moment only increased their misery and wants, as
their cattle and herds having been swept away
(these being still in the hands of the Zulus) and
having been prevented from cultivating any lands,
they were not only exposed to the greatest want,
but were actually in a state of famine, when some
liberal minded countrymen of theirs at the Cape,
hearing of their distressed condition, sent them
supplies of food, medicine, and other necessaries
of life, which helped them through the miseries of
the winter of 1838, during which season, want,
disease, and famine stalked over the land, making
fearful ravages among them.

" Dingan ever watchful when to attack his foe
with advantage, being fully informed of their
wretched condition, made another attack upon
them in August 1838; but, on this occasion, the
Emigrant Farmers (having their scouts always out
to give them timely intimation of his advance)
were every where prepared to give him a warm
reception, and at every *laager* the Zulu forces
were driven back and defeated with great loss,
only two or three lives having been lost among the
Emigrants during several successive engagements."

Though the Boers were thus victorious, they had
to contend with great difficulties. Various small
parties who joined them brought little effectual
assistance ; but, before the end of the year, a num-

ber of young men descended from what was lately
the Sovereignty, while Andries Pretorius was
added to their number. Having been formerly
a field-cornet in the Graff-Reinet District, he
became extremely popular among the Emigrants,
and four hundred and sixty fighting and mounted
men put themselves under his command. "They
were powerfully aided by the brave and sterling
Carl Landman, who joined them with all those
Emigrants who had already commenced settling
themselves down near the Bay; and these combined forces, profiting from the experience of the
past, advanced with great caution, securing their
position every evening, so that, when they had
nearly reached the Umhlatusi River, they were
fully prepared, as at the earliest dawn of day on
Sunday the 16th December, 1838, the whole of
Dingan's forces, about ten or twelve thousand
strong, attacked their position with a fury far
exceeding all their former attacks. For three
hours they continued rushing upon them, endeavouring to tear open all their defences and force
the Emigrant camp; until Pretorius, finding the
Zulu forces concentrating all their efforts upon one
side of the camp and their own ammunition nearly
failing, ordered two hundred mounted men to sally
forth out of one of the gates at the rear of the
line which the Zulus were attacking; and these
mounted warriors, charging both flanks and pouring their deadly volleys upon the immense masses
which were gathered together within a small space,
at length beat them off with a fearful loss. The

Emigrants assert that nearly three thousand Zulus licked the dust before they retreated; and their defeat must have been complete, as Dingan fled quite panic stricken, set fire to the whole of his town of Umkungunghlovu, and hid himself, with the remnant of his force, for a considerable time, in the woods skirting the Umfolosi River.

"The Emigrants, having had only three or four men killed and as many wounded in this decisive engagement (among the latter of whom was Pretorius himself), advanced upon the town of Umkungunghlovu, which they still found partially burning; and, on the awful hillock out of the town, they beheld, on one vast pile, the bones and remains of Retief and their one hundred companions in arms, who, ten months before, had fallen victims to Dingan's treachery, but whose deaths they were then in fact avenging. Many of the straps or *riems* by which they had been dragged to this place of slaughter, were still found adhering to the bones of the legs and arms by which they had been drawn thither. The skulls were frightfully broken, exhibiting marks of the knob-kirries and stones with which they had been fractured; and, singular to relate, the skeleton of their ill-fated leader, Retief, was recognized by a leathern pouch or bandoleer, which he had suspended from his shoulders and in which he had deposited the deed or writing formally ceding this territory to the Emigrant Farmers, as written out by the Rev. Mr. Owen, on the day previous to his massacre, and signed with the mark of Dingan, by which

he declared 'to resign to Retief and his countrymen the place called Port Natal, together with
all the land annexed: that is to say—from the
Tugela to the Umzimvubu River, and from the
sea to the north, as far as the land may be useful
and in my possession.' These are the very words
of the original document, which was found still
perfectly legible, and was delivered over to me
by the Volksraad in the year 1843, and is now
(or ought be) among the archives of the Colonial
Office here." Having interred the remains of
their unfortunate countrymen, the Boers sent out
a strong patrol which was unexpectedly attacked
and escaped with difficulty. In consequence of
this, the Dutchmen retired from Dingan's country
taking with them, it is said, some five thousand
cattle.[14]

After their return, the farmers entered into a
treaty with the Zulu king, "at his instance," by
which he agreed to restore the horses, cattle, and
guns which had fallen into his hands, and relinquished
the country south-west of the Tugela river. The
British Commandant was concerned in the negociations which led to this convention; but interfered
no further "than by using his good offices in the
attainment of some arrangements," which he
thought would probably prevent further bloodshed.[15]

Not long after the treaty had been formed,
Dingan's brother, Pande, thinking his life in
danger, left the Zulu-country, and took possession

of some land on the Umvoti. He was accompanied
or followed by a large portion of the Zulu forces.
From the Umvoti he sent messengers to the
Farmers, soliciting their support and protection.
It was at first suspected " that this was a deep-laid
plot between him and Dingan, to inveigle them
into the Zulu-country; but, after repeated con-
ferences, a formal treaty of alliance, offensive and
defensive, was concluded with him; by the terms of
which the Emigrant Farmers pledged themselves to
support and defend Pande; while he, on the other
hand, promised to support them in any attack upon
Dingan."

In 1840, the Boers mustered a force of four
hundred mounted men, under the command of
Pretorius. These joined Pande's army, about four
thousand strong; and the combined force entered
the Zulu-country, the Farmers keeping themselves
at some distance from Pande's people.

When the Dutchmen were collecting their forces
at Pieter-Maritzburg, Tambuza arrived with an
offer of peace. "He was, however, seized, with his
attendant Combizana; and, upon being rigidly
questioned, frankly admitted that he had also been
sent with a view of reporting to Dingan the state
of the combined army of Emigrants and Zulus
under Pande. The latter, evidently embittered
against this person (one of Dingan's principal
counsellors), charged him with having been the
chief cause of the murder of Retief and his party;
that he had plotted and advised his (Pande's)
death; and in short brought such a series of

charges against him that (contrary to every usage
of civilized life) he was taken along with the army
as a prisoner, until they reached the banks of the
Buffalo or Umzinyati River, where a court martial
was formed, which under the excited feelings of the
occasion, soon passed a sentence of death upon the
unfortunate prisoners, and which was carried into
execution within a few hours after; Tambuza not only
nobly upbraiding his executioners with the viola-
tion of all usage towards messengers, even amongst
savages, but expressing his perfect readiness to die,
he only implored (but in vain) mercy on behalf
of his young attendant, who was only a camp
follower, and had thus been but doing his duty in
following his master. This may be said to have
been the only blot which seriously reflected upon
the conduct of the Emigrant Farmers in their several
engagements with the Zulus, for they otherwise
constantly endeavoured to spare the women and
children from massacre, and have uniformly conducted their wars with as much discretion and
prudence as bravery."[16]

A few days after the execution of Tambuza,
Pande's army defeated the forces of Dingan.
When the Farmers heard of their ally's success,
they followed it up with great vigour, drove
Dingan over the Black Folosi, and thence to the
Pongolo. Having crossed the latter river, he
attempted to pass through the Amaswazi-country,
with his children, his cattle, and a small force; but
was murdered by that people, who (according to
Pande) kept all the royal children, with those of

Senzangakona and several of the great men, and many of the royal cattle. Pande subsequently required the children and cattle to be restored; but the feet of the messengers were worn out in vain—no redress was given.[17]

IV.—Having no doubt that Dingan was dead and his army dispersed, the Farmers "assembled in great state on the banks of the Folosi, February the 14th, 1840; and there, under the discharge of their guns, Andries Pretorius proclaimed Pande the sole and acknowledged king of the Zulus." In a proclamation issued by Pretorius and the other commandants, the Boers "declared their sovereignty to extend from the Black Umfolosi and St. Lucia Bay to the Umzimvubu or St. John's River; and in fact, by their proceedings of that day, assumed a certain authority or sovereignty over Pande himself: from whom they received, as their indemnity, thirty-six thousand head of cattle." Of these, fourteen thousand were given to the farmers from beyond the Draakensberg who had come to the assistance of their friends.

It does not fall within the province of this work to relate the subsequent history of the Farmers, their strife with the British troops, and the annexation of Natal to the colonial possessions of this country. Pande's proceedings have not been productive of events calculated to interest the general reader; but the conduct of his sons, Cetwaya (or Ketshwaya) and Umbulazi, lately detailed in the newspapers, requires some notice.

It was known to the traders, during November, 1856, that Zulu politics were in a critical state, and that Pande's sons were preparing to engage in a contest for the sovereignty. Cetwaya and Umbulazi, being each at the head of an army, approached a spot about seven miles from the Tugela —the boundary between Natal and the Zulu-country. Cetwaya's followers amounted, it is supposed, to twenty thousand, while those of Umbulazi did not exceed eight thousand. The latter, wishing to obtain assistance from the colony, had applied to the nearest British official, who very properly said that he had no authority to interfere. It appears, however, that his interpreter "volunteered to cross the river, with a small body-guard, to endeavour to negociate terms of peace between the belligerent parties. The proposal was unfortunately acceded to, and the Kafir-police attached to the station, with the uniforms and arms supplied for their use by our Government, besides a number of Hottentots and other natives, collected and armed for the purpose, proceeded on their dangerous mission— their leader (Mr. Dunn) being also armed to the teeth. The very appearance of such a force (it numbered sixty men) was calculated to irritate already excited savages; and it is not surprising that no answers were returned to repeated messages sent to Cetwaya with a view to open negociations—more especially if it be true, as positively affirmed, that Mr. Dunn and his men took up their quarters with Umbulazi, thus apparently at least, ranging themselves on one side, and, therefore, being disqualified as arbitrators between the two. At length Mr. Dunn proceeded in person towards Cetwaya's position, when he was fired upon and the ball passed near his head. On this, the party were drawn out and ordered to fire; and thus commenced the horrors of the day. A Dutchman named Gouws (a settler in Natal) was professedly supporting Umbulazi at another point. Mr. Dunn's little party thrice momentarily repulsed the huge mass of Cetwaya's army, and gallantly stood their ground for a time; but against such terrible odds resistance was hopeless; and the whole army of Umbulazi took to flight, as well as the Dutchman and his party. No battle therefore was fought, but the scene was a rout and a wholesale slaughter." The fugitives ran towards the colony, where alone they could find safety.

" Followed by a mighty mass of infuriated and triumphant savages, multitudes fell fainting by the way, and were quickly despatched by assagais; and multitudes more fell beneath the deadly thrust of that weapon while running for their lives. The women and children, who had taken refuge in *kloofs* and ravines, prior to the actual attack, were enclosed and mercilessly butchered. Still several thousands of men, women, and children, reached the Tugela, and plunged into its swollen stream; where again the spear of their brutal pursuers helped the deep and rapid current in the work of destruction. The river was reddened with blood, where it was not blackened with the shrieking forms of innumerable savages; and some idea of

the number of corpses that shortly encumbered
the water may be formed from the fact that they
obstructed the action of the oars and the passage
of the boat that conveyed the few who were able
to avail themselves of it. Of Mr. Dunn's party
of sixty, only eight or ten returned to tell the tale
of horrors; and the number of Zulus that perished
by spear or water, in their terrible massacre, is
estimated to be at least six thousand. Notwithstanding all this sacrifice of life, fully three thousand miserable half-drowned or wounded wretches
succeeded in reaching the Natal side; and, since
the day of the slaughter, Umbulazi himself (who
at first was said to be killed, but who, it seems,
had succeeded in concealing himself) came over
with one hundred of his followers, the remnant of
his army, and is now under British protection, as
well as a lad, one of Pande's youngest sons."

Some English traders (who observed a strict
neutrality) "escaped across the river with the
utmost difficulty and peril. But the whole of their
property was carried off by the victorious army;
twelve wagons were entirely stripped and sacked,
and no fewer than one thousand six hundred head
of cattle belonging to the traders were carried off.
Six of the wagons, with about one thousand head
of cattle, had been taken in safety over the Zulu
side of the river to an island in the centre; yet,
even here, on this neutral ground (if it be not
actually British territory) they were emptied of
their contents and the cattle driven off. The value
of property and cattle thus seized is not less than

four thousand pounds, whilst a large amount of the property and cattle of traders still remains in the interior of the country at the mercy of the victorious savages. We have the concurrent testimony of the most respectable and experienced traders for the belief that but for the unfortunate attempt of Mr. Dunn and his party, clothed, in the apprehension of ignorant savages, with the authority of the British Government, no white man's life would have been endangered, no wagon plundered, and if any trader's cattle had been taken away in the foray they would have been promptly returned on application. Up to the eve of the catastrophe, and during the known preparations, the traders had mixed freely in friendly and business intercourse with both parties, and the continued observance of a strict neutrality on our part would, it is fully believed, have prevented any loss or danger to Englishmen, as well as the very serious complications which have now arisen."

The victor is said to have divided his army into three parts, which scoured the country in all directions, putting to death not only those who favoured his rival, but all who were neutral or doubtful. Elated with his success, Cetwaya praised his young men, saying that they, and not the *amadoda*, were the warriors. Offended at this and fearing for their lives, Mapite and another old and influential chief deserted with their numerous followers and returned to Pande. Masipula, his principal general, a supporter of Cetwaya, had reached the Great Place before them; but it was only to watch the king until the arrival of the rebel army. The appearance of the two chiefs was therefore peculiarly opportune, and Pande immediately told them to slay Masipula. This being done, Pande and his old warriors collected all their people, gave battle to the usurper, and put his "boys" to flight.

Pande appears to have obtained help from the Boers, to whom he made over the region lying between the White Folosi and the Colony. " The large slice of the Zulu-country thus ceded," says the Natal Mercury, " comprises the most healthy and fertile portion of the whole, flanking the Natal border along its entire length, and having a commercial outlet on the coast at St. Lucia Bay. We have not heard what is to be done with Cetwaya, but presume he will share the fate of the weaker, now that a stronger than he has taken the field. The Boers, it is stated, are hunting him from his hiding-place. Boers came in to the number of from four hundred to five hundred—strong enough to dictate their own terms; and we understand the ceded country will be speedily occupied by a large number of settlers from the Buffalo district and the more remote and inconvenient districts of the Trans Vaal. This new turn in Zulu affairs considerably complicates the difficulties of our colonial statesmanship, though we do not in the least apprehend that it increases, but rather diminishes, the danger of inroad or collision."[18]

CHAPTER X.—ZULU WARFARE.

I.—MILITARY POLITY.   II.—MODE OF WARFARE.   III.—AN
EXPEDITION.

I.—THE Zulu army (the organization of which is due to Tshaka) consists of two classes, namely "men" and "boys"—the former being those entitled to wear the head-ring, and the latter all others.[1] Both classes are divided into regiments, each of which assembles at one of the royal kraals. Under ordinary circumstances the men attend there when they please; but, if the number present be too small, the *in-duna* sends for as many as he may think necessary. The regiments bear the same name as the kraals where they assemble. Two or three years ago, Pande's army embraced the following. (1.) Of OLD "MEN," he had four regiments, namely *Tuguza, Isiklepini, Imbelibeli, Nobambe* (the last being particularly ancient people). (2.) Of YOUNGER "MEN" (*ama-kehla*) he had six regiments, namely *Bulawalo, Nodwenge, Dumazulu, Lambongwenya, Swongindaba, Indaba-ka-aumbi.* (3.) The "BOYS" were distributed into four regiments, *Tuluana, Isangu, Ingulubi Hlambehlu.* (Some of the Hlambehlu "boys" were thirty-five years of age). Tshaka "established a force of nearly one hundred thousand men, about fifty thousand of whom were warriors in constant

readiness for battle." A European, who saw
Pande's army setting out on an expedition, estimated it at twenty thousand.[2]

Tshaka is said to have supplied his soldiers, when
assembled at his kraals, with all the food they
required; but Pande only gives them an ox or
two now and then. Whatever additional food
they need must be sent from their own homes.
The officers bring cows to supply themselves with
milk. The troops have no pay. Beads and
blankets are occasionally given to the "men," but,
with the exception of a few favourites, the "boys"
receive nothing. I do not know whether Pande
is more generous after a successful foray, unless
it be to those who have slain an enemy; but
Tshaka made a liberal distribution of the spoils
taken in war.

When Tshaka's soldiers were defeated, he killed
them. "After an expedition his troops were permitted to retire to their respective kraals for a
short period, to recover from their fatigue; whence,
in a short time, the chiefs were called to collect the
people, to hear the details of those operations in
which the warriors had been engaged; at which
time all who had evinced cowardice were selected,"
and put to death. An entire regiment was sometimes massacred. It is easy to see how much
Tshaka's practice in this respect, must have contributed to render his troops desperate, if not
courageous. Pande has put men to death for
defeat or cowardice; but I have been told that, when
he was proceeding to destroy several in succession,

some of his great officers interfered to prevent the massacre.

The normal weapon of the Kafir tribes is the assagai *(um-konto)*, which consists of a double-edged iron-blade inserted in the thicker end of a tapering stick—the whole being about five feet long. It is used principally as a dart; but, having no other offensive weapon, a prudent warrior reserves his last assagai to be employed as a stabbing instrument. Tshaka abolished the use of the assagai as a missile; but, before he directed his followers to depart from the usage of their forefathers, he ordered a mock fight between two regiments, reeds being substituted for more dangerous arms. The one regiment was told to follow the old-fashioned practice, and cast their reeds at the enemy; the other, each man having a single reed, was to rush upon the opposing rank and use their fragile weapons at close quarters. The latter having gained an easy victory, the people were willing to lay aside their darts; each soldier was supplied with a short, stout spear, the loss of which in battle was made a capital offence. The Zulu forces owed much of their original success to this new weapon; but, afterwards, when contending with the Farmers, they discovered that it was of little use against a mounted foe, and resumed the old assagai. The war-shield is of ox-hide, nearly oval and strengthened by means of a stick down the centre. It almost covers the body—a circumstance from which, as previously mentioned, the Zulus obtained their Bechuana appellation of *Matabele*, those who disappear. (A smaller shield is used for dances.)

It is stated by Mr. Isaacs, that Tshaka maintained a "system of espionage, by which he knew at all times the condition and strength of every tribe around him, both independent and tributary." Spies were also sent out before an expedition. Thus, when he had determined to attack the Amampondo, persons were despatched to examine the country, find out the enemy's strong-holds, and ascertain how these might be approached from some point whence an attack would be least expected. The same practice is still observed.

It was Tshaka's custom to conceal the destination of his army, until the moment before starting. "When all was ready," says Isaacs, "for entering upon their march, he confided to one general his design, and to him he entrusted the command, should he not head his army in person. . . He made it an invariable rule to address his warriors at their departure; and his language was generally studied, to raise their expectations and excite them in the hour of battle. He particularly detailed to them the road his spies had pointed out, inducing them to believe that they were going to attack any party but the one actually designed." Concealment was intended to prevent treasonable communications being made to the enemy; though, as is evident from the fact already mentioned in connexion with the expedition against Sotshangana, it was not always successful.

There can be no doubt that, speaking generally, these people are deficient in courage, and that the conquests achieved by Tshaka were due in a far greater measure to himself and the discipline he established, than to the bravery of his soldiers. Their celibacy contributed to foster a martial spirit, but they "fought to avoid being massacred, and triumphed more from the trepidation of their opponents than from the use of their spears." The affair at Ingoma, in which he was engaged, convinced Isaacs that they possessed no innate courage. The following anecdote will show how a few resolute men have defeated a much larger number. Dingan having sent a force against a tributary chief, the latter was surprised and fled. A considerable body of the Zulu soldiers were driving away his cattle, when his brother, not aware of the circumstances, seized his weapons; and, running in advance of a few followers, chased the plunderers. He rushed singly to the attack; killed several in the enemy's rear; and, when his handful of supporters came up, put the entire body to flight. Having recovered from their consternation, they turned upon their pursuers; but again gave way; and it was only when one of Tshaka's noted regiments came up that the brave little party was defeated.

Medicine and superstition are conspicuously associated with Zulu warfare. Before an expedition sets forth, the king takes medicine, into which is introduced some personal article belonging to his enemy. The belief in the efficacy of this is so confirmed that, if a chief is obliged to retreat, the floor of his hut is scraped; and, I suppose, it was for the same reason that Dingan, when he fled before the Boers, set fire to his kraal. The doctor who prepared Tshaka to go against Pagatwayo, made cuttings in various parts of his body, and placed medicine in them. During Pande's preparations for encountering Dingan, a celebrated practitioner cut off the fore-leg of a heifer and left the animal to die; what use he made of the limb I do not know, but the proceeding is believed to have contributed very materially to Pande's victory.

Medicine is administered to the soldiers. A young bull having been slain, they take with their fingers a decoction of medicine; and subsequently pieces of the beef are rolled in powdered medicine, thrown into the air, caught by the warriors, and applied to their mouths, as at the Feast of First Fruits. Taking from the fire a root or stick of medicine, the doctor blows sparks from it towards the soldiers, who are then dismissed to the bush and directed not to wash themselves until morning. Next day they take copious draughts of a decoction—apparently an emetic—and, having left the kraal, vomit into a large hole. A medicine called *mabopi (ama-bopi?)* is used. Standing in the midst of the warriors, the doctor takes it in both hands and elevates it several times, saying: " Here is the *mabopi (Nangu mabopi)*; do you see it?" Their united voices reply, in a tone of thunder, " We have seen it." They are then fumigated with the medicine. The doctor's words, " *Nangu mabopi*"—the first being several times repeated—form a war-cry: " *Nangu, nangu, nangu, nangu mabopi.*"

It is uttered not only when the men rush to battle, but when they are about to ford a deep and dangerous river. In addition to his other ceremonies the doctor sprinkles them with some mysterious preparation, using the tail of a gnu. Pande's wives also sprinkle them with water, employing for that purpose small household brooms. An offering having been previously made, the king addresses the Spirits that they may bless and prosper the expedition.[3]

The army is accompanied by doctors, who carry bundles of medicine with which to prepare the soldiers again before they engage the enemy. Mr. Isaacs says that the doctors prepared the Zulus for an attack at Ingoma, by sprinkling them with some decoction, which the recipients carefully rubbed over their persons in the belief that it would render them invulnerable and victorious. When the same writer was wounded, a young heifer was killed—he says as a sacrifice for the patient's speedy recovery, but I was assured by a distinguished warrior that the beast is not, on such occasions, offered to the Spirits. Some of the small entrails being parboiled with gall and medicine, the mixture was given him to drink. His olfactory sense had been so much affected during the preparation, that he refused to taste the abominable compound. The doctor was furious—unless he drank of the mixture he could not be permitted to take milk, lest the cows should die—if he approached the king without having used the charm, his Majesty would become ill. Finding expostulation vain and being

too feeble to resist, Isaacs yielded to the wish of
the doctor, who had directed him to take three sips
and sprinkle the remainder over his body. He
was then told to spit on a stick, point it three times
at the enemy, and then throw it towards their position. This done, the doctor gave him an emetic,
to eject the nauseous mixture he had swallowed.

III.—The following narrative relates to an expedition sent by Pande to recover the cattle which
the Amaswazi had taken from Dingan.

About the month of April (the rivers being then
low) the soldiers were summoned to Nodwenge.
After a grand dance, they received cattle for
slaughter, and repaired to the bush to feast and
pass the night. Next morning another dance took
place, and the doctors began the ceremonies
previously described. When Pande addressed the
warriors, he told them (following Tshaka's system
of deception) that they were going against the
Usutu, a tribe living beyond the Amaswazi. To
excite their enthusiasm, he described the Usutu as
having abundance of cattle—his spies had been
among them and seen their large herds. The
"boys" clamoured to be at once dismissed, and
asked why the king had not sent them before.
Observing the "men" silent, they charged them
with cowardice and insinuated that they preferred
the society of their wives and children to the perils
of war and the king's honour. The accused were
not slow to resent the imputation and vindicate
their prowess—who but they had gained the

victories of Tshaka and Dingan and built up the
kraal of Senzangakona—what did the "boys"
know about war? Pande was indignant that
the "men" should talk of his predecessors, and
show more regard for Tshaka and Dingan than
for him. The "boys" seconded the king's denun-
ciation, and the dispute soon ceased to be a war
of words. The "men," with their sticks, attacked
the "boys," who vigorously returned the blows;
nor did the battle cease until Pande and his
principal officers had rushed among the bel-
ligerents and beaten them into order. To prevent
a repetition of the fight, the "boys" were ordered
to leave the kraal. The "men," being now upbraided by the king, explained their unwillingness
to go—they had heard that there were Dutchmen
among the people against whom they were to be
sent—they feared to encounter enemies of whom
they had learned so much in Dingan's time.
Pande did not believe that they would meet with
many Boers; and attempted, by other arguments,
to overcome their fears. He failed, however; and,
telling them to remain at home if they were afraid
to go, retired in high dudgeon to his palace. In
the evening oxen were again given to the "boys,"
but the "men" received nothing.

Next morning, the boys having entered the
kraal, Pande addressed them, saying (among other
things) that, if they met with any Dutchmen, they
were not to attack them; but if attacked, they
were to defend themselves and kill their opponents.
The women now sprinkled them with water; Pande

invoked the Spirits and the various regiments were ordered to march. The "men," being still in the bush, were not sent; but, feeling that it would be disgraceful to remain behind or dreading Pande's wrath more than the Farmers' guns, they set forward to join the "boys." This being reported to the king, he followed his repentant *ama-doda*; and, having had them duly prepared by the doctors, addressed the Spirits in their behalf. The entire army now proceeded, the "men" and the "boys" being in separate divisions. Masipula, the general-in-chief, accompanied the former.

While passing through Pande's dominions the soldiers helped themselves to food at the various kraals. In one locality the women, who expected a visit, had removed as much as they were able and concealed it in the bush. The hungry warriors were therefore obliged to be content with a scanty supper and to leave the kraals without breakfast. Arrived at another place, they searched the huts in vain; neither corn nor milk was to be found; and it seemed as if the neighbourhood had been visited by a famine. They were more successful when they turned their attention to the cattle-folds, and sought the subterranean granaries constructed there. The women wept and wailed at the rifling of these precious stores, and fled to the bush that they might not witness the consumption of their children's food. Having gorged themselves to their satisfaction, the warriors broke the cooking-vessels they had used; and, being now near the frontier, carried away more corn than they had eaten, as some provision for the journey.

Having entered the Amaswazi-country, they found that the people had retired, with nearly all their movables, to the caves. The first night they slept in some deserted kraals, having previously enlarged the doors of the huts that they might the more easily escape if attacked. Next morning they set fire to the houses which had afforded them shelter, and proceeded. They now travelled a considerable distance without seeing any evidence that the country was inhabited. As they crossed the valleys or peered into them from the heights above, they could discover neither cattle nor kraals; the footprints which occurred near their track were those of wild animals alone; nor could they, by the utmost straining of their eyes, descry even a distant curl of smoke to indicate the presence of a human being. At length one of their number declared that he had heard the crowing of a cock; and in a short time they came unexpectedly within view of a kraal. Having approached it silently, they hoped to surprise the inhabitants, but were happily disappointed; the huts were deserted and empty. The "boys" discovered an underground granary; but they would not permit the "men" to touch its contents, nor could Masipula himself prevail on them to yield. Having few facilities for cooking, they were obliged to eat the corn in a half-crude state, while at the same time they imprudently drank a great deal of water. Many in consequence became ill, and several were left behind—to be destroyed by the Amaswazi. The *ama-doda* were indulged with beef.[4] Next morning the host advanced, without burning the kraal (which would have alarmed the people on their route), and ultimately reached another deserted habitation. Here they found milk scattered on the ground, and two slaughtered cows. The latter were tempting, but they did not doubt that poison had been introduced. However, having cut away large portions about the wounds (which the very dogs of the kraal refused) they ventured to eat the rest. Maize was also discovered; but the officers, remembering the evil which had resulted from using it half-cooked, forbade the corn to be eaten.

Being now not far from a kraal belonging to the chief of the Amaswazi, the army was prepared for action by the doctors; Masipula and the other great officers invoked the spirits; and the soldiers learned for the first time that they had been sent to plunder the Amaswazi. When the order was given to proceed, the "boys" were directed to follow the "men," whose experience rendered it desirable that they should advance first to the attack. The "boys," however, would not consent to give place to the others—the "men," they said, had no business there at all—who had sent the cowards? After a good deal of wrangling, the "boys" cut short the dispute by setting forward. Masipula, who knew how to deal with them, ordered the "men" not to follow; and waited until a little reflection should have cooled the ardour of the thoughtless warriors. His policy was justified by the event, for they soon returned, and consented to follow their seniors to the fight. No battle, however, was to take place, for when the kraal became visible it was burning. A messenger, whom Masipula had sent forward to deceive the Amaswazi, and who had been given up for dead, now arrived. On reaching the chief's kraal, he had represented himself as coming from Pande, to request that Dingan's oxen might be restored and, in case of refusal, to threaten an invasion. The chief said that an army was already coming; and thought it quite reasonable to keep Dingan's oxen, since both he and Tshaka had stolen plenty of theirs. Some of his soldiers wished to kill the Zulu; but he would not allow them to violate the custom of the nation, by slaying the messenger of a chief. Scouts having returned to report the near approach of the invaders, he sent his young men to guard the cattle; while he and the remainder withdrew to the caves, leaving a person to scrape his floor and burn the kraal.

Two Dutchmen, whom the messenger had seen at the chief's, visited the Zulu army and told them to go home. The "men," finding their worst apprehensions likely to be realized, desired to return; but the "boys" were resolved to push forward, and next morning resumed their march. The officers followed and attempted to beat them back; but the effort was fruitless, and the "men," afraid to face Pande alone, had no alternative but to proceed. Guided by the footprints of the Amaswazi chief's cattle and passing some deserted habitations, the united force advanced as far as the river Umkomazi. From the appearance of the trail the generals now judged it necessary to return, and invoked the Spirits to grant them success. That done, the army went back in two divisions—the " men" scouring the country to the right and the "boys" that to the left.

The latter were not very successful at first, but ultimately captured a magnificent herd of cattle and a large flock of goats. Subsequently they picked up a few more; but were obliged to pass a great number which had been driven to places difficult of access and well defended. One of these overlooked a kraal which had been occupied by the chief's father. Men, standing on the top of a pre-cipice, bade the marauders not go home and tell Pande they were unable to find Dingan's oxen— "here they are, come and take them." Girls, having shields and assagais in their hands, taunted the Zulus with cowardice and dared them to scale the heights. The reckless "boys" wished to do so; but they had been rejoined by a regiment of " men," who dissuaded them from the dangerous attempt—even Tshaka and Switi had been con-tent to pass the place—one of Dingan's regiments was nearly destroyed in endeavouring to storm it. Their reasoning prevailed, and the "boys" proceeded. Soon afterwards they were joined by the remaining regiments of men, who had captured many cattle and several young women. The "boys" wished to kill these " calves of the Amaswazi." The army then passed a number of caves, in which the people had taken refuge, and where they had also secured the cattle. Near one of the caverns was a dead ox, which had not been able to enter, and which its owners, rather than allow it to wander, had slain. The beast was remarkably fat, and some of the soldiers wished to eat it; but the officers suspected that poison had been introduced into the carcass, and commanded them to refrain. Some of the "boys," notwithstanding the order, had to be beaten away. When the army reached home Pande was angry that they had not brought Dingan's oxen, and within a few months sent them again.[5]

CHAPTER XI.—ARTS AND MANUFACTURES.

I.—MEDICINE. II.—IRON. III.—MISCELLANEOUS

I.—LIKE all other trades, that of medicine is hereditary—a doctor communicating his secrets to none but his children or relatives. I have heard it said that, if he were to teach the art to a younger son, the eldest would be entitled to his brother's fees. When the profession descends to a female, she is allowed to have the absolute control of all cattle received in the exercise of her calling.[1] It sometimes happens that a family has derived from its ancestors the knowledge of a particular medicine. "Hence," says Mr. Fynn, "on a native being attacked by disease he obtains the opinion of a doctor as to the nature of his complaint and is recommended to apply to the family which possesses a knowledge of the appropriate remedy for the fever, dropsy, rheumatism, or whatever the complaint may be. But the doctors frequently purchase a knowledge of such remedies for their own practice." The people generally are very slightly acquainted with medicines.

It is said by Mr. Fynn (who has frequently bought a knowledge of native herbs) that the doctors have a considerable acquaintance with medicinal plants, of which some are really valuable. These, he adds, are usually mixed with others which possess no healing qualities—a practice originally adopted, doubtless, to disguise the nostrum and prevent its becoming known, though "the useless additions are now believed to be an essential part of the remedy." Medicine is sometimes administered in the form of a decoction, and sometimes as a powder. In the latter shape it is not only taken internally, but is also introduced into small wounds cut on the surface of the body.

A species of cupping is frequently practised, and I know not that the people have any other method of bleeding. The operation is effected by making incisions in the skin, and then applying a horn, through the small perforated end of which the blood is sucked by the doctor. "Should the blood not flow freely, the affected part is beaten with a stick." Broken limbs are bound up with the assistance of dried hide or bark; and sometimes a cradle is formed of reeds. Another method is described by Captain Gardiner on the authority of a European who had benefited by it. The patient having broken his arm, a party of men assembled with a doctor at their head and scooped a deep hole in the ground. This being partly filled with soft clay, "the whole arm, with the hand open and the fingers curved inwards, was then inserted; when the remainder of the clay that had been prepared was filled in and beaten closely down. Several men then steadily raised his body perpendicularly to the incased arm, and drew it out by main force. By this simple but somewhat painful method his arm was perfectly reset; and, had he retained the native bandage, would doubtless have grown perfectly straight."

II.—Iron is abundant in the region occupied by these people; copper has been found in Natal; and some description of white metal seems to exist in the Zulu-country. During one of his journeys, Isaacs observed, in places where the rain had washed away the surface, a glittering mineral, which apparently possessed some metallic properties. He dug a large quantity, but could not induce the natives to carry it. They said that, some years before, a mineral was dug which turned to a beautiful glossy white colour when melted. The chiefs had ornaments manufactured from the new metal, abandoning the old fashioned iron rings to their people. Several of the former having died, the prophets at first ascribed the circumstance to poison; but, when the malady continued, notwithstanding the destruction of many suspected "evildoers," they attributed it to the ornaments lately adopted by the chiefs. The individuals who had discovered the metal were slain; those who had made the rings shared their fate; the ornaments were buried where the ore had been found, and orders were given that no one, on pain of death, should again dig up the pernicious metal.[2]

When a blacksmith wishes to smelt iron ore, he provides himself with a sufficient quantity of charcoal. He then digs a hole to serve for a furnace, and buries a short tube of coarse pottery, one end of which communicates with the furnace, while in the other extremity he inserts a horn, and in *that* the nosle of his bellows.   By this means

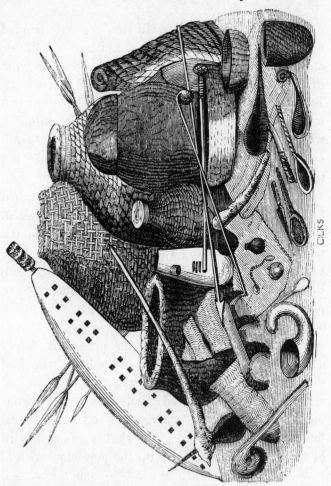

the blast is directed under the fire.   Several bellows are sometimes used.   The brass (obtained through the Amatonga from the Portuguese at

Delagoa Bay) is melted in crucibles of coarse sand-stone, which are sunk in the glowing charcoal. The metal is then " either run into bars for forming throat-rings and armlets, or into smaller clay moulds for the knobs and studs with which the women frequently ornament their girdles and petticoats."[3]

Picks or hoes, axes, and assagais are the prin-cipal articles manufactured by the smiths. Picks are now extensively introduced from England, and sold at about one and sixpence each, whereas the native smiths would probably not have been con-tent with less than the present equivalent of half a sovereign. Small axes are also bought from the traders. Many of the brass ornaments for-merly made by the native artists are obtained from European traders.

III.—To make the leather used for a married woman's dress, the skin of an ox or cow is steeped to facilitate the removal of the hair; grease and friction are employed to soften it; the inner side is scratched with a piece of prickly branch, until a long nap is raised; it is then blackened with charcoal, and looks like a piece of shaggy cloth. Shields are made of dried hide with the hair on.

Wooden vessels are not much needed by people who possess the calabash, and I do not remember to have seen more than the milk-pail and some large spoons. The former, which is deep and narrow, is hollowed from a piece of wood. The " pillow," sticks, hoe-handles, etc., do not require special notice here.

Baskets are made of grass, some being so close in texture as to be capable of holding liquids. Mats are manufactured for various purposes.

The women make their own cooking-pots of clay, and burn them on a small fire of sticks, brands being also placed inside the vessel.

To procure malt for beer, the grain (maize or millet) is wetted, wrapped in a mat, and left to sprout. It is then ground into meal; and, having been boiled, is placed into a large pot to ferment. During the fermentation, which continues for some days, the scum is removed with an instrument made for the purpose. When poured out for drinking, it passes through a strainer.[4]

APPENDIX.

SKETCH OF NATAL.

I.—THE Colony of Natal extends from the Umzimkulu and one of its branches to the Tugela and Umzinyati, and from the sea to the Draakensberg. The land gradually rises from the coast to the foot of those mountains, which form the ascent to the great plateau of South Africa.

A strip of strongly undulating ground, with an average breadth of about ten miles, runs along the coast; and, at its inland-edge, terminates abruptly. The surface of this region presents throughout " an almost painful succession of hills and vales, rising and falling in endless monotony. The traveller fords a stream, ascends a hill, descends, crosses a brook. If he sees ahead of him (as he does in the vicinity of Natal Bay) a level plain, he hails with joy this interruption to the fatiguing monotony of grass-covered hills and ravines." The inland-edge of this coast-region is, in many places, precipitous. At various intervals it has been cleft, to afford a passage to the rivers, which sometimes flow between perpendicular walls of rock, " from five hundred to two thousand feet high."

The precipices bounding this district overlook " a deep gulf between the first and second range of table-lands." This depression is an exceedingly broken country. In some parts occur isolated mountains, with flat tops several acres in extent and covered with grass. Others appear as sharp or rounded peaks, others again being "carved into a thousand fantastic shapes." The spaces between these detached mountains " are nearly filled with innumerable round, grass-covered hills, rising from one hundred to two thousand feet high. The appearance of these valleys as viewed from the surrounding heights, has been compared to the ocean stirred from its depths and then suddenly congealed." Near Esidumbini, an American Mission station, is " a granite boulder, thirty feet thick, one hundred and forty feet long, and ninety-five feet broad, extreme measure. One end is elevated thirty-four feet from the ground, and the other end about ten feet, resting on three rocks not more than four to eight feet in diameter. The rocks on which it rests are split into shivers, as if the boulder had fallen from above and partially crushed them."

Beyond the " gulf" the land continues to rise gradually " and stretches out in broad table-land often cut deep by ravines and rivers, and sometimes interrupted by ranges of mountains. As we penetrate inland about fifty miles, the peaks of Draakensberg, are visible in the distance."

The Draakensberg, was described by the late Surveyor-General as consisting of two parts, having different directions and different geological features. The one forming the N.W. boundary of Natal, he called the Small Draakensberg. It "is of the average altitude of five thousand feet above the sea, and about one thousand five hundred feet above the general level of the country at its base. The outline is in general round and soft, presenting some remarkable features, and occasionally high table-lands with precipitous sides. These mountains are composed of beds of sandstone cut through by veins of trap, and diminish in height as they advance to the N.E. until at some distance beyond the source of the Umzimyati, they appear to terminate in low hills. They are passable almost at any part by horses and cattle; but there are only three passes in use by the Boers." That portion which forms the western boundary (the

Great Draakensberg) joins the other about the source of the Tugela. "These mountains are much higher than the others, and quite impassable, presenting a rugged outline and bold and precipitous escarpments." From a distant view of their outline the Surveyor concluded them to be granite.

Natal abounds in streams. The Tugela (the largest river-system in the country), the Umkomazi, and Umzimkulu rise in the Draakensberg. Cascades and falls are frequent. The Umgeni-Fall, near Maritzburg, is two hundred and seventy-six feet in perpendicular height. None of the rivers are navigable; and most of them are closed, during the greater part of the year, by sand-banks at their mouths. Though low in the dry season, most of them are perennial. Their water "is soft and clear; and, running over beds of granite and trap rock, is but slightly impregnated with minerals. It is said, however, that the waters of several rivers (as the Umgeni and Umhloti) are slightly alkaline."

II.—The geology of the country is but little known; "yet some features are manifest to the most cursory observer. The perpendicular sides of the table-lands and mountains, in the coast division, generally present *strata* of red sandstone; and what, perhaps, strikes a foreigner most, is the perfect horizontalism of these *strata*. In several places, the mountains seem to have been worn by water up to the very top of the rocks. One can hardly resist the impression, that the widest valleys have been washed out, or, at least, have once been filled with water. Many of the rounded hills in these valleys are *moraines*. Nearly all the streams flow over beds of gneiss, granite, or trap rock; and in their channels abound large boulders of those rocks. All the varieties of quartz are found in the beds of the streams, and on the lower hills. As we pass along the beach, we may travel a few miles on *strata* of sandstone;

then intervenes a couple of miles of basalt or pudding-stone, gneiss, or granite. All of these are found in distinct sections along the coast, each occupying in succession from fifty rods to five miles. From the Ilovo river to the Umpambinyoni—a distance in latitude of perhaps eighteen miles—at an elevation of three hundred or four hundred feet above the sea, is a continuous mass of greenstone conglomerate, surmounted, towards the northern part, by Ifumi Hill—a mass of sandstone, some three miles in circumference, and two hundred or three hundred feet high above the surrounding country. Imbedded in this greenstone are fragments, both angular and worn, of quartz, granite, porphyry, jasper, sienite, varying from the size of a pea to that of a bushel measure. Adjoining this formation on the north, and also in other places in the district, is found slate-stone. But little lime, and none of pure quality, has been discovered near the coast, except in the form of shells and corals. There are seen large banks of shells in several places, many feet above the present level of the sea." Coal has been found. "On the Umtwalumi river is found a black oxide of iron, resembling lava, in which are cemented particles of coarse siliceous sand and pebbles of quartz. No fossils, except a few ammonites, have as yet been discovered."

III.—A thick bush extends along the coast, "varying in width from two rods to as many miles." Bush is also found along the numerous streams of the coast region, "through almost every part of which, wagons can find their way, without their owners being required to bestow labour in making the roads." There is a thick bush on the Berea heights behind Port Natal. The table-lands beyond the "gulf" are almost destitute of trees, though the mountains which have been described as interrupting them, are clothed with forests. Timber abounds in the valleys on the S.E. side of the Small Draakensberg.

The botany of the country " is but little familiar to the public." Trees exist in great variety. The most singular in appearance is the *euphorbia,* which has been compared to a cactus grown to the height of thirty feet. A variety of the castor-oil tree abounds; as well as the mimosa, which yields gum. "A singular tree called by the natives the *umtombi*—from the quantity of milky juice which exudes from its bark when pierced—fastens itself, when young, upon another tree; and, after a few years, completely envelopes and kills it in its embrace."

IV.—Many of the quadrupeds of Natal have been previously mentioned. Serpents are numerous and some of them very poisonous. Birds of beautiful plumage occur in great variety, nor are they all without song. Hawks steal your fowls; and, when their appetite is sharpened by a cold day, are amazingly impudent; the secretary-bird stalks among the grass in search of the serpents on which it preys; vultures approach within a few yards of your house; while the eagle soars aloft, and would be scarce visible even as a speck but for the bright light in which he moves. Scorpions, hornets, flies, and ants, are some of the disadvantages to be balanced against the beautiful climate; but more troublesome than these are the *ticks,* which, during the warm weather, abound in the region near the coast. "On every spire of grass, they await the passing of some living creature, to which they tenaciously cling, bury their heads in the flesh, and while they suck the blood infuse a subtle poison, which excessively irritates the skin and causes painful and obstinate sores." Some are so small as to be scarcely visible until swollen by the blood they have extracted. Those which fasten on the cattle thus enlarge until they become as big as the end of a man's little finger. When they fall off the blow-flies attack the sore. Neglected cattle sometimes lose their ears and are occasionally killed by the maggots which result.

V.—The temperature of the coast region is rather high in summer, but in winter is everything a reasonable person can desire. Inland, it is, of course, modified by the gradual elevation of the ground. The rain falls chiefly between September and March—most copiously in December and January. The extreme of moisture thus coincides with the extreme heat—a circumstance which gives a surprising impetus to the progress of vegetation. After a fortnight's absence at this period, I have been hardly able to recognize my own garden.

MISSIONARY OPERATIONS.

I.—In 1834, the late Captain Gardiner visited South Africa, to endeavour "to open a way whereby the ministers of the gospel might find access to the Zulu nation." Travelling through Kafir-Land and the Amampondo-country, he reached Port Natal, and thence proceeded to Umkungunghlovu. Dingan treated him well, but would not allow his people to be taught—a determination which was doubtless, in a great measure, due to the story Jacob had invented. Having, on his return to Natal been assured by the Europeans that missionary operations there should have their support, the Captain selected a spot on the heights near the Bay, as the site of a missionary establishment. He named the station Berea, "since, notwithstanding my ill success with Dingan, the word has here been gladly received." He subsequently visited England.

Meanwhile, the attention of the American Board of Commissioners for Foreign Missions having been attracted to the Zulus, they determined to send agents not only to them but to the people of Umzilikazi. Those who went to the Matabele obtained Umzilikazi's permission to settle in his dominions; and, in 1836, took up their residence at Mosega. Their prospects, however, were blighted when the Boers attacked that chief, and compelled him to remove farther to the north. Of the missionaries who were sent to Natal, the Rev. A. Grout visited Dingan (December, 1835) and obtained permission to build in his dominions. After a visit to Algoa Bay, he proceeded to the Zulu-country, and erected a house, "frequently visiting Dingan at his capital." Other stations were established by Mr. Grout's brethren near Port Natal.

In 1837 Mr. Grout went to America; and, during his

absence, Captain Gardiner returned with the Rev. F. Owen, of the Church Missionary Society. Mr. Owen went to Dingan's, and was there during the massacre of Retief. The events following that terrible deed affected the missionaries in common with the other white people ; and, " in the year 1838, all the stations were abandoned." The American mission was afterwards revived, Mr. Grout returning to the Zulu-country. Owing, I believe, to information that Pande intended to destroy the people of his station, he removed to Natal, after about sixteen months' residence in Pande's territories.

In 1843 (Natal had passed into the hands of the British) the American Board thought it advisable to discontinue their missions in that country, and sent instructions to their agents to withdraw. Mr. Grout sailed for America ; but, on his arrival at Cape Town, a strong desire was manifested both by the public and the government that the mission at Natal should be continued. An address was forwarded to the Board begging them to reverse their resolution ; a subscription was raised to defray Mr. Grout's expenses ; the governor and his secretary entered warmly into the matter ; Mr. Grout soon returned to his labours with a grant of land from his excellency ; and the Board decided to continue their operations. A great addition was made to the number of missionaries then employed. In their Report for 1851, the Board stated that they had in Natal eleven stations and six outstations ; fourteen missionaries (one a physician) ; one male and sixteen female assistant missionaries ; and three native helpers.

The Wesleyans extended their South African missions to Natal ; and in 1843 a Norwegian Missionary, Herr Pastor Schreuder, with a lay assistant, arrived. He resided some time at an American station, twice visiting Pande and seeking permission to build in his country and teach his people. The king refused unless the

Missionary would first kill the people who had deserted him and were living at Mr. Grout's station on the Umvoti. Mr. Schreuder subsequently established a station in Natal near the Zulu frontier. While he resided there, his medical skill became known to Pande, who was suffering from gout. The missionary, having been sent for, succeeded in subduing the despot's pain and renewed his original request. He received permission to select two places for building, and established a station, Empangeni, near the mouth of the Umhlatusi. Afterwards he commenced another, Entumeni, higher up the river. Missionary operations are now conducted in connexion with the diocese of Natal.

II.—The practice of selling their women in marriage presents a serious obstacle to the conversion of these Kafirs. It is too profitable to be given up; and, lest the girls should acquire notions which might render them indisposed to be objects of bargain and sale, they are withheld as much as possible from intercourse with the Europeans. It is well known, in Natal, that native female servants can rarely be obtained—those found in service being generally orphans. "And why does the Kafir not give his girl in service? It is because he fears to lose her. With civilised people the girl might soon become civilised and opposed to that trade." For the same reason, Kafir parents prevent their girls attending at the mission services. Many say: "Children you are too young to resist the power of the word of God—you might become converted; but we old people can go and hear, because our hearts are hard and strong enough to resist." A few may perhaps allow their daughters to go, but not until they have previously endeavoured to prejudice them against the gospel. Girls have sometimes "been brought to missionaries for service or medical purposes, but with strict injunctions not to allow themselves to be taught; and, as soon as the parents perceived that their child was instructed, they took it away." Girls expressing a desire to become Christians have been cruelly treated by their parents, who ceased their ill usage only on the interference of the Diplomatic Agent.[a]

Polygamy has been found a great hindrance to the progress of Christianity—the missionaries having required their converts to retain only one wife. Polygamy, says a member of the American Mission, is the "peculiar and idol institution" of the Kafirs; "and, as the gospel strikes at the root of this sin, they hate it with their whole hearts."

"I am sick," said a native to a missionary.

"How are your wives and children?"

"They are sick, and suffering from cold. Give them blankets. Why do you, our teacher and king, refuse?

"You say you are sick; but what is your disease, and where is it situated?"

"In my head, feet, and all over my body."

"Why do you not wear clothing then, if you are so very ill?" Why are you out this cold day with only pieces of sheep-skin about your loins?

"Teacher! Where shall I get clothing? Have I not asked you for it and been denied?"

"Why do you not purchase it?"

"But have we black people any gold and silver? Do we know how to coin money?"

"And have you no cows that you could dispose of for money, and buy clothing for yourself and family?"

"No, I have no cows; and my wives and children are at this moment suffering for want of corn and milk."

"It is all true that you say, I presume; and the same may be said of nearly all the men in the kraals about us. But is it not your own fault that you are thus troubled? Have you not just bought a seventh wife; and have not ten of your best cows, those on which you have hitherto de-

pended for milk, been driven past my door to yonder kraal
to pay for that wife. Did you need an additional wife as
you need food and clothing, with a respectable house to
live in? Have you not sinned in buying wives? And is
not your trouble a natural consequence of this sin? Why
do you, an able-bodied man of fifty years, come to me to-
day naked, begging clothing, money and food, while all
your time, energy and property are devoted to self-gratifi-
cation?"

After a short silence the man said, " Teacher, you speak
the truth. But we are black people; and this custom has
descended to us from our fathers. *We love polygamy, and
cannot abandon it.*"

III.—Notwithstanding the various obstacles with which
they have had to contend, the missionaries have met with
some success. In their Report for 1850, the American
Board state that " there were churches at nine of their
eleven stations, containing one hundred and twenty-three
members, thirty-six of whom were received during the
year." We must not however estimate the result of
missionary labour merely by the number of converts.
The people are becoming gradually enlightened; " and
we believe that the seed sown will not be altogether lost.
Many of them already know enough of the gospel to come
to Christ, whenever the Spirit of God shall bring home
his word with power to their hearts."

It is not surprising that the missionaries have to lament
the infirmities of some of their converts. " It is characteristic of the natives of this country," says the Rev. —
Lindley, one of the first missionaries sent to South Africa
by the American Board, " and, for ought we know, it may
be characteristic of all the heathen, to talk very much and
very loud, to scold and wrangle and brawl about trifles.
With their tongues, as also with their hands, armed not
unfrequently with sticks of various sizes, they make a

great ado about a little matter. No effort is made by them to restrain their anger. And some of our church members have been quite faulty in this respect. A little child that could crawl about with some facility, unobserved by its mother, pulled its father's best coat down into the dust to play with it. For this act of the child, the mother received a severe scolding, with a few heavy blows from the father. Sometimes the chickens of one person have found their way into the garden of another; and this trespass of the poor fowls, that have literally to scratch for a living among the heathen, has been the occasion for a war of words hot enough to roast them, feathers and all. Thoughtless little children, cows, calves, dogs, &c., have all furnished cause or opportunity for these perverse disputings. One poor woman received a hard slap on the mouth from her husband, because a well-meaning person told him that he ought not to scold his wife, as he was then doing, for not having his food prepared just when he was ready to eat. His excuse for this barbarous act was, that he wished to let others see that she was *his* wife. The feeling of his heart was probably: "I paid cattle for you, to serve my pleasure; and you shall serve it." Widows, living with their married sons, feel at liberty to scold their daughters-in-law as much as they please, with or without cause. Anger has, with one exception, caused all the difficulty that we have had since my last report. We have frequently preached against it in public; and in private we have talked against it to the individuals most concerned; and once the members of the church were assembled, that we might hear from all what they had to say on the subject, and that I might be heard by them all in general, and by some of them in particular. Apparently there is some improvement. I should be sorry, however, to have it supposed that all our church members are prone to indulge their angry passions. We live much more amicably than our brawling neighbours, the heathen. Five of our church members have, in our opinion, deserved and have received reproof, with exhortations to keep their tongues and tempers with greater dilligence. In regard to one of these five, I have but faint hopes of improvement." With several of his converts, however, Mr. Lindley continued to be well pleased. With most, indeed, he saw no cause to find serious fault, yet his experience during the past year (I quote from the Missionary Herald of April, 1854) had tended to weaken his "confidence in the religious professions of this people. They do not give such evidence as I could wish of a thorough change of heart. And this question, always a difficult one, has now become painful; 'How much allowance ought to be made for imperfection in the Christian character of those who have barely, and but lately, emerged from the depths of a truly degrading heathenism?'"

IV.—The following extract from a letter of the Bishop of Natal (dated March 22, 1856) relates to a very interesting and unexpected circumstance:—"The central institution at Ekukanyeni (Place of Light) has by the course of events been brought into active operation much sooner than I had at all anticipated, though it was always my hope that we should eventually succeed in making it available for the purpose to which it is now devoted, viz. the education of a number of Kafir lads, from five to fourteen years of age, all sons of chief men, or their indunas, who have been committed into their hands by their parents in the most confiding manner, to be taught and trained in any way we think best. My hope was that, from our different stations scattered about the country, we might, after a year or two, be able to procure a few lads whose parents would allow them to be removed from their native kraals and their abominations, and be brought up under our care. But on proceeding to find a station with the chief Geza, shortly after Sir George Grey's return from his visit to this colony, we (Mr. Shepstone and myself) were led by circumstances to make a proposal to the tribe, that they should send their children to me for education. The experiment was so utterly novel and untried, that Mr. Shepstone (whose influence with the Natal Kafirs is most remarkable) had never before thought of the plan as possible; and indeed proposed it to them with considerable hesitation as to the probability of their assenting. However, he explained to them fully the advantages of such a measure; and their confidence in him was such, that with one voice they agreed to do what he recommended, and to send their boys (it will be a more serious matter to get the girls, but we must try for that in due time) as soon as I should be ready to receive them. Happily we had almost completed at Ekukanyeni a residence for the principal of the institution (whoever it might be), with outbuildings for barn and stabling, all which might be adapted for our present necessities. And, accordingly, we promised to be ready in a fortnight; and they might send their children as soon after that as they pleased. To the great trial, however, of our faith and patience, three months elapsed before any children came, and it appeared that meanwhile great discussions had been carried on within and without the tribe of Geza (which for the present was principally concerned in the proposal) as to the object for which the children were required. Geza himself and his chief men were firm in their resolution. The former declared that 'his two boys should go, if they went alone.' But in all the tribes of the district, to whom the intelligence was soon conveyed, there were serious misgivings as to the consequences of such a measure; and by many Geza and his people were called fools for trusting their children wholly into the hands of the white man. However, these fears and suspicions, from which perhaps their own hearts, if the truth were told, were not wholly free, were so far overcome at last, that on a day, of which due notice was given us, nineteen young boys were brought to the station by their friends, who formed a long procession of men and women, some leading the little ones by the hand, others bearing them upon their shoulders, and with much ceremony and some speech-making, delivered up into our hands. 'We might do what we liked with them—take them over the sea to England if we pleased, as many people said we should, though they sincerely hoped we should not.' Since that time we have received eleven more, and it is quite possible that in the course of a few months our numbers may steadily increase to fifty or one hundred children. They feel very much the change from the warm, close Kafir hut to the airy and draughty European house, more especially in wet weather, when they suffer a good deal from cold. This requires us to pay careful attention to the matter of clothing, and entails of necessity no inconsiderable expense.

"In order to break as much as possible, especially during the first winter, their change from Kafir to European habits, I have been obliged to order this day the construction of a first-class Kafir hut at the institution, where on a wet evening the children may sit around a fire in the centre, and feel a little of the warmth and comfort of home. And in order to provide for their better accommodation at night I have had constructed a wooden building of some extent, which must serve for the present as chapel, school-room, and dormitory, while we proceed to erect other buildings where the lads may have each his little stretcher and separate bed at night, and so be accustomed by degrees to the decencies and the wants of civilized life. At present they sit around upon the floor for their meals, which consist mainly of meal porridge with beef, and at night a cup of coffee on Sundays. Never was a lesson of order and patience taught more

expressively than by the appearance of these thirty lads
at meal-time. The old Kafir woman, whom the tribe
chose at my request as their attendant, standing in the
middle, ladles out the porridge with provoking deliberation, generally going the round twice to equalize the
portions, though the little ones always tell her when they
have enough on their plate. Not a movement is made
towards the food, however hungry they may be, till this
process is duly completed; then they say their little grace
in Kafir, and, at a given signal, the meal proceeds."

TRIBES OF THE ZULU-COUNTRY AND NATAL.

THE ZULUS (Uzulu) are a branch of an older tribe (Amantombela) now extinct; and, through it, connected with the AMALANGA and QUABIES (Uquabi). The ZULUS, who remain chiefly on their original site, embrace the following divisions; viz. Amampongosi, Amambani, Bakwabiyele, Amanhlagazi, Abasemgazini, Amahlabiza, Amatelezi, Amaxulusi, Amazuza. The AMALANGA lived on a ridge near the Umhlatusi, where some remarkable trees stand. Tshaka's mother was of this tribe. It is said that he fought a severe battle with them in the early part of his career. They are now dispersed. The Amagwaza, Amantshali, and Amasimangu were divisions of this tribe. The UQUABI lived from the Umhlatusi to the Tugela. A spring near the mission station Entumeni bears the name of Ukonhlo, the father of Pakatwayo. I am not certain about the names of the families of this tribe. " It was a powerful tribe, excited the jealousy of the aspiring Amazulu, and was one of the first to suffer at the hands of Tshaka, in the early days of his reign. Being disturbed and overcome, some passed over to the west of the Utugela and went down as far as the Amampondo a full quarter of a century since. These were followed by others at different times, who built along the coast from the Utugela to the Umkomazi, chiefly at first about the mouths of the Nonoti and Umvoti, and afterwards on the Umpongodwe and Amanzimtote, being joined by some of those who had fled before them to the Amampondo. Different companies passed over at different times and settled at different places, from the days of Tshaka or before, until the arrival and residence of the Boers in Natal and perhaps until the country became a British colony, for, if we mistake not, Mawa who came, we think in 1843, either originally belonged to this tribe or else joined it after her arrival here. They are now residing, some at the Umona and Umtongati and Umvoti, under the chief Umusi, and some at the Umvoti under Umanfongonyana; and some in other parts of the colony. In 1847 the number of kraals belonging to this tribe, then living upon the Umona and Umtongati, where they had then been for seven or eight years, was about one hundred, besides sixteen or seventeen kraals at the mouth of the Umhloti, and fourteen or fifteen more on the Uhlanga. Of this tribe there are now ninety-six kraals (338 huts) belonging to the Inanda location."

The DWANDWES (Undwandwe) believe themselves to be connected with an ancestor of the Zulus, named Inkosi Enkulu (Great Chief). They lived on the Black Folosi and beyond, and were partly intermixed with the Zulus. They included the *Xnumayo* a considerable division now in Natal; Abakwansimbi; Abakwakumayo; Abasimangcwangeni; and, I have been told, the tribe of Umzilikazi. Usikonyana, is said to be still living, near Sotshangana. The UMTETWA (Tetwas) lived on the low ground beginning at the Umlelas. They included the Abakwasibata; Abakwambogazi; Abakwamcaya; Abakwamcnubi; Abakwamkunzi; Abasimaclambini; Abakwasiyana; Abasihlambeni; Abakwadubi; Abakwampugunyoni; Amakoba (?); Abakwasigoti, the tribe of Sotshangana, who lives near Delagoa Bay, on the Paüla (Lipalule?); Abakwamsweya, whose chief, Mandeku, is near Sotshangana; while Uxnaba, of the Abasimansimeni, is in the same neighbourhood.

The Quabies, Tetwas, Dwandwes (who are distinguished as Amatefula, an opprobrious term) spoke a dialect somewhat different from that of the Zulus.

The following is a list of tribes who dwelt in the present colony of Natal (or very near it) at the time of the Zulu invasion, and are again found there in something of a tribal state under their respective chiefs. The sites which they occupied when disturbed by the Zulus are indicated, but it has not been thought necessary to note the particular localities they now occupy.[3]

AMANGWANE lived near the sources of the Umzinyati and the Tugela. The notorious Matuana was chief of this tribe. After his defeat by the colonial forces, he returned with some followers and made terms with the Zulus, but was subsequently killed by Dingan. The *Amahlubi*, who separated from the Amangwane, lived between the Tugela and Umzinyati. Disturbed by the Amacunu, and afterwards by the Zulus. F. *Amabomvu*, said to be a branch of the Amangwane. Inland on the Umzinyati. Not much disturbed by Tshaka, but fled before Dingan. *Amabele*, a branch of the Amahlubi, high up on the Impafana (Mooi River). Some in Faku's country; some in Natal. F. (I have been told that the Amangwane were related to the Zulus).

AMAGOBA, AMABAZO, ABAKWAZWANA, AMALATA, AMA-QANYENI, AMAXIMBA. Beyond Umzimyati. AMACUNU: said to be a branch of the Quabies. Once lived at Eganhla, below and beyond the Umzimyati.

AMANYUSWA OR AMANGCOBO. On the Emambo, a trib. of Tugela on its left bank. Served Tshaka. *Amacadi*, a branch of the Amanyuswa. Lived on the Insuze, trib. of Tugela on its left bank, nearly opposite Kwamapumulo. *Amagongoma*, a branch of the Amanyusa, on whom they were dependent until Dingan's time.

AMANCOLOSI. Originally above Kwamapumulo on the Umambulo south of Tugela. Many destroyed, some fled, some submitted.

AMAHLANGU, or Inhlangu or Enhlangwini. Originally near the junction of Tugela and Umzinyati, towards Noodsberg and Isidumbi. Fled to S.W. part of Natal.

ABASEMBU or Abambu. Branched from the Quabies.

Lived near the junction of Tugela and Umzinyati. Routed by Tshaka.

INATI. Both sides of the Tugela. Fled to the bush, but afterwards submitted to Tshaka.

ABATEMBU, on the Umtshizi, N. of Tugela, far inland.

AMAOSIANA. Originally near Kwamapumulo.

AMASEKUNENE. Kwamapumulo. Nearly destroyed by Tshaka. F.

AMAKABELA. Near the mountain Untunjambile, on the Tugela, not far from Kwamapumulo. Became tributaries in skins.

AMAFOZE or Amafuti. Originally between Tugela and Umyinyati.

ABAKWAMKULISA. Lived near Job's Berg.

AMAMEMELA. Lived above Job's Berg.

AMAMPUMUZA. Lived on the Umpanza, a trib. of the Impafana.

AMASEPEPETA. Lived near the hill Episweni between the Umvoti and Tugela.

AMANGANGA. Lived near the sources of the Nonoti.

AMASOME. Lived near the sources of Nonoti.

AMAKANYA. Lived near Nonoti.

AMAHLONGWA. Lived on the sources of Umvoti. Some became herders of Tshaka's cattle on the Umzimkulu.— *Amahlala*, a branch of the former, lived in the same neighbourhood. *Amalanga*, another branch of the same. Lived on the Umvoti and Ihlimbiti. *Amapumulo*, another branch, who resided near Kwamapumulo. *Amandelu*, or Amabahlela, separated from the Amahlongwa and lived on the Umvoti.

AMALULEKA. On the Umvoti. Once subject to the Amahlongwa. Present chief banished for "witchcraft."

AMACELE. Lived near the Umvoti, Tongati, and Inanda. At first all lived near the mouth of the Umvoti. Two sons of the chief quarrelled and divided the tribe. Some never left the country.

AMANDWAYANA. Lived at Esidunjini in the region of Isidumbi.

AMATSHANGASI. At Emanhlatoti, above Kwamapumulo.

AMADUNGA. At Epasiwe, between the Umvoti and Tugela inland. Near them lived a branch of the tribe, *Amabombo*; while the *Amanyafu*, another branch, dwelt near Noodsberg, Umvoti, and Isidumbi.

AMABACA, lived high up on the Umgeni.

AMATULI. See page 261.

AMATOLO. Inland on the Umkomazi.

AMEKUZE. On the Umkomazi. Some say that they dwelt beyond the Tugela before Tshaka. F. (I have heard them spoken of as allied to the Zulu tribes).

The following tribes originally lived in Natal, but have no tribal existence there now. The *Amahlanga* dwelt on the Umgeni, inland, in Tshaka's time. They were slain or dispersed by the invader Some fled to the Amabaca, who were then with the Amaxosa. Some now live with the Amabaca; some with the Inhumbi tribe on the Umtwalume; some on the Umgeni sources, and some with other tribes. Their hereditary chief is Umgada, said to be living not far from Pietermaritzburg. The *Amandhlovu*: there seem to have been two distinct tribes or branches called by this name. Some lived on the west of the Umtongati, some on the west of the Umgeni, near the sources of the Umhlatuzana, and further inland. Of the former there are now four or five kraals living on the Umpongodwe and Isipingo. The latter fled far inland at the time of the invasion. A few are now living on the Umkomazi, near Udumisa. There are also some of this name, amounting to twentynine or thirty kraals, living with Ukofiana on the Uhlanga, and on the Inanda location. The *Amageni* dwelt near Isidumbi. They were destroyed and driven off to the southwest by the Amazulu. There are a few still living in the colony, chiefly on the Umhlatuzana. The *Amazilemu* for-

merly lived in the region of the Umtongati. When they
fled before Tyaka many perished through famine; some
escaped to the Amamponda land, whence they have not
returned in any considerable numbers. A few, however,
may be now found living on the Umtwalume, among them
is the chieftess Uvunhlazi. They were the parent of the
Amabaca. *Amakamyao*, lived formerly on the Uhlanga
and Umhloti. They shared the same fate as the Amazilemu. A few took refuge with the Amatuli at the Bluff,
and were saved. There are five at least now living under
the chieftain Uvunhlazi on the Umtwalume. The *Ama-
hlungele*, an off-shoot from the Amazilemu, dwelt on the
Uhlanga at the time of the Zulu invasion. The greater
part were slain. Some fled to the bush, and some died of
famine. The *Kwalanga* tribe dwelt on the Umgeni, inland, and were mostly slain by the Zulus. Some were
carried away captives, and some escaped to the Kwahlamba mountains. As a tribe they are extinct; but a few
live near Table Mountain, and a few others are scattered
in other parts of the colony. The *Amatshibi* anciently
dwelt on the Umzinyati, but emigrated to the Umvoti,
near the Isitemtu Mountain, before the days of Tshaka.
They were originally an off-shoot from the Amancolosi.
They were dispersed by Tshaka. Some, however, still
remain in the district of Natal; some are with Fodo, some
with the Amabaca, and some just this side of the Umzimkulu, under Ungobozi. The *Amazotsha* built in ancient
times on a plain south-west of Table Mountain. They
were subdued by the Amabaca and many of them incorporated with that tribe. Some now dwell high up the
Umkomazi, and some on the west side of the Umvoti, not
far from the sea. The *Amantuluzela* dwelt on a tributary
of the Umtwalume. Many were destroyed. A remnant
now resides near the Kwahlamba Mountains. F. The
Amanzobe dwelt on the Umvoti. Their chief, Undabane,
was slain by the Zulus. Some saved themselves by flight

to the west. The remnant now resides on both sides of the Umzimkulu. The *Amakulu,* or Iminkulu, anciently lived inland on the Umhloti, at a place called " Ozwatini," under the chief Umambane. Some are now found in the country scattered among other tribes. There is a remnant on the Umkomazi; but the royal family is extinct. The *Amazizi,* it is said, formerly lived above Pieter Maritzburg, and that some are still living near their old home, while some are scattered among other tribes. F. Some of the *Amajïvane* tribe, which once lived between the Umzumbi, and Umzimkulu, are said to be residing now near the Umgeni, under Ukofiana. Some of the survivors of the *Amahloko,* who once built on the Umhlale, are now incorporated with the Amacele. The *Amajuzazi,* who dwelt on this side of the Umzinyati; the *Amabane,* who dwelt on the Umvoti; and the *Amansipo,* who dwelt on the Umona, were nearly all destroyed by the Zulu invader, or driven whence they have not been heard from by us. Of the *Abatwawo,* or Abatshwawu, F, who formerly lived around the mountain, Inhlazuka, near the Ilovo; of the *Amantshele,* and of the *Amatshobene,* a few survivors may be found in the colony incorporated with other tribes. Of the *Amambibi* also, who once lived between the Umkomazi and Umzumbi, there are still a few in the colony.

The names also of a few other tribes once inhabiting the Natal district, may be given here, of which a few individuals also may be found scattered here and there in different parts of the Natal colony, of which are the *Amanjilo,* who once lived west of the Umgeni, about the sources of the Umlazi, under the chief Usali; the *Amalumba,* once lying on the north of the Umhloti; the *Amanjale,* on the same river, inland; the *Amankomo,* not far from the last named; the *Amamtambo,* on the Umkomazi, inland; the *Amazodwa,* on the Umkomazi also, inland; the *Amampofana,* near the same river ; and the *Amantozake,* near the Umzumbe, inland. F. A few kraals, belonging to all the above tribes and to a few others of ancient residence in Natal, but now nearly extinct, especially as tribes, are still to be found in different parts of the colony incorporated with other tribes.

THE KAFIR LANGUAGE.

I.—A SUBSTANTIVE consists of a *root* and a *prefix*—the latter being a particle with no separate meaning. E.g. *umu-ntu*, a man; *i-hashe*, a horse. The name of *inflex* has been given to the prefixed particle, because by changes of it the modifications of the noun for number and case are effected, as in Latin and Greek they are effected by means of *terminal* particles, or inflexes set after the root. Thus, in the Latin word, *hom-o*, the root is *hom* and the inflex *o*, which is changed to *ines* in the plural, the whole word becoming *homines ;* just as the singular words *umu-ntu* and *i-hashe* become, in the plural, *aba-ntu* and *ama-hashe*. There are eight singular inflexes, six having plural forms; and thus we have eight species of nouns, two of which want the plural. Some of the inflexes are abbreviated; e.g. *umu* occurs in the shorter forms of *um* and *u ; ili* becomes *i*. Both the full and abbreviated forms are given below.

I.	*umu*,	plural,	*aba ;* ....as *umu-ntu*,	man,	*aba-ntu*,	men.
	um,	plural,	*aba ;* ....as *um-fazi*,	wife,	*aba-fazi*,	wives.
	u,	plural,	*o ;* ....as *u-dade*,	sister,	*o-dade*,	sisters.
II.	*ili*,	plural,	*ama ;* ....as *ili-zwe*,	land,	*ama-zwe*,	lands.
	i,	plural,	*ama ;* ....as *i-hashe*,	horse,	*ama-hashe*,	horses.
III.	*im*,	plural,	*izim ;* ....as *im-azi*,	cow,	*izim-azi*,	cows.
	in,	plural,	*izin ;* ....as *in-kabi*,	ox,	*izin-kabi*,	oxen.
	i,	plural,	*izi ;* ....as *i-tunga*,	pail,	*izi-tunga*,	pails.
IV.	*isi*,	plural,	*izi ;* ....as *isi-nkwa*,	loaf,	*izi-nkwa*,	loaves.
V.	*umu*,	plural,	*imi ;* ....as *umu-ti*,	tree,	*imi-ti*,	trees.
	um,	plural,	*imi ;* ....as *um-sebenzi*,	work,	*imi-sebenzi*,	works.
VI.	*ulu*,	plural,	*izim, izin ;* as *ulu-to*,	thing,	*izin-to*,	things.
	u,	plural,	*izim, izin ;* as *u-tango*,	hedge,	*izim-tango*,	hedges.
VII.	*ubu*,	no plural,	as *ubu-kosi*,	greatness.		
VIII.	*uku*,	no plural,	as *uku-lunga*,	righteousness.		

There is a fragment of each inflex, which is found to be of great consequence in grammatical construction. It has been called the *characteristic* of the inflex. Thus, in the first species, *umu, um, u,* are represented by *u,* and *aba* by *b.* The characteristics (singular and plural) of each species are as follows:—I. *u, b.* II. *l, a.* III. *i, z.* IV. *s, z.* V. *u, i.* VI. *lu, z.* VII. *b.* VIII. *ku.* (*U* and *i* before a vowel become *w* and *y.*)

The Vocative Case is formed by eliding the initial vowel. E.g. *'ba-ntu* people.

The Possessive is formed by prefixing the characteristic of the inflex of the governing noun with the connecting vowel *a.* E.g. *umuntu wa-ilizwe* would be a man of the country; but *a* coalesces with *i,* and the correct form is *umuntu welizwe.* (The vowels *a* and *u* would coalesce into *o;* *a* and *a* into *a.* E.g. *wa-umzi* would become *womzi; wa-abantu, wabantu.*) Proper names of persons drop their initial vowel and prefix *ka,* to which again is prefixed the last syllable of the inflex of the governing noun, whenever that is dissyllabic. E.g. *umfazi ka-Tshaka,* wife of u-Tshaka ; *aba-fazi baka-Pato,* wives of Pato.

The Locative or Oblique Case is that in which a noun is put when it follows a verb, of which it is not the direct object; and will be expressed in English by *in, to,* or *from.* It is formed by changing the initial vowel into *e;* and the final, if *a* or *e,* into *eni*—if *i* into *ini*—if *o* into *weni*—if *u* into *wini.* E.g. *imi-hla,* day, *emihleni.* Proper names of places merely change the initial vowel into *e.* E.g. *em Voti,* from *um Voti.* The locative takes a euphonic *s* before it when preceded by a monosyllable.

II.—ADJECTIVES take the inflex of the substantives they refer to. (1.) When an adjective accompanies a substantive as an epithet (e.g. the white man), it follows it, with the full inflex of the substantive—the first vowel of the inflex being prolated (by the change of *i* into *e,* and *u* into *o*). Thus (*kulu* signifying great) *in-kosi en-kulu*—a great chief. (2) When an adjective is separated from its substantive and used as a predicate (e.g. the man is white) the last syllable only of the inflex of the substantive is prefixed. E.g. *in-kosi in-kulu ; ili-so li-kulu.*

*** As will be seen hereafter, the adjectival inflexes in the one case are relative pronouns; and in the other personal pronouns. (1.) *Ili-so eli-kulu*=the eye which (is) great=the great eye. (2.) *Ili-so li-kulu*=the eye it (is) great=the eye is great. These may be called, respectively, the relative and personal inflexes.

III.—The personal PRONOUNS, of the first and second persons, are *gi* (*ngi* after a vowel), I; *u*, thou. Those of the third person (the personal inflexes) are the last syllable of the inflexes of the nouns to which the pronouns refer. Personal pronouns have a Possessive, and a Prepositional case—the latter being the form in which they take a preposition and corresponding to the objective case of nouns. There is also an Emphatic form of these pronouns which may be used when emphasis is required instead of any of the other forms or in addition to either of them.

Personal pronoun of the first person: *Gi*, I or me; *ami*, of me; Prepositional, *mi*, as *ga-mi*, by me; *ku-mi*, to me; *na-mi*, with me. Emphatic form, *mina*. PLURAL: *Si*, we or us; *etu* of us; *ti*, as *ga-ti*, by us; *ku-ti*, to us; *na-ti*, with us. Emphatic, *tina*.

Second person: *U*, thou or thee; *ako*, of thee; *we*, as *ga-we, ku-we, na-we.* Emph. *wena*. PLURAL. *Ni* you; *enu* of you; *ni*, as *ga-ni, ku-ni, na-ni.* Emph. *nina*.

*** The characteristic of the governing noun, with *a*, is prefixed to the genitive of the pronoun as of a substantive. E.g. *uku-hla kwami, kwako, kwetu, kwenu ;* my, thy, our, your food.

The forms or cases of pronouns of the third 'person vary, according to the inflex of the substantive they refer to. Thus, if the latter belong to the first class of substantives, of which the inflex is *u ;* the pronoun will be *u, a, e ;* possessive, *ake ;* prepositional, *ye ;* emphatic, *yena.* If of the second class, the inflex being *ili,* the simple form will be *li ;* possessive, *alo ;* prepositional, *lo ;* emphatic, *lona.*

Relative pronouns. First person, *o ;* plur., *aba, esi.* Second person, *o ;* plur., *aba, eni.* Those of the third person are the same as the relative inflexes, *i.e.* they are the complete inflexes of the noun they refer to, with their initial vowels prolated. E.g. *ili-zwe eli,* the land which ; *aba-ntu aba,* the people who. These serve for the nominative ; but the possessive and accusative are expressed by the personal pronouns. *E.g. umuntu ilizwe lake li-n'amanhla,* the man, his word is powerful=the man whose word is powerful.

Domonstrative pronouns are formed from the relative by prefixing *l* to signify *this* ; by prefixing *l* and changing the final vowel to *o,* to signify *that ;* by prefixing *l* and affixing *ya,* to signify *that there, i.e.* further off. E.g. *leli ilizwe, lelo ilizwe, leliya ilizwe.*

IV.—Verbs, besides their simple form, have the following : (1.) A FORMAL PASSIVE, formed from the simple by adding *kala,* or changing its final vowel to *eka.* Ex. *bona,* see, *bonakala,* become seen, appear ; *tanda,* love, *tandeka,* become loved. (2.) CAUSATIVE, formed by inserting *is* before the final vowel. *Hamba,* go ; *hambisa,* make to go. (3.) OBJECTIVE (so called because it generally expresses that the action of the verb is done for or towards some object) is formed from the simple by inserting *el* before the final vowel. *Sebenza,* work ; *sebenzela,* work for. (4.) The REFLECTIVE form prefixes *zi. Tanda,* love ; *zitanda,* love one's self. (5.) The RECIPROCAL inserts *an* before the final vowel. *Tanda,* love ; *tandana,* love one another. (6.) The Simple, Causative, and Objective forms have each a Passive, formed by inserting *w* before their final vowel. *Tanda, tandwa; tandisa, tandiswa; tandela, tandelwa.*

The Verb is used in *six* Moods— Imperative, Infinitive, Indicative, Potential, Optative, Subjunctive.

The IMPERATIVE *Second Person Singular*, is the Root of the Verb. *Ex. tanda*, love thou, *tanda-ni*, love ye. The other persons of the Imperative are formed by means of the particle *ma*, (from the verb *ma*, stand,) and the Subjunctive. *Ex. ma-ngi-tanda*, let me love.

The INFINITIVE consists of the Simple Verbal Root Form, preceded by *uku*, and generally ends in *a. Ex. uku-tanda*, to love, *uku-hamba*, to walk.

In the INDICATIVE there are *ten* Tenses, four of which are *Simple*, and six *Compound, i.e.* formed by help of the auxiliary verbs, *ya* or *za*, go, *ba*, be.

Every action, whether in *Present, Past,* or *Future* Time, may be regarded as, at the moment spoken of, either just *beginning to be*, or *already in progress*, or *just finished*. Thus we shall need *three* Tenses for each species of Time, to express the action as *commencing, continuing,* or *completed* (perfect). Hence we have the following Scheme of Tenses :—

(1.) Commencing Present, *gi-ya-tanda, I love*, now begin to love.

(2.) Continuing Present, *gi-tanda, I love or am loving*, have been, and still am loving.

(3.) Completed Present, *gi-tandile, I have loved*, have done loving.

(4.) Commencing Past, *ga-tanda*, I *loved*, then began to love.

(5.) Continuing Past, *gi-be ngi-tanda, I was loving*, had then been, and still was, loving.

(6.) Completed Past, *gi-be ngi-tandile, I had loved*, had then done loving.

(7.) Commencing Future, *gi-ya-ku-tanda*, *I shall come to love*, shall then begin to love.

(8.) Continuing Future, *gi-ya-ku-be ngi-tanda*, *I shall be loving*, then, as before.

(9.) Completed Future, *gi-ya-ku-be ngi-tandile*, *I shall have loved*, shall then have done loving.

Besides which there is the *Imperative Future*, which is only used when an idea of *positiveness, authority, command*, or *compulsion*, is to be expressed.

(10.) Imperative Future, *go-tanda*, I will love.

Three of the Simple Tenses are the same in form with the Root, but take the prefixed pronouns with different vowel-sounds, as *gi-tanda*. I love, *ga-tanda*, I loved, *go-tanda*, I will love. The fourth is formed from the Root by changing the final vowel into *ile*; as *gi-tandile*, I have loved.

The *Simple* Forms are also used as *participles*, each with its proper shade of meaning. *Ex. gi-tanda*, I loving (now), *ga-tanda*, I loving (then, in past time), *gi-tandile*, I having loved.

The Compound Tenses are formed by means of the tenses of the auxiliaries, and the simple participles of the verb.

gi-ya-tanda, (probably, for *gi-ya ngi-tanda*, I am going loving,) I love.

gi-ya ku-tanda, I am going to love, I shall love.

gi-be ngi-tanda, I was loving, *gi-be ngi-tandile*, I was having loved, I had loved.

gi-ya-ku-be ngi-tanda, I shall be loving.

gi-ya-ku-be ngi-tandile, I shall be having loved, I shall have loved.

N.B. *be* appears to be the tense of the verb *ba*, which corresponds to *tandile* from *tanda*.

So too the Future Imperative may be expressed in three Forms, by means of the auxiliary *ba* and the participles.

Ex. Commencing, *go-tanda*, I will love.

Continuing, *go-ba ngi-tanda*, I will be loving.

Completed, *go-ba ngi-tandile*, I will have loved.

The *Compound* Forms are also used as *participles*.

The Future Compounds are also found with *za* instead of *ya*, and then the action is intended to be expressed as more *immediate*. *Ex. u-za-ku-fa*, he is just about to die,

The above tenses are all made *negative*, by the use of the negative particles *a* and *nga*, which are inserted as follows, with a change of the last vowel of the root in the present to *i*, and in the past to *anga*. (In the *Compound* Futures the change of vowel takes place, it will be seen, in accordance with the above rule, in the verb *ya*, The Future *Imperative* has no negative form.)

Present.	*Past.*
1. *a-ngi-tandi.*	4. *a-ngi-tandanga.*
2. *gi-nga-tandi.*	5. *gi-be ngi-nga-tandi.*
3. *a-ngi-tandile* (or *tandanga*).	6. *gi-be ngi-nga-tandanga.*

Future.

7. *a-ngi-yi-ku-tanda.*

8. *a-ngi-yi-ku-be ngi-tanda.*

9. *a-ngi-yi-ku-be ngi-tandile.*

There are *five* Tenses in the POTENTIAL Mood, formed by means of the particle *ga* or *nga*, introduced into certain tenses of the Indicative, as follows :—

1. *gi-nga-tanda*, I may or can love.

2. *gi-be-ngi-nga-tanda*, I might or could love.

3. *ga-ngi-tanda*, I should or would love.

4. *ga-ngi-tandile*, (or *tandanga*), I might, could, should, would, have loved.

5. *ga-ngi-ya-ku-tanda*, I may or might &c. come to love.

The three tenses of the OPTATIVE are formed from the First Tense Potential, by prefixing to it the Present, Past, and Future, Simple Tenses, of the verb *ga* or *nga*, to wish.

1. *gi-nga-gi-nga-tanda*, I wish I may love.

2. *ga-nga-gi-nga-tanda*, I wished I might love.

3. *go-nga-gi-nga-tanda*, I shall wish I might love.

The one tense of the SUBJUNCTIVE is formed from the Present Indicative, by changing the final *a* into *e*.

Ex. (*ukuba*) *gi-tande*, (that) I may love.

A verb is always used with pronominal prefixes (the usual personal pronouns). Thus, in the Commencing

Present of the Indicative Mood: *Gi-ya-tanda*, I love; *u-ya-tanda*, thou lovest. The prefix of the third person depends on the nominative case; and will be, according to the species of the noun, *u, li, i, si, u, lu, bu, ku, ya-tanda:* Plural: *Si-ya tanda*, we love; *ni-ya-tanda*, ye love; third person *ba, a, zi, i-ya-tanda.*

The accusative of a pronoun, referring to the object of the verb, is inserted between the verb and pronominal prefix; and the Emphatic form is often put, as an expletive, after the verb, in apposition to the accusative before it. E.g. *ba-m-sabe yena*, they him frightened, him.

(N.B. *m* is an accusative form of the pronoun, third person, first species.)

The preceding sketch of some of the more prominent features of the Kafir language, is compiled, generally verbatim, from the Elementary Grammar of the Bishop of Natal.

PRONUNCIATION OF NATIVE TERMS.

A to be pronounced as in *father ; e,* as *a* in mate; *i,* as *e* in seen; *o,* as in *bone; u,* as *oo* ; *au,* as *ow* in *how. C, q, x* are clicks—*c* being the *dental, q* the *palatal,* and *x* the *lateral,* which are uttered, respectively, by thrusting the tongue against the *top of the front teeth,* the *roof of the mouth,* and the *side teeth,* and suddenly withdrawing it. The accent to be placed on the penultimate. The prefixes of the substantives are usually distinguished, in the preceding pages, by hyphens.

NOTES.

CHAPTER I.

[1] THE eye is sometimes turned up at the outer corner.

[2] The Amatonga are said to be very dark—a statement confirmed by Captain Owen's assertion that the people of Mapoota are all jet-black. (*Pritchard's Researches*, vol. ii. p. 322.)

[3] Red hair occurs among the natives of Kongo. (*Id.* 324.)

[4] Lam. v. 10. See also Job xxx. 30.

[5] The Amampondo wear a head-ring, but do not shave the hair outside it. I think the Amalala practice was similar. (Young men sometimes trim their hair like a bishop's wig.) The Amaswazi partially shave their head. The Makua (coast of Mosambique) "dress their hair fantastically; some shave one side of the head, others both sides, leaving a hairy crest from the forehead to the nape of the neck, while others wear only a knot on the top of their foreheads." Some or all of the Amalala tattooed themselves—a practice which Tshaka forbade to the captives. Some cut off a joint of a finger—a custom not unknown among the Frontier Kafirs. The Amatonga and Makua tattoo.

CHAPTER II.

[1] Kraal, generally supposed to be Hottentot, was first written *corael* and *crael*, and is regarded by the editor of the Cape Documents as a corruption of the Spanish *corral*.

[2] From *umnini* a proprietor, and *umzana* a place.

[3] Stone fences for kraals are found in the upper country, where bush is rare. Anciently, when catttle-stealing was common, two kraals would, I have been told, be built near together with a short passage between them, for mutual security.

[3] The Kafirs cultivate Maize, Millet, three seed-bearing plants, viz. *inyaloti* or *inyauti*, *donqa*, and *upoko;* two Gourds, Calabash, Pumpkin, Water-Melon, Underground Bean, Kidney-Bean, Kidney-Potatoes, Sweet Potatoes, an Arum, a Yam; Sugar-Cane; a Sweet Reed (*imfi*); Tobacco; Bananas grow in various parts and are supposed to have been planted.

[4] When the grass is large and not dry enough to burn, the land is picked or dug before the sowing.

[5] *Um-takati*, is usually translated witch. It signifies an evildoer. See p. 141.

[6] Mr. Gordon Cumming states that, a piece of dry dung having been ignited by the patch from his rifle, an elephant turned aside and smelt it with his trunk. It was night.

[7] Isaacs, vol. ii. p. 52. In this and other quotations, I have, for the sake of uniformity, departed from the author's mode of spelling native terms.

[8] Arbousset, p. 221.

[9] A missionary asked Pande's doctor what took place in connection with the death of the black bull, but the official would not tell him. Isaacs mentions little more than that the king breaks three calabashes " as indicative of his command for the people to garner and eat the new food." (This may be the principal part of the original ceremony.) Mr. Fynn thinks that Tshaka added the war-ceremonies that his troops might be ready to march when the rivers should be down.

[10] I once detected a Kafir, who had placed a pot of meat on the fire, eating a very bitter root. He said it was to prevent his jaws aching; but afterwards confessed that *rich* men used it as a provocative.

[11] This description of Pande's cattle is on the authority of Europeans who have seen them. Horns are bent by being scraped on one side, and (it is said) softened with water. The three horns could have been produced only by splitting one or both of the others—a practice alluded to by Mr. Anderssen, who says (Lake Ngami) that some African tribes take much pains to form the horns of their oxen " of a certain shape. This is effected either by sawing off the tips, *splitting* them, bending them forcibly when tender, and so forth."

[12] A circumstance which may be due to the abolition of cattle-stealing by Tshaka. See p. 155.

[13] Murray's Africa. Cattle are fond of the shoots of reeds. A fact which may deserve consideration in connexion with Genesis xli. 2, 18, where the meaning of the original of " meadow" is uncertain.

[14] This animal is not very common in Natal. In the Zulu-country it occurs chiefly near the coast.

[15] Arbousset's Narrative.

[16] Isaacs' Travels.

[17] The Amatonga are said to catch fish in a sort of basket.

[18] Notes to Pringle's Poems.

CHAPTER III.

[1] Mr. Fynn's Evidence.

[2] My informant belonged to the Dwandwes.

[3] This has been considered a Jewish usage, but it must be remembered that the practice of taking a deceased brother's wife prevailed before the time of Moses. Gen. xxxviii. 8. " Resemblances to this usage have been traced in India; among the Athenians; among the ancient Germans; and among the modern Egyptians."

[4] The custom appears to prevail between a husband and his wives' mothers, (a man calls his father's wives his mothers); between a wife and her husband's father (until she have a child?) and the father's brothers; between a

father and his sons' wives (in the same hut*); between a
mother and her daughter's husband (and his brothers?);
between an uncle and his nephew's wives and niece's
husband's wives, but not *vice versâ* (?) The asterisk
indicates that the *igama*, in this case, is not within the
custom. See p. 221.

⁵ Mr. Peppercorne, magistrate of the Pafana Location,
appears to be speaking of the tribes generally, when he
says, (" Evidence ") that the consent of the chief must be
obtained by a young man before his marriage, which consent the chief frequently withholds as long as possible.

⁶ See Mr. Dohne's Evidence.

⁷ Tshaka, says Mr. Fynn, ordered a merely nominal
price to be given; but the people have now reverted to
the normal usage.

⁸ See Mr. Dohne's Evidence.

⁹ Mr. Dohne's Evidence.

¹⁰ See Mr. Fynn's Evidence.

¹¹ This may explain such a statement as the following :
" The amount of cattle does not compel the female to
accept a husband whom she may dislike."

¹⁰'Mr. Dohne's Evidence.

¹¹'Though the marriage becomes valid by the slaughter
of the ox, the guests would be indignant if it were
considered so, while any beef remained unconsumed.

¹² See Gen. xxx. 33, (margin); " So shall my righteous-
ness answer for me *to-morrow*." See also Exod. xiii. 14.
Josh. xxii. 24.

¹³ See p. 107, note 9.

¹⁴ Mr. Peppercorne's Evidence.

¹⁵ Mr. Peppercorne.

¹⁶ See note p. 46.

¹⁷ It is implied, in the remark of Mr. Isaacs, that the
women work up to the very time of their delivery—a
circumstance to which it may be owing that children are
sometimes born in the garden. I have heard that women

sometimes retire to it, as a quiet place. See Canticles viii. 5.

[18] Circumcision—a usage so extensively prevalent in Africa—is still retained by the Frontier tribes, and was practised by those of Natal and the Zulu-country before the time of Tshaka. That conqueror interdicted the practice—an innovation which some of the ancient people regret; the men of the present day, they think, are not so strong as their fathers, while the hair becomes gray sooner than before. Isaacs tells us that the rite was attended with some ceremony; the youths were admitted to the rank of manhood after the operation; and for three months succeeding it were permitted unlimited indulgence, in dancing, singing, and other amusements. I am not aware that there is any ceremony which now marks the period when a boy ceases to be regarded as a child. It is otherwise as to the females; Tshaka's orders did not extend to them; and a ceremony is still practised at about twelve years of age. " From this time forth the girl is allowed to associate with the class of women;" previously she had nursed the younger children; but she now she learns to do her mother's work—whether in the house or in the garden or in bearing burdens—and thus begins her training for the duties of a wife.

" There is, strictly speaking, no fixed time of majority of males and females respecting marriage; all depends on circumstances. The female is thought fit a year after that period above mentioned; the male as soon as he is able to to pay the requisite number of cattle." It is doubtful whether the last remark would apply to the people in their normal condition; for the chief would probably withhold his consent to the marriage of a very young man. In Natal, however, where the chief's consent is not necessary, the young men are in the habit of marrying as soon as they have obtained sufficient means. Nor are these difficult to procure; wages can be always earned from the colonists; and if a boy begins to work early, he may easily be married in his teens. I know one man, who could hardly have passed his 21st year, when he took his third wife.

[19] Great men are addressed as father.

[20] If a young man have no cattle, and his relatives will not furnish him with any to purchase a wife, he sometimes procures them by attaching himself to a wealthy person. In Natal the young men work for Europeans.

[21] I have been told that the master claims a portion.

[22] See Mr. Fynn's Evidence.

[23] Mr. Fynn's Evidence.

CHAPTER IV.

[1] Fynn's Evidence. *Isi-funda* and *um-funda* applied, with a difference of signification, to the subjects of a chief, appear to be connected with *funda* to learn. A chief has various titles. The Zulu king is called Elephant, Lion, Father, Great Mountain, You who are black, &c

[2] Mr. Fynn's Evidence. The term *in-kosi,* chief, has been explained to signify the Fountain of Mercy.

[3] See Appleyard's Kafir Grammar.

[4] Bishop of Cape Town's Journal.

[5] Isaacs' Travels.

[6] See p. 46, respecting the custom of *hlonipa*

[8] Mr. Fynn's Evidence.

[9] Commissioners' Report. Dr. Livingstone discovered people who hold their women in high estimation. If a man were asked to go anywhere or to agree to any arrangement, he would say, " I must go home and ask my wife," If she said " no," it was impossible to get him to move. Women sit in their councils; and, while a Bechuana swears by his father, these people swear by their mother Many of the women become chiefs. (Speech at a meeting of the R. G. S.) The Damaras swear by the tears of their mothers. Their tribes are divided into " castes," having

different rites. If a man of one caste marry a woman of another, the offspring adopt the rites of the mother.

[10]Arbousset's Narrative.

[11]When the natives saw the first cannon at Port Natal and enquired their use, they were told that they would learn *by and bye.* Hence the name.

[12]He is not peculiar to the Zulus.

[13]The black isi-gohlo is the part appropriated to the king's wives and concubines. The white is occupied by his mothers, etc.

[14]The property of an " evildoer " is taken to the king.

CHAPTER V.

[1]Blue Book.

[2]" The spirit of revenge, as among all savage nations, is very strong; but it can neither be implacable nor inexorable, for in many places in this district the bitterest enemies of former times are living together as neighbours, cultivating the same fields, and mixing together in daily social intercourse." (Mr. Shepstone's Evidence.) As to the cowardice of the people, see p. 341.

[3]A gentlemen, long acquainted with the people, suspected it; one of the author's cows died with apparent symptoms of strychnine; a plant yielding that poison grows in Natal.

[4]The pamphlet has been acknowledged by the author of the History of Natal.

[5]The Kafirs appear to think that an " evildoer " always knows an antidote to his poison. The " Vandoux," a mysterious and dangerous community, found chiefly in Mexico and Texas, is supposed to be of African origin. Its " members possess or pretend to possess important secrets respecting the properties of several more or less known plants. They prepare poisons capable of producing various effects : some kill slowly, some quick as lightning; some stupify the brain, some destroy the reason. They know also the proper antidotes." See " Clerical Journal," April 8, 1857.

CHAPTER VI

[1] Mr. Fynn's *Evidence.*

[2] Among the Frontier Kafirs *Uhlanga* is sometimes used for the Supreme Being. (See p. 199.) Arbousset says that the following legend is very current in the S. of Africa: " The Lord sent in the former times a gray lizard with this message to the world : *Men die ; they will be restored to life again.* The chameleon set out from his chief, and arriving in haste, he said : *Men die ; they die for ever.* Then the gray lizard came and cried, ' The Lord has spoken, saying, *Men die ; they shall live again.* But men answered him, the first word is the first; that which is after is nothing." A tradition among the Namaquas states that the moon sent the hare to man with this message : " As I die and am born again, so ye shall die and be again alive." The hare made a mistake and said : " As I die and am *not* born again, so you," &c. When he returned, the moon, being angry at his error, threw a stick at him and split his lip. The animal then fled and is doing so to this day.

[3] Bishop Colenso's Ten Weeks in Natal, from which the fact respecting Zikali in the previous paragraph is taken.

[4] The Damaras believe that the spirits of the deceased appear after death, usually in the shape of a dog. A belief in transmigration has been suspected to exist among some of the Bechuanas. The " Mucarongas" " hold monkeys were in times past men and women, and call them the old people."

[5] A white man who had a particularly fine ox which became sick, sold it to a Kafir for a trifle. The beast having recovered, he would gladly have purchased it, but the owner, much to his surprise, could not be induced to part with it.

[6] The Frontier Kafirs burn fat in some cases as a sacrifice. Mr. Fynn told me that a war offering made before a battle is burnt. What remains of the black bull at the Feast of First Fruits is burnt with the skin and bones.

[7] See p. 221.

[8] " According to a horrible law of the Zulu despots, when a chief [important man ?] is put to death, they exterminate his subjects : *" Your father is dead ; who will be able to support you, is all that is said."* (Arbousset.) When an "evildoer" is killed, those supposed to be acquainted with his poison are slain.

[9] See Mr. Fynn's Evidence.

[10] The natives seem to ascribe dreams in general to the spirits ; the prophet's heir is distinguished by the number and peculiarity of his visions.

[11] A misprint for *change*. *Twasa*, a verb used to signify the change of the moon to the new, and the changing of the year to spring, is applied to a prophet in his novitiate.

[12] Mr. Fynn. The belief that they can discover a misdoer, must tend to prevent crime to some extent; if, therefore, we destroy their influence without supplying some other motive for obedience, we shall make the people worse than they are.

[14] After remaining there a year, Makanna, with a few followers (Kafirs and slaves), disarmed the guard and attempted to escape in a boat, but was drowned. (Pringle's Narrative, from which the account of Makanna is taken.)

[15] This account of Umlanjeni is from a narrative of the war published in Graham's Town, and King's Campaigning in Kafir-land.

[16] From the newspapers It was stated in April that the apprehensions lately entertained respecting the safety of the colony, existed no longer.

[17] See p. 4. The bow of the queen is, of course, the rain-bow.

[18] Animals, whose names are in italics, are abstained from among the Frontier Kafirs.

[19] From a Cape periodical.

[20] Arab women in N.-Africa give their male children a piece of the lion's heart to eat to make them courageous.

[21]See Bell's Geography, vol. ii. p. 532.
[22]See Mr. Backhouse's work.

CHAPTER VII.

[1]The first vowel of a proper name is usually omitted. The final vowel is sometimes omitted, as Dingan, for Dingane.

[2]From a statement of Isaacs in a Cape paper.

[2]Kafirs from a distance have applied to me for food, alleging that their brethren in the neighbourhood (of another tribe) would not give them any.

[3]The leader of the dance walks about while speaking.

[4]Appleyard's Grammar. *Bush* is figuratively a refuge; the *blind* are mankind or the heathen; the *trumpet* is the church-bell.

[5]Facts mentioned by Backhouse.

[6]When a man is killed at Pande's, the executioners wash.

[7]This seems the case among the Amaxosa.

[8]Soldiers cut their hair after an expedition in which any of them have been killed or perhaps died.

[9]Arbousset says that some Zulus burn the dead, while some others expose the corpse of a chief on the branches of a tree, and afterwards burn it, throwing the ashes in the river. It is said that cremation is practised at Benguela; and that in Loango, the bodies of great men are dried before burial.

[10]See Bishop Colenso's Ten Weeks in Natal.

CHAPTER VIII.

[1]Gardiner's Journey.

[2]Mr. Fynn as quoted in a Cape periodical, where the visitor is supposed to have been Dr. Cowan.

[3]Isaacs.

[4]One account says that Tshaka joined him.

[5] His policy was, at first, not to destroy people, but to subdue and incorporate them with his own subjects (Rev. L. Grout.)

[6] A MS. says that Tshaka was hiding many months.

[7] Mundiso is said to have ridiculed Tshaka.

[8] Tshaka seems to have had regiments of " men," though unmarried.

[9] See Mr. L. Grout's Evidence.

[10] Fynn pleaded hard for the lives of some captives, but in vain—the only time he ever failed.

[11] Mr. L. Grout's evidence.

[12] People condemned by Pande are said to thank him.

[13] Tshaka related this imposture to Isaacs.

[14] " Birds of prey darken the air in the neighbourhood of Dingan's kraal." MS.

[15] In 1838 it had amounted to 10,000 souls.

[16] The Amangwane are said to have been living in huts, and to have cultivated the ground !

[17] Isaacs. Natives say that Sotshangan poisoned the water—a possible fact, there being much stagnant water in the region. See p. 23.

[18] Arbousset.

CHAPTER IX.

[1] " He pledged his word to us to recal those scattered by Tshaka." MS.

[2] Arbousset. The Malutis are the Draakensberg.

[3] Isaacs. Mr. Moffat visited Umzilikazi in 1855, at Matlokotloko, and describes his dominions as reaching the Zambeze.

[5] I have omitted parts of the poem as given by Arbousset.

[6] The Sagacious One is the elephant.

[7] This refers to the " medicine " taken after Tshaka's death by his relatives. Arbousset says they consist of milk and water and the juices of certain bitter herbs.

[8] The plural of a man's name expresses his people.

[9] Fynn was made chief of Natal at his suggestion.

[10] They would receive nothing through Cane.

[11] Isaacs, who is said to have subsequently taken up his abode on an island on the W. coast.

[12] Lectures on the Emigration of the Dutch Farmers, by the Hon. H. Cloete, L.L.D., Recorder of Natal.

[13] Holden's History of Natal.

[14] Cloete, and despatch of British Commander at Port Natal.

[15] From his despatch.

[17] Message from Pande in the Blue Book.

[18] From the newspapers.

CHAPTER X.

[1] " Men " ordinarily implies married men, but Tshaka, who allowed so few of his warriors to marry, seems to have had regiments of " men."

[2] There were none but old men left behind.

[3] Green enumerates (MS.) an emetic, sprinkling, and incense (mabopi?) among the preparations for war.

[4] Tshaka gave his army cattle for food during the march, but Pande seems to send very few. Other oxen are sent to assist in finding and driving away the enemy's cattle.

[5] The Amaswazi-country, more extensive than Natal, was described as without population in 1853.

CHAPTER XI.

[1] The same rule applies to a prophetess.

[2] A European has heard a similar story.

[3] Captain Gardiner.

[4] A stimulating plant is said to be added.

APPENDIX.

[1] The quotations are from Holden's History and Blue Book.

[2] See Mr. Dohne's Evidence.

[3]The rest of this article is founded on the valuable list in Mr. L. Grout's Evidence. It has not been thought necessary to distinguish quotations. F, added to the account of a tribe, signifies Fingo.

THE END.